Crossing Over

MĀNOA 19:1   UNIVERSITY
OF HAWAI'I
PRESS

HONOLULU

Crossing Over

PARTITION LITERATURE

FROM INDIA, PAKISTAN,

AND BANGLADESH

Frank Stewart

EDITOR

Sukrita Paul Kumar

GUEST EDITOR

Attock Bridge, Pakistan, 1900.
Silver gelatin print by unknown
photographer. Courtesy of Pump
Park Vintage Photography.

Editor Frank Stewart

Managing Editor Pat Matsueda

Production Editor Brent Fujinaka

Associate Editor Leigh Saffold

Designer and Art Editor Barbara Pope

Fiction Editor Ian MacMillan

Poetry and Nonfiction Editor Frank Stewart

Abernethy Fellow Brandy Nālani McDougall

Staff Samantha Cosentino, Jennifer de Jesús, Bruce Leong

Corresponding Editors for North America
Barry Lopez, W. S. Merwin, Carol Moldaw, Arthur Sze

Corresponding Editors for Asia and the Pacific
CHINA Howard Goldblatt, Ding Zuxin
HONG KONG Shirley Geok-lin Lim
INDONESIA John H. McGlynn
JAPAN Leza Lowitz
KOREA Bruce Fulton
NEW ZEALAND AND SOUTH PACIFIC Vilsoni Hereniko
PACIFIC LATIN AMERICA H. E. Francis, James Hoggard
PHILIPPINES Alfred A. Yuson
WESTERN CANADA Charlene Gilmore

Advisory Group Esther K. Arinaga, William H. Hamilton, Joseph O'Mealy, Robert Shapard

Founded in 1988 by Robert Shapard and Frank Stewart.

Text permissions can be found on page 218.

Mānoa gratefully acknowledges the continuing support of the University of Hawai'i Administration; the support of the University of Hawai'i College of Languages, Linguistics, and Literature; and grants from the National Endowment for the Arts and the Hawai'i State Foundation on Culture and the Arts. Thanks also to the Mānoa Foundation.

Mānoa is published twice a year. Subscriptions: U.S.A. and Canada—individuals $22 one year, $40 two years; institutions $40 one year, $72 two years. Subscriptions: other countries—individuals $25 one year, $45 two years; institutions $40 one year, $72 two years; air mail, add $24 a year. Single copies: U.S.A. and Canada—$20; other countries—$20. Call toll free 1-888-UHPRESS. We accept checks, money orders, Visa, or MasterCard, payable to University of Hawai'i Press, 2840 Kolowalu Street, Honolulu, HI 96822, U.S.A. Claims for issues not received will be honored until 180 days past the date of publication; thereafter, the single-copy rate will be charged.

http://manoajournal.hawaii.edu/
http://www.uhpress.hawaii.edu/journals/manoa/

CONTENTS

Partition Literature from India, Pakistan, and Bangladesh

Editors' Note

Crossing Over is the most recent volume in the series from *Mānoa: A Pacific Journal of International Writing,* published by the University of Hawai'i Press. For two decades, *Mānoa* has been featuring contemporary literature from countries and regions in Asia, the Pacific, and the Americas. Many of these works have never before appeared in English translation, or have not been readily accessible to American and other English-speaking readers.

According to the Bowker Global Books in Print database, works of translation account for about three percent of all books published in the U.S., and almost three-quarters of those translations are nonfiction. American readers are thus not only deprived of the abundance of fine international literature, but also of the insights and intimate knowledge of other people which only literature can provide. Given recent U.S. intervention in global affairs, there may have never been a time when reading the literature of America's transnational neighbors has been more important.

Crossing Over comprises stories from three South Asian countries—India, Pakistan, and Bangladesh—with a combined population of over two billion. The works here focus on the cataclysmic experiences of Partition in 1947 and its aftermath, including the Bangladesh War of Independence in 1971. The selection is by no means exhaustive. At best, it serves as a sample of a rich and vast body of literature being produced in many languages of South Asia. The purpose of gathering these stories, however, has been neither to offer solutions to intractable political and social issues nor to assign collective blame. Instead, the stories in *Crossing Over* depict the responses and emotions of ordinary people caught in a tragic turning point in history, when tolerance, respect, and compassion broke down. Written by some of the region's finest writers, these works make us aware that such responses are not exclusive to South Asia. They are possible everywhere.

During the last few years, renewed attention has been given to what is called Partition Literature. These works of fiction, poetry, and memoir describe and explore the events that occurred when the British colonial government departed South Asia, and the nation of Pakistan was created by hastily drawn borders that carved out portions of eastern and western India. Pakistan gained independence just after midnight on August 14, 1947, and India on August 15. This caused frantic Hindus, Muslims, Sikhs, and other communities to cross the newly formed national borders in both directions in a massive migration, as sectarian violence broke out immediately.

In the tumultuous hours and days following the British exodus, more than a million people experienced unprecedented horrors: communal rioting, murder, rape, abduction, disease, and starvation. The tragedies of Partition, however, did not end with the migrations and resettlements; they continue today. On several occasions, open warfare has broken out between Pakistan and India, and communal violence and riots continue to erupt in parts of the Subcontinent. Partition also has had ramifications beyond the region, not the least being the precedent it set for other nations locked in communal strife.

Authors writing about the enormity of the social violence and the complexity of individual experience of Partition were, and continue to be, challenged by a difficult task. The shock of incomprehensible barbaric acts drove many to silence, denial, rage, guilt, lamentation, and despair. What is there to say, and how should it be said? To whom can an author speak about such things without giving in to the temptation of assigning blame to a particular community, or of withholding sympathy and compassion for all who suffered, regardless of religious or ethnic affiliation? How can storytelling give us the courage to accept our complicity in creating a world where atrocities are committed and endured by people very much like ourselves? How can stories tell what "really happened" while also giving us reason to believe that an ethical, humane future is possible?

An aesthetic shaping of the incidents of Partition has been of deep concern to the authors in *Crossing Over*, especially those who lived through the events. Their subject was and continues to be the working of the human mind and heart at the collective, as well as the individual, level. The great task they have faced has been to describe and attempt to comprehend how normal human beings could so easily be swept into barbarism. Their approach does not derive from sociology, history, or political science. The best writers work in a more subtle realm, where the truth is revealed in a nonpartisan narration of life experience, and where such essential human values as social justice, compassion, and love are not put aside. At the same time, these writers do not flinch from the reality of combative feelings, criminality, vengefulness, and cruelty. Some have rendered events with stark realism; others have created parabolic stories; and still others have explored the psychic responses that give rise to nostalgia, the wish to recall and value a lost connectedness that transcends communal strife. Prafulla

Roy's Bengali story "Where There Is No Frontier" comes to mind in this context, along with Mohan Rakesh's Hindi story "The Claim," which ends with the driver of a horse-drawn carriage reminiscing about the mango tree he has had to leave behind—as well as his missing wife. Blessing his old horse, he says, "If God keeps you well, Afsar, the old days will return again."

Researchers have accumulated statistics—the numbers of migrants and refugees, rapes, murders, and so forth; they have reexamined the political debates and scrutinized the positions and motives of leaders during and after Partition. Other researchers have concluded that, for millions of individuals who were involved, the intensity of experience was so deep and powerful that quantification and theorizing alone cannot provide a true calibration of the events. These tools of the academic and the researcher hardly begin to yield a comprehensive and satisfactory description of what so many individuals endured. For many years, people from all professions and facets of society seem to have made a deliberate effort to bury the stark truth of those experiences in their subconscious—to engage in a collective amnesia. From what depths would the refugee or the victim of rape, or the person who might have killed his neighbors, be capable of mustering the fortitude to confront the gruesome past, especially when the present demands his or her full energy to construct a new home and a new identity? Collective amnesia has always served as a survival strategy for individuals, communities, and nations.

Slowly, however, the repressed memories have risen to the level of consciousness. Novelists Khushwant Singh *(A Train to Pakistan)*, Bhisham Sahni *(Tamas)*, Joginder Paul *(Sleepwalkers)*, Intizar Husain *(Basti)*, and others describe Partition as a rupture that was never healed and was therefore followed by reenactments of the same events. The project of engineered forgetting—whether conducted by the individual, the society, or the state; whether through censorship or simple denial—comes under scrutiny in the powerful literary works of these authors, and reveals the awesome and multifarious colors of Partition.

The numbness in the psyche of those aversely affected by Partition has been like the numbness that sets in after a devastating storm or earthquake: bewilderment, disorientation, silence, and a sense of helplessness. On the one hand, Partition meant the aspiration of Indian and Pakistani nationhood after independence had been attained: hundreds of people had become martyrs in the struggle for independence, and there had been countless idealistic, selfless acts by freedom fighters, which were celebrated. On the other hand, there had been unimaginable acts of cruelty and injustice. The euphoria of freedom and the horror of the riots could not be experienced simultaneously. In these contradictory circumstances, a profound emotional, psychic, and moral confusion ensued. Some novelists—as if to salvage a sense of humanity or to recover elevated emotions of solidarity and communal harmony—produced nostalgic journeys into a beautiful past, the recalling of which might restore harmony in the present. A convincing and authentic reliving of that past is found in Krishna Sobti's magnum opus, the novel *Zindaginama,* which brings to life an era of peaceful cohabitation among several communities of the earlier decades of the twentieth century; the author delves into recapitulation, not amnesia. *Aag ka Darya* (The River of Fire), a novel by the eminent Urdu writer Qurratulain Hyder, also traces the long history of the composite culture of the Subcontinent disrupted so violently in 1947. Similarly, Kamleshwar's Hindi novel *Laute hue Musafir* portrays communities re-forming after Partition. These are but a few of many fictional narratives that have attempted to counter the era of violence by recollecting the time of peace.

Indeed, nostalgia and forgetting appear together in some examples of Partition literature. In many Hindi and Urdu stories, the protagonists struggle to remember and to overcome memory in order to recover. The intense process of remembering enables them to put their fragmented, bruised selves back together, to recover a dignified identity. In Lalithambika Antharjanam's story "A Leaf in the Storm," the protagonist must purge herself of the memory of her brutal rape in order to make space in her psyche for the birth of the baby in her womb. The immediate sensations of the baby quickening in her body connect her with her new self and a new life.

On the other hand, many characters in Partition fiction are doomed because they cannot forget or because they cling tightly only to sweet memories, hoping to escape the pain of the cruel present. In "The Thirst of Rivers," an Urdu story by Joginder Paul, an old woman cannot part with a set of keys to the *haveli* (residential compound) she and her family had to abandon when they migrated across the border. Unable to forget, she believes she will be able to open the locks of her son's new house with those keys, and in this way, she remains a prisoner of her past.

A number of Partition authors have skillfully intermixed subjective memory with collective memory, and further mixed them with centuries-old historical events and with larger, non-linear cultural mythology. In his novel *Basti,* for example, the Urdu writer Intizar Husain uses the term *hijrat* (emigration) to describe the massive displacement of populations that occurred first in 1947 and then in 1971, when civil war destroyed East Pakistan and created the independent nation of Bangladesh. In *Basti,* the protagonist, Zakir, is a Shiite Muslim professor of history who moved to Lahore with his family in 1947; the present-tense action of the novel takes place in 1971, in the months preceding the dissolution of East Pakistan. Zakir is aware (as are the novel's readers) that the term evokes the Hijrat of the Prophet Muhammad, when the Prophet fled persecution in Mecca in

622 C.E. and founded the first all-Muslim community in Medina. In that crucial moment in Muslim history, hardship was quickly converted into victory. The "emigrations" of 1947 began hopefully but on many levels became tragic. *Basti* alludes to the long history of changes in the fate and status of Muslims in South Asia, through eras of secular and sacred time, many of them colored by suffering as much as by glory. In the excerpt printed in *Crossing Over,* Husain skillfully intertwines the past and present, the individual and the communal. "Basti" is a word that can refer to any dwelling place, and thus the protagonist's city is given a mythic quality. "Zakir" means "one who remembers." The name of his beloved childhood sweetheart, Sabirah, means "patient" or "enduring"; as the excerpt suggests, their love—and the hopefulness of childhood—is never fulfilled. Neither person is able to cross over the borders to the other.

"What place do you come from?" After the initial greetings, this is a question asked whenever refugees, now a very senior generation of people, meet each other in India or Pakistan. The question underscores the lingering desire to reestablish some contact, if not with the place, then at least with someone who might have come from the same town or city. Identification with place could hardly be depicted more powerfully than in Saadat Hasan Manto's story "Toba Tek Singh." The narrative begins in a madhouse and ends on the newly created border between India and Pakistan— which, the story suggests, is itself a creation of insanity. In his confusion, the pitiful protagonist no longer differentiates among himself, his name, and the town he is from and to which he wishes to return. By altering his physical relationship to home, Partition has made his psychological ties all the stronger, and his insanity perhaps all the more intractable.

Similarly, Joginder Paul's Urdu novella, *Sleepwalkers,* begins with the words "This is Lucknow." As we discover, however, the city being referred to is not Lucknow, India, but Karachi, Pakistan; the *mohajirs* (migrants) who left Lucknow because of Partition transported their home city "within the folds of their hearts" to Pakistan and rebuilt it, more splendidly, in Karachi. The people's sense of their home territory consists not merely of buildings and streets; it encompasses their specific ancestry, social norms, moral order, and deep communal identity. The massive migration of people in 1947 resulted in many stories with themes of exile and cannot be understood without knowledge of the profound significance "home" has to people in South Asia. Even a pile of rubble that had once been a house, as we see in the story by Mohan Rakesh in *Crossing Over,* has extraordinary psychic meaning to the man who once lived there.

Many of the migrants who exited their homelands in large *kafilas* (columns) had no specific destination; theirs was a journey into exile and homelessness. For people who cherished and found meaning in long-established neighborhoods, extended families, and cultural networks, the exodus was traumatic. The oral-history narratives in Urvashi Butalia's collection *The Other Side of Silence* reflect what she calls "the layers of silence" of survivors and their anguish as a result of keeping their stories secret for decades. In the words of Intizar Husain, their journey into the inner self remains forever an "unwritten epic." In Prafulla Roy's Bengali story "Father," the eighty-year-old protagonist bolts himself in his room and refuses to come out when his daughter, abducted thirty years earlier, locates him at his house in Calcutta. He would rather hide in the darkness than open the door to hear her story of what happened to her.

The Partition riots of 1947 and the subsequent riots in East Pakistan in 1971 were particularly brutal for women. Sexual assaults, abductions, and suicide (or martyrdom) are recorded frequently in Partition literature. Deeply seated notions of honor, purity, and chastity created a situation in which women were targets of savage abuse; many of those who survived abduction or rape, as in "Father," were often accused of bringing dishonor upon their families. After the riots subsided, the governments of Pakistan and India established programs to find abducted women and return them to their relatives. These so-called rehabilitation programs could not decondition the mindsets of people who condemned the women for having survived. Thus, "rehabilitated" women who were returned to their families were often victimized a second time. Rajinder Singh Bedi's Urdu story "Lajwanti" is particularly powerful because of its poignant irony. Lajwanti—her name is the same as that for the mimosa or touch-me-not plant—has been abducted and raped. While she remains missing in Pakistan, her grieving husband becomes secretary of the city's Committee for the Rehabilitation of Women and participates in demonstrations for the acceptance of those women who are found and returned. When at last Lajwanti is returned, her husband not only treats her with excessive care, but begins to address her as Devi (goddess). The painful irony is that, despite the best intentions, Lajwanti and her husband are unable to restore their past happiness. As Bedi tells us, "She had returned home, but she had lost everything."

Soon after Partition, journalistic writing thrived on descriptions of savagery and indulged in what came to be called "pornography of violence." Some important fiction writers, such as Saadat Hasan Manto, wrote stories that were so vivid in their depiction of violence that the writers were banned from publishing—or, as in Manto's case, prosecuted for obscenity. But Manto and other skillful writers shaped their stories so powerfully and memorably that such savagery is ultimately redemptive.

In an age when fanaticism, communal strife, and the politics of identity and "otherness" are increasingly destructive, it becomes imperative to seek an unbiased understanding of inter-community and inter-national relationships. The politics of divisiveness has been shown to have only tragic results, and yet political interests and religious fanaticism make us blind. Wise and perceptive stories restore our sight and enrich our understanding. How could one not be moved by the fate of the little boy in Bhisham Sahni's "Pali," who undergoes religious conversion twice and is trapped in the meaninglessness of dogmatic religious affiliations? Reading the literature of Partition is bound to arouse comparison with present times; and having read it, we will perhaps be less inclined to dismiss a nostalgia for multiethnic, multireligious cohabitation as sentimentalism. Where will we find the wisdom to create a new future? *Crossing Over* suggests some answers, and the consequences if we fail.

A Karachi Family Album

Throughout *Crossing Over* are photographs from the family album of Teresa Vas Mansson, born and raised in Karachi (in present-day Pakistan) and now living in Hawai'i. Her family story is in some ways a counterpoint to the others in *Crossing Over*. For instance, her family did not suffer the level of violence that befell many of the real and fictional families described here, and thus her story might seem less dramatic and troubled. But there is no need to compare degrees of suffering. What unifies her experience with that of others in *Crossing Over* is the disruptive effects of Partition, the separation of close-knit extended families, the abandonment of beloved homes, and the scattering of friends and kin. Through her story, we realize that we need the narratives of many individuals to begin to comprehend the meaning of history.

Teresa was born to Cyril and Sophia Vas in 1927. Her grandfather had migrated to Karachi, possibly in the 1870s, from Goa, a verdant region comprising about 1,400 square miles on India's west coast. Goa and Karachi are strikingly different. Goa is moist and fertile, while Karachi is hot and dry. Since the early sixteenth century, Goa was separated from the rest of India, colonized by Portugal rather than Britain. In this Portuguese enclave, Goans developed a distinct identity. For example, a large minority of Goans were Roman Catholic rather than Hindu (today Christians still comprise about thirty percent of Goa's population), having been converted, sometimes by force, by the Portuguese. At the same time, many of the converted Goans maintained their Hindu culture. The language of the upper classes was Portuguese instead of the English spoken in the rest of India by the British colonists and those who worked for them. Most Goans in Goa, however, spoke Marathi or Konkani. In addition, many Goans took Portuguese surnames. Similarly, many towns and districts acquired Portuguese names; for example, the major port city is called Vasco, after Vasco Da Gama.

By the mid-1800s, large numbers of Goans were moving to Karachi to find work under the British. When the Suez Canal opened in 1869, the city

Teresa Vas
Pakistan, circa 1948

became South Asia's closest major port to Europe, and by 1900 Karachi had become the biggest wheat-exporting port in the British Empire. Like other Goan migrants who hoped to do well, Teresa's Roman Catholic grandfather would have had to learn to speak English. While this was somewhat of an obstacle, Goans wanting to work for the British in Karachi had several things in their favor: Goans were predominantly Christian, they had long been familiar with European culture, they got along with everyone, and they were hard workers. Their British employers favored them, and Goans prospered. Moving up in the British civil, government, and defense services, they built homes and started families. They lived in communities with names such as Depot Lines, Soldier Bazaar, Cincinnatus Town (now called Garden East), Camp (later known as Saddar), and Catholic Colonies. By the time of Partition, Catholic Colonies and Saddar had become the city center of Karachi.

Religion played an important role in creating a cohesive Goan community. There was no church in Karachi when the large migrations began, so with support from the Irish Fusiliers and other Roman Catholic soldiers and individuals, the Goans built St. Patrick's chapel, which became a church and eventually an impressive cathedral. When St. Patrick's was completed in 1881, it had high vaulted ceilings, stained glass, and marble paving, and could accommodate 1,500 worshipers. With a fine private school supported by the church, St. Patrick's became a center for the entire Catholic community; adults and children gathered there for social events, as well as for religious services and festivals.

In 1886, the community was large enough to establish a library, which became the Goan Portuguese Association. Later, as the community outgrew this facility, the name was changed to the Karachi Goan Association. In 1905, the association completed construction of a lavish stone building that had Belgian tiles and teak flooring, used for cultural, sporting, and other gatherings. The building, called variously the Goa-Portuguese Hall and Goan Gymkhana, was one of the most elegant and prominent structures in the Saddar Bazaar, an area of sprawling shops with expensive imported goods, food markets, and sellers of all manner of merchandise. The area included the Empress Market (named after Queen Victoria, Empress of India) and Elphinstone Street (now Zaibunnisa Street), which had the largest number of shops of any street in the bazaar. Across Bunder Road (now M.A. Jinnah Road) was a forty-three-acre park, laid out by the British in 1874, called Government Garden or Rani Bagh (later Gandhi Garden, and now the Zoological Garden). The park had a large bandstand as well as grounds set aside for cricket and croquet. The Goan community thrived in Karachi, and many Goans became entrepreneurs, business managers, and professionals.

Teresa's grandfather also did well in Karachi, rising to the post of Customs Inspector. Members of his large, cultured family became prominent among the ranks of the military and professional classes. The oldest son, Joseph Anthony, born in 1875, was the first Goan to pass the Indian Civil Service exam and had an outstanding career in the Service. After attending D.J. Sind College in Karachi (established in 1887), Joseph received degrees from King's College, Cambridge, in 1898. He was then posted to Bengal, where he died at age forty-six. He was survived by his wife, Mattie.

Joseph's brother Alec joined the British Indian Army during World War I, perhaps encouraged by the fact that Karachi was then the headquarters of Allied Operations in the Middle East and a major supply depot for British troops. It was Alec who changed the spelling of the family name from "vaz" to "vas," to increase his chances of being taken for an Anglo-Indian, desirable for recruitment into the British Indian Army. At the time, the British Indian Army was the largest volunteer army in the world, and Alec was one of approximately 1.4 million Indians sent to help the allies in World War I. He was killed about 1915, possibly at the Second Battle of Ieper in Belgium, and buried in what has become known as Flanders Field.

The daughters of the family included Matilda, affectionately known as Mitz, and Gilomena. And there were three more sons: Alfie, Cyril, and Fred.

Cyril graduated from Grant Medical College, Bombay, in about 1915 and became a doctor. Soon afterwards, he married Sophie, and they had four children: Patricia, Ken, Eric, and Teresa.

Teresa's brother Eric, born in 1923, joined the British Indian Army and was commissioned in 1942. He would have been on duty during Partition, as trains filled with fleeing immigrants were crossing the Indian and Pakistani borders. Later Eric went through the Staff College, Wellington, and the National Defense College, New Delhi. He became a highly decorated commandant and rose to the rank of lieutenant general before retiring.

Teresa's other brother, Ken, married a Karachi woman named Yolanda; after Partition, the couple opted to stay in Pakistan, despite their not being Muslim.

Cyril and Sophie Vas raised their young family in the area called Depot Lines, in a house directly across from the Karachi Goan Association Hall. In many of the family photographs, the large stone building is visible in the background. During these years before Partition, Karachi was relatively tranquil, clean, and well regulated, despite the city's rapid growth as an important British seaport. But the period was not without sorrows for the Vas family. Teresa's mother, Sophie, died in 1932, and the family moved in with Cyril's widowed sister, Matilda, and her son, Bude (Vincent). They lived in the nearby area called Cincinnatus Town, named after a prominent Goan, Cincinnatus D'Abreo. In anticipation of marriage, Bude built a large house, Greyholme, for the extended family.

In the sweltering summers, many Goans, including Teresa's family, took vacations back in Goa, where the weather at the seashore was mild.

Another getaway was the resort in Nainital, a town in the foothills of the Himalayas. Established in 1841 as an exclusive refuge, or hill station, for the use of British dignitaries, by 1925 it began to be used as a retreat by Indian professionals and high-ranking members of the British civil service. Located at an elevation of nearly 7,000 feet, the town was set between the snowy Himalayan range and the broad plains to the south. Teresa remembers vacationing there with her friends in the 1940s, after graduating from high school.

Partition dramatically and irrevocably altered Karachi. Before 1947, it was regarded as one of the most prosperous and well-planned cities in British India. Out of a total population of 400,000, Muslims comprised forty-two percent, while Hindus comprised fifty-one percent. Karachi had become the capital of Sindh Province in 1937, and the citizens were proud of their orderly city. Compared to cities in the part of the country that became Pakistan after Partition, Karachi—far to the east of the new border—was peaceful. When the riots began elsewhere in August 1947, migrants (known as *mohajirs*) streamed across the border into the newly created Pakistan, and within months more than 600,000 had reached Karachi. The numbers and desperation of the *mohajirs* put intense pressure on the local authorities to house and accommodate them, and many of the refugees found themselves having to live in refugee camps and squatter settlements *(katchi abadis)*. Hindus were slow to leave at first, feeling somewhat secure in their numbers and their good relationships with the local Sindhi population. However, they soon felt overwhelmed by the newcomers, mainly Urdu-speaking, who needed shelter.

By early 1948, tensions were reaching the breaking point. In January, 200 to 300 Sikhs inexplicably arrived in Karachi by train. When the news spread, a mob of *mohajirs,* armed with hatchets and swords, surrounded the train cars. The Sikhs managed to lock themselves in a Sikh temple near the train station. When the mob could not break down the doors, they set the building on fire, burning alive most of the men, women, and children. Those who escaped the blaze were butchered as they fled. The riots quickly spread to other areas of the city, and many non-Muslims were raped and murdered. Rioting and looting continued for two days.

The incident shocked the local residents. Some—including a large number of the Sindhi-speaking population, who were of various ethnicities and held diverse political and religious points of view—had grown to resent the unruly refugees. In referring to themselves as *mohajirs,* the refugees were using the term adopted by the Prophet Muhammad's followers, who had fled to Medina in the sixteenth century to avoid persecution. In this sense, the refugees considered themselves the founding fathers of Pakistan. They were the ones who were sacrificing all for the new nation, and they felt themselves to have a special privilege over the Sindhis, whom they looked down upon as uneducated rural farmers.

The January riots led to a massive exodus from the city of 170,000 of the remaining Hindus, Christians, and other imperiled citizens. Further demographic changes occurred in May 1948, when, over the objections of the Sindhi population, Karachi was federalized and declared the capital of the new nation of Pakistan. Karachi's change of status meant that numerous senior officials and some 4,000 clerks who were needed to run the country were added to the congestion. In addition, Karachi's status as Sindh's provincial capital, having been superseded by the federal administration, resulted in the new government taking over buildings and land. Between 1947 and 1951, Karachi's population grew by 432 percent, as 815,000 new immigrants raised the population to 1.2 million. By 1951, the Muslim population was more than ninety percent of the total, and the Hindu and Sindhi-speaking populations less than ten percent. Today, the population of Karachi is 15 million and growing by 2 million per year.

These events took their toll on Teresa's family, as they did on many others. In addition, her father died in 1948, leaving only Teresa and Matilda at home; her brother Ken had already married and moved into a house of his own. Teresa had been working since 1944, starting with her joining the Women's Royal Indian Naval Service (WRINS), so she was out during the day. Left at home by herself, Matilda could not cope with the stress of ethnic tensions spreading through the city, and she was sent to Bombay, into the care of her extended family.

In 1945, Teresa took a shore-based position in the Royal Indian Navy. In November of that year, Indian recruits in the Indian Civil Service and armed forces had staged a mutiny in Bombay. In the following months, the mutiny spread among the air force and navy, leading to street riots in sympathy for Indian independence. The mutinies may have hastened Britain's realization that its Indian colony was ungovernable. Military trials and inquiries ceased after Partition, and Teresa went to Bombay to join her extended family. She kept up her ties with Karachi, however, and even took a temporary job at the Indian consulate there before moving away for good.

In 1943, Teresa's cousin Alexander Athaide, known as Alec, married Phyllis de Lima. Alec was a sportsman of some repute in Karachi, but hardly on the level of his athletic wife. Born in Bombay in 1914, Phyllis was a national champion in several sports, particularly tennis, badminton, and table tennis. Having no opportunity to compete overseas, she played matches against world champions who passed through Bombay. As a young woman in her twenties, she left Bombay in 1942 to become an art teacher in Karachi, where she met and married Alec. In 1948, Alec and Phyllis moved to Bombay where they shared their two-bedroom apartment with displaced family members: Alec's parents; his sister, Kitty; his aunt

Matilda; and perhaps others as the need arose. The help that the extended family gave to one another was crucial in these difficult times.

In 1950, Teresa moved to London, encouraged by expatriate friends, Anglo-Indians from Singapore whom she had met in Karachi. She worked with her friend Coral in the East End and lived in a boardinghouse in Finsbury Park. Eventually, she got a job at the Indian consulate in London, allowing her to travel frequently to Bombay. Access to her home city of Karachi, however, was almost impossible. Her brother Ken died in Karachi, survived by his wife, who still lives there. Her brother Eric is now retired but continues to be active in international relations, writing for various journals and newspapers on the subjects of national security and peace.

Cyril Vas, Teresa's father
Karachi, circa 1915

The Train Has Reached Amritsar

There were very few passengers in the compartment. The Sardarji, sitting opposite me, had been telling me stories about the war. He had fought on the Burmese front, and every time he talked about the white soldiers, he laughed at them derisively. There were also three Pathan traders in the compartment. One of them, dressed in green, lay stretched out on the upper berth. He was a jovial man who had joked throughout the journey with a frail-looking Babu. That Babu seemed to be from Peshawar, because at times they talked to each other in Pushto. On the berth opposite me and to my right sat an old woman whose head and shoulders were covered. She had been telling the beads of her rosary for quite some time. There may have been other passengers in the compartment, but I can't remember them anymore.

The train moved slowly, the passengers gossiped with each other, the wheat fields outside swayed gently in the breeze, and I was happy because I was going to Delhi to watch the Independence Day celebrations.

When I think back on those days, they seem to be shrouded in mist. Perhaps the past always seems hazy. And as the future opens up before us, the past becomes even more indistinct.

The decision to create Pakistan had just been announced, and people speculated about the shape of things to come. But no one could foresee the future clearly. The Sardarji, sitting opposite me, asked me repeatedly whether I thought Jinnah Sahib would continue to live in Bombay or move to Pakistan. My answer was always the same: "Why should he leave Bombay? What would be the point? He can always go to Pakistan and come back." There was speculation about which side of the border Lahore and Gurdaspur would find themselves. Nothing had changed in the way people talked to each other or joked together. A few people had abandoned their homes and run away, while those who had chosen to stay back had merely laughed at them. No one knew what to do, what steps to take. Some people rejoiced at the creation of Pakistan; others rejoiced at India's independence. In a few places there had been riots, but in other places preparations were being made for the celebration of freedom. Given the country's history, everyone felt that after Independence the riots would automatically stop. However, the golden glow of freedom was surrounded by uncertainty and darkness. Only occasionally did one catch a glimpse of the future through the surrounding haze.

Soon after we crossed the Jhelum, the Pathan sitting on the upper berth untied a bundle, took out chunks of boiled meat and nan, and offered them to the passengers. In his jovial way, he invited the Babu sitting next to me to share them with him. "Here, Babu, eat. You will become strong like us. Your wife will be pleased. Eat it, dalkhor. You are weak because you only eat dal."

Everyone in the compartment laughed. The Babu smiled, shook his head, and said something in Pushto.

The other Pathan joined in the teasing and said, "Oh, zalim, if you don't want it from our hands, pick it up yourself. I swear it's only goat's meat and nothing else."

The Pathan sitting on the upper berth chuckled and added, "Oh, son of a swine, no one will know. We won't tell your wife. If you share meat with us, we'll drink dal with you."

Everyone laughed. The Babu smiled, shook his head, and said something in Pushto again.

"How can we let you sit there and stare at us while we eat? It's not courteous." The Pathans were in a good mood.

"He doesn't want to take food from you because you haven't washed your hands," the fat Sardarji said and tittered at his own joke. He was reclining on the berth, and half his belly had spilled over. "The Babu doesn't want to accept meat from your hands because you have just woken up and have begun eating. There is no other reason." As he said that, he looked at me, winked, and tittered.

"If you don't eat meat, you should travel in the ladies' compartment. Why sit here?" Again, the whole compartment laughed. There were other passengers in the compartment, but a sort of informality had grown among those of us who had been together since the beginning.

"Oh, zalim, come and sit, sit with me. Let's tell each other stories," one of the Pathans said.

The train stopped at a station, and lots of new passengers pushed their way in.

"What station is it?" someone asked.

"Wazirabad, I hope," I replied, looking out of the window.

The train didn't stop there for long. But before it left, there was a minor incident. A man had stepped down from the next compartment to get some water. He had just begun to fill his pot when he suddenly turned around with a start and ran back. Some water spilled out of his pot. But the manner in which he had been startled was revealing in itself. Others who were standing around the tap also ran back towards their compartments. I had seen people run in fear like that before. Within a few seconds, the platform was deserted. Inside our compartment, however, people were still laughing and joking.

"Something is wrong," the Babu sitting next to me muttered.

Something was certainly wrong. But none of us was able to find out what had happened. Since I had seen many riots, I could sense the slight change in the atmosphere. The sound of doors shutting, people standing on rooftops, and an eerie silence—they were all the signs of a riot.

Suddenly, there was an altercation at the door opposite the one that opened onto the platform. Some passengers were trying to get in.

"There is no room in here. Don't try to force your way in!" someone shouted.

Shut the door! Can't you see there is no room! People think they can push their way in! Many passengers shouted at the same time.

As long as a passenger outside tries to force his way in, people inside oppose him. But the moment he gets in, all opposition subsides and he becomes a part of the inner world of the compartment, and at the next station he begins to shout and scream at other passengers trying to get in. "There is no room here—go to the next compartment! People think they can walk in!…"

The commotion at the door increased. A man who had a drooping moustache and was wearing tattered clothes was trying to squeeze his way into the compartment. From his filthy clothes, it appeared that he worked in a halwai's shop. Without paying attention to the protests of the other passengers, he turned around and began pulling in an enormous black trunk.

"Come on, climb in!" he shouted to someone behind him. A thin, frayed woman climbed up, followed by a young, dark girl of sixteen or seventeen. People continued to scream at them. The Sardarji had to get up and sit on his berth.

Shut the door! People barge in as if they are walking into their father's house! Don't let anyone else in! What are you doing? Push him out! Everyone shouted at the same time.

The man continued to pull his trunk in while his wife and daughter stood against the restroom door.

Couldn't you have found another compartment?…Did you have to bring women in here too?…

The man was breathless, and his clothes were soaked through with sweat. Having pulled in the trunk, he began hauling in a bundle of wooden legs for his cot.

"I have a ticket. We are not travelling without tickets. I was lucky to reach the station." Suddenly all the passengers fell silent.

But the Pathan sitting on the lower berth yelled, "Get out of here! Can't you see there is no room?" Blind with rage, he suddenly got up and tried to kick the man. Unfortunately, he missed him, and the kick landed on the wife's stomach. She screamed with pain and collapsed on the floor.

The man had no time to argue with the passengers. He was much too busy collecting his luggage. But an ominous silence descended on the compartment. The man began pulling in large bundles packed with his things.

Seeing that, the Pathan sitting on the upper berth lost his patience and yelled, "Throw him out! Who does he think he is?!" The Pathan sitting on the lower berth got up and threw the man's trunk out the door of the compartment. It fell at the feet of a coolie in a red uniform.

No one interfered. Only the old woman sitting in a corner muttered, "Have some pity. Be kind to them and let them come in. Come, child, come and sit next to me. We'll somehow manage! Leave them alone, you scoundrels, let them in."

Before the man could pull all his baggage in, the train began to move.

"My luggage! My luggage has been left behind!" he screamed in despair.

"Father, our luggage is still outside," said the girl as she trembled with fear.

"Get down, down!" shouted the man in despair. He threw the rest of his luggage out and, holding the iron bars of the door, jumped down himself. His terrified daughter and his wife, who was still groaning with pain, followed him.

"You are cruel people—that was an awful thing to have done," the old woman protested loudly. "There is no pity left in your hearts. He had a young daughter. You are cruel, pitiless people. You pushed them out."

The train sped past the deserted platform. There was an uneasy silence in the compartment. No one had the courage to defy the Pathans.

Just then, the frail Babu sitting next to me touched my arm and whispered, "Fire. Look, something is burning."

The train had left the city behind. We saw flames leaping out of the clouds of smoke that rose above the city.

"A riot. That is why people were scared at the platform. There has been a clash somewhere."

The city was in flames. The passengers in the compartment rushed to the windows to catch a glimpse of the fire.

After the train left the city far behind, there was silence in the compartment. When I turned around to look at the passengers, I noticed that the Babu's face was pale and that his forehead was covered with sweat. He looked deathly pale. I realized then that each passenger was nervous and suspicious of his neighbour. The Sardarji got up from his seat and sat down next to me. The Pathan on the lower berth climbed up to join his two companions on the upper berth. Perhaps the conditions in the other compartments were the same. Everyone was tense. The lights had been turned off. The old woman was telling her rosary. The three Pathans on the upper berth quietly watched everyone below. The passengers were alert to everything around them.

"What station was that?" someone asked.

"Wazirabad," another person replied.

The name produced a strange reaction amongst the passengers. The Pathans became less tense while the silence amongst the Hindus and Sikhs became more ominous. One of the Pathans took some snuff out of a small box and sniffed it. The other Pathans did the same. The old woman continued to tell her beads over and over again and mutter something in a hoarse voice.

There was an ominous silence at the next station where the train stopped. Not even a bird was in sight. A mushqee, however, walked across the deserted platform with a bag full of water on his back, offering some to the passengers. "Water, come and drink water," he cried. The women and children sitting in the ladies' compartment stretched out their hands.

"There's been a communal riot here. Many people have been killed." It appeared as if he was the only man who had stepped out to do a good deed.

As soon as the train began to move, people pulled their windows down. One could hear, over the clatter of the wheels, the loud rattle of windows being pulled shut in compartments far away.

The Babu was so terrified that he jumped up from his seat and lay down flat on the floor. His face was tense with fear. Seeing him thus, one of the Pathans on the upper berth mockingly said, "Oh, coward, are you a man or a woman? Don't lie there on the floor. You are a disgrace to all men." Then he added something in Pushto and laughed. The Babu lay on the floor without saying anything in reply. The other passengers sat in tense silence. The atmosphere in the compartment was charged with fear.

"We won't let a coward stay in our compartment. Oh, Babu, get out at the next station and go sit in the ladies' compartment."

The Babu's lips were dry. He stammered something and then fell silent. After some time he got up, dusted his clothes, and resumed his seat. I didn't know why he had decided to lie on the floor. Maybe when he heard the sound of the shutters being pulled down, he thought that people outside were either throwing stones or firing at the train.

I was confused. It was possible that one person had, in panic, pulled the shutters of his window down and that others had instinctively followed his example.

Tense and nervous, we continued on our journey. The night outside grew darker. The passengers watched each other suspiciously. Whenever the train slowed down, they stared at each other apprehensively. Whenever it stopped, the silence became unbearable. Only the Pathans seemed to be unconcerned. After a while, however, they too stopped chatting because no one was in the mood to talk to them.

A little later the Pathans began to doze, while the other passengers continued to stare anxiously into nothingness. The old woman covered her head, folded her legs up on the seat, and went to sleep. One of the Pathans, climbing onto the upper berth once again, pulled out his rosary and began counting the black beads mechanically.

The moon had appeared in the sky by then, and the world outside seemed even more mysterious and threatening. In the far distance, we

Alex Cordeiro, Teresa's cousin
(Karachi Goan Association
Hall in background)
Depot Lines, Karachi, circa 1920

Mattie Vas (front row, left),
Teresa's aunt
circa 1910

occasionally saw flames leaping up into the sky. Cities were burning all around us. There were times when the train screamed through the night; at other times, it crawled for miles.

Suddenly the Babu, who had been looking out the window, shouted excitedly. "We have crossed Harbanspura!" All the other passengers were startled by his shrill voice. They turned to look at him.

"Oh, Babu, why are you screeching?" the Pathan with the rosary asked in surprise. "Do you want to get down here? Shall I pull the chain?" He continued to make fun of the Babu. It was obvious that he neither had heard of Harbanspura nor was aware of its importance to the passengers.

The Babu didn't say anything in reply. He merely shook his head, looked at the Pathan, and turned around to look out the window again.

Everyone in the compartment was silent. The engine blew its whistle and slowed down. There was a loud clatter of the wheels. Perhaps the train had changed tracks. The Babu continued to lean out the window and stare ahead.

"We have arrived!" he shouted again in excitement. "We have arrived in Amritsar!" He leapt up, whipped around to face the Pathan, and began shouting, "Come down, you bastard! You son of a bitch!…May your mother…"

The Babu began to hurl filthy curses at the Pathan. With the rosary in his hand, the Pathan turned to look at the Babu and said, "Oh, Babu, what's the matter? What have I said?"

Seeing the Babu greatly agitated, the other passengers sat up.

"Come down, you son of a bitch!…You dared to kick a Hindu woman, you bastard!…"

"Oh, Babu, stop cursing and screaming. I'll cut your tongue out, you son of a pig."

"You dare to abuse me! May your mother…" The Babu shouted as he stood on his seat. He was trembling with rage.

"Enough, enough," the Sardarji said. "Don't fight. We don't have far to go now."

"I'll break your legs! You think the train belongs to you?!" the Babu continued to shout.

"Oh, Babu, what have I said? Everyone wanted to throw them out, so I pushed them. Why curse me alone? If you don't stop, I'll cut out your tongue."

The old woman pleaded, "Please sit down and be calm. Please, in the name of God, be calm."

The Babu seemed to be possessed and was muttering something incoherently. He continued to shout, "You pretend to be brave like a lion in your own backyard! Now talk, you son of a bitch!"

The train slowly pulled into the Amritsar station. The platform was crowded. The people who peered into the compartment wanted to ask only one thing: "What's happening back there? Where have the riots broken out?"

The entire platform was buzzing with talk about the riots. The passengers in the train had pounced upon the few hawkers on the platform. They were hungry and thirsty.

A few Pathans appeared at the window of our compartment. The moment they spotted the Pathans inside, they began talking to them in Pushto. I looked around for the Babu. He was nowhere in sight. I was disturbed. He had been trembling with rage. I didn't know what he would do. The Pathans in our compartment collected their bundles and left with the other Pathans to sit in a compartment further up. This segregation, which had taken place earlier in our compartment, was now taking place in the entire train.

The crowd around the hawkers began to thin out. People started walking back towards their compartments. I suddenly saw the Babu. His face was still pale, and a lock of hair had fallen across his forehead. As he came closer, I noticed that he was carrying an iron rod in his hand. I didn't know where he had found it. Before entering the compartment, he hid the rod behind his back, and as he sat down on the seat next to mine, he slipped it under the berth. When he raised his eyes, he was startled to find that the Pathans were no longer sitting on the upper berth.

"The bastards have run away. The sons of bitches…they have all escaped." He stood up and started shouting angrily, "Why did you let them escape?! You are all impotent and cowardly!"

The train was very crowded. Many new passengers had boarded it. No one paid him any attention.

The train began to move, and once again, he sat down on the seat next to me. But he was very upset and continued muttering to himself.

The train lurched forward. The passengers who had travelled with us had eaten as many puris as they could and had quenched their thirst. The train was now passing through a region in which there was no danger to their lives and property.

The new passengers were gossiping. The train had begun to move at a steady pace. Soon the passengers began to doze. But the Babu continued to stare into space. He repeatedly asked me where the Pathans had gone after getting down from the berth. He seemed to be possessed.

Soon even I was lulled to sleep by the rhythmic movement of the train. There was no space to lie down, so I slept where I sat. My body swayed with the train. Sometimes when I woke up, I heard the Sardarji lying on the opposite berth snoring comfortably. He looked like a corpse. Indeed, I felt, looking at the awkward postures people were reposing in, that I was travelling on a train full of dead bodies. The Babu, however, was restless. He sometimes leaned out of the window and sometimes sat still, his back erect against the wall.

Whenever the train stopped at a station and the clatter of its wheels ceased, a deep silence fell over everything. In such a silence, even the sound of something falling, or the footsteps of someone getting down, startled me out of my sleep.

Once when I woke up, I noticed that the train was moving slowly. It was dark inside the compartment. All the lights had been switched off. I looked out of the window and saw the red light of a signal glowing somewhere far behind. We had just passed a station, but the train had not yet picked up speed.

I heard a vague sound outside the compartment. Then, still half asleep, I saw the shadow of something moving. I stared at it for a while and then forgot about it. It was nearly dawn.

Suddenly, I heard someone outside bang on the door of the compartment. I turned around to look. The door was shut. I again heard someone bang on the door. It seemed as if someone was hitting the door with a stick. When I leaned outside the window, I saw a man on the footboard of the compartment. He had a lathi in his hand and a bundle over his shoulder. His clothes were dirty, and he had a beard. When I looked down, I saw a woman running barefoot alongside the train. She was carrying two bundles in her hands. Because of their weight, she couldn't run fast. The man standing on the footboard urged her again and again, "Come on, climb up!"

The man banged on the door with his lathi and called out, "Open the door! In the name of Allah, open the door!"

He was breathless. "In the name of Allah, open the door! There is a woman with me. She'll be left behind…"

I saw the Babu jump up from his seat, rush to the window, and ask, "Who is it? There is no room in here."

The man outside pleaded, "For the sake of Allah, she'll be left behind…"

The man pushed his hand in through the window and groped for the latch.

"There is no room in here. Get down from the train!" the Babu screamed, and in the next instant he pulled the door open with a jerk.

"Ya Allah," I heard the man exclaim with relief.

At that very instant, I saw the iron rod flash in the Babu's hand. He gave the man a sharp blow on his head. I was so shocked that I couldn't move. At first I thought that the blow had had no effect. The man still held on to the bars of the door. The bundle had slipped down his shoulder and hung on his arm.

Two or three thin streams of blood began to flow down the man's face. In the faint light of the morning, I saw the man grimace with pain. He uttered "Ya Allah" a few times, groaned, and staggered. He looked at the Babu with eyes that were barely open, as if trying to ask his assailant what crime he had committed. The shadows of the night scattered. I saw terror on the man's face.

The woman, who was running along the track, was shouting and cursing. She didn't know what had happened. She thought that her husband had staggered under the weight of the bundle he was carrying. Running beside him, she kept trying to place his feet back on the footboard of the compartment.

Suddenly, the man's grip on the door handles loosened, and he fell to the ground like a tree that had been chopped down. As soon as he fell, the woman stopped running, as if both of them had reached their journey's end at the same time.

The Babu stood at the door like a statue. The iron bar was still in his hand. His arm didn't seem to have the strength to throw it away. I was afraid and sat unnoticed in my corner, staring at him.

After some time, the Babu stirred. A strange impulse made him lean out the door and look back. Somewhere far behind, next to the railway tracks, lay a dark heap. The train continued on its journey.

The Babu roused himself out of his trance. He threw the iron rod out the door, then turned around and cast his eyes over the passengers. They were all asleep. He didn't notice me.

He closed the door shut. After examining his clothes carefully, he checked both his hands and sniffed them to see if they smelled of blood. After that, he walked quietly across the compartment and sat down on his seat.

Slowly, the morning sun dispelled the darkness. Bright and clear light spread over everything. No one had pulled the chain to stop the train. The body of the man who had fallen had been left miles behind. The wheat fields swayed gently in the breeze.

The Sardarji woke up and scratched his body. The Babu sat quietly with his hands behind his head and stared into space. There was a shadow of a beard on his face.

Seeing the Babu sitting opposite him, the Sardar laughed and said, "You look frail, Babu, but you are brave. You showed real courage back there. The Pathans got scared of you and ran away. If they had stayed here, you would have smashed the heads of all of them."

The Babu smiled in reply—a terrifying smile. He continued to stare at the Sardar's face for a long time.

Translation from Hindi by Alok Bhalla

Sophie Vas at family home
Depot Lines, Karachi, circa 1915

Joseph and Mattie Vas (rear)
Fred Vas, Joseph's brother (front)
Karachi, circa 1915

Toba Tek Singh

Two or three years after the Partition, it occurred to the governments of India and Pakistan that along with the transfer of the civilian prisoners, a transfer of the inmates of the lunatic asylums should also be made. In other words, Muslim lunatics from Indian institutions should be sent over to Pakistan, and Hindu and Sikh lunatics from Pakistani asylums should be allowed to go to India.

It is debatable whether this was a judicious step. Nonetheless, several high-level conferences took place, and the day of the transfer was fixed. Following a great deal of initial investigation, those inmates who had relatives in India were retained there, while the rest were transported to the border. Since there were no Hindus or Sikhs in Pakistan, the question of retaining anyone there did not arise. All the Hindus and Sikhs in the asylums were taken to the border in the custody of the police.

What happened in India is not known. But here, in the Lahore asylum, the news of the transfer resulted in interesting speculation among the inmates. One man, who had been reading *Zamindar* regularly for nearly twelve years, was approached by a friend.

"What is Pakistan?"

"A place in India where they manufacture razors," he answered after much deliberation.

His friend appeared to be satisfied by the answer.

A Sikh lunatic asked another Sikh, "Sardarji, why are we being sent to Hindustan? We can't even speak their language."

"But I know the language of the Hindustanis," the first one interjected with a smile, adding, "Hindustanis are devilish, they strut about haughtily…"

During the course of a bath one morning, an inmate shouted, "Pakistan Zindabad!" so loudly that he slipped on the floor and fainted.

Some of the inmates were not deranged at all. Many of them were murderers whose relatives had bribed the asylum authorities to keep them there so that they would be safe from the hangman's noose. These men had some idea of what was going on and knew something about Pakistan. But they did not have all the facts. Not much could be ascertained from newspapers alone, and since the guards on duty were illiterate for the most part, little information could be gained by talking to them. All they knew was that there was a man, Mohammed Ali Jinnah, who was known as Quaid-e-Azam, and that he had founded, for the Muslims, a separate country called Pakistan. Where was Pakistan? What were its boundaries? They did not know. For this very reason all the inmates who were altogether mad found themselves in a quandary; they could not figure out whether they were in Pakistan or India, and if they were in Pakistan, then how was it possible that only a short while ago they had been in India when they had not moved from the asylum at all?

For one lunatic, the entire issue of Hindustan-Pakistan and Pakistan-Hindustan resulted in further disorientation. One day, while he was sweeping the floor, he suddenly suspended his task and climbed onto a tree, where he remained for nearly two hours. During that time, he lectured extensively and nonstop on the matter of Pakistan versus Hindustan. When ordered by the guards to come down, he climbed higher still; when threatened with force, he said, "I want to live neither in Pakistan nor in Hindustan—I will live on this tree."

He descended from the tree when his fever cooled somewhat, and embracing his Hindu and Sikh friends, he cried bitterly. He was saddened by the thought of their impending departure to India.

One morning, a Muslim engineer who used to spend most of his time walking back and forth in a particular part of the garden suddenly took off his clothes and began running about naked.

A fat Muslim from Chiniot, who had once been an active member of the Muslim League and who bathed at least fifteen times during the day, suddenly gave up bathing altogether. His name was Mohammed Ali. One day he announced that he was Quaid-e-Azam, Mohammed Ali Jinnah. Following his example, a Sikh in his enclosure announced that he was Master Tara Singh. Blood would have been spilled, but luckily both men were declared to be dangerous and were confined to separate quarters.

There was a lawyer in the asylum, a young man from Lahore who had lost his sanity over a tragic love affair. He was deeply grieved when he discovered that Amritsar had become part of India, because the girl he had been in love with was from there. She had rejected this young lawyer, but despite his mental state, he still cared for her. And he cursed all the leaders, both Muslim and Hindu, who were responsible for splitting Hindustan in two. His beloved had become a Hindustani while he was now a Pakistani.

Some of the other inmates tried to comfort the lawyer. They told him he would be sent to Hindustan, where his beloved lived. But he did not wish to leave Lahore, for he felt that his practice would not thrive in Amritsar.

In the European Ward were two Anglo-Indians. When they heard that the English had given Hindustan freedom and then left, they were devastated. In the course of several secret meetings, they discussed the future of their status in the asylum. Would the European Ward be retained? Would they continue to get breakfast? Would they be forced to eat the bloody Indian chapati instead of bread?

A Sikh who had been in the asylum for fifteen years used to mutter constantly to himself. "Oper di gur gur di annexe di bay dhania di mung di daal di of laltain," he kept saying, over and over again. He slept neither at night nor during the day. According to the guards, he had not slept at all in fifteen years. He did not lie down either. Sometimes he leaned against a wall.

His feet and ankles were swollen from standing too much, but in spite of the bodily discomfort he experienced, he refused to rest. With great seriousness he listened to all the talk about the matter, then assumed a solemn air and replied, "Oper di gur gur di annexe di bay dhania di mung daal di of di Pakistan government"—his usual gibberish.

Later on "of di Pakistan government" was replaced by "of di Toba Tek Singh government." Now he began asking people where Toba Tek Singh was, for that was his hometown. But no one could answer that question for him. And if someone did make an attempt to figure out the present status of Toba Tek Singh, more confusion would follow. It had been rumoured that Sialkot, which was once in Hindustan, was now in Pakistan; who could say where Lahore, which was in Pakistan today, would be tomorrow, and was there anyone who could guarantee that both Pakistan and Hindustan would not disappear someday?

This man's kesh had become thin and straggly, and since he seldom bathed, his kesh and his beard had become glued together, giving him a ghoulish appearance. But he was a harmless man. In fifteen years, he had not once been involved in a brawl with the other inmates. The guards only knew that he was from Toba Tek Singh, where he owned land. He had been a well-to-do landowner. Then, without warning, he had gone insane. His relatives had bound him with iron chains, brought him to the asylum, and admitted him.

They visited him once every month, inquired after his well-being, and then left. Their visits continued until the disturbances began.

His name was Bishan Singh, but people now called him Toba Tek Singh. Though it was apparent that he was impervious to the passage of time, he waited for the visits from his relatives and was ready for them when they came. Before their arrival, he would tell the guard his "visit" was coming; he bathed, scrubbed his body with soap, oiled his hair and combed it, put on his best clothes, which he had reserved for this occasion, and then went to see his visitors. He remained silent when they addressed him. Sometimes, however, he muttered, "Oper di gur gur di annexe di bay dhania di mung daal di of laltain."

He had a daughter who was grown up now. As a child, she cried whenever she saw her father, and she continued to cry for him when she was a young woman.

When the disturbances began, Bishan Singh started asking the people at the asylum where Toba Tek Singh was, and since he was unable to receive a satisfactory answer, his curiosity increased. His "visits" had also stopped. He had been able to sense the impending visits of his relatives. But now it seemed the little voice in his heart that had told him they were coming was stilled.

He longed for his visitors, who had been sympathetic and had brought him gifts of fruit, sweets, and clothing. He was convinced they would be able to tell him if Toba Tek Singh was in Pakistan or in India, his conviction stemming from his belief that his family came from Toba Tek Singh.

In the lunatic asylum there was a man who believed that he was God. Bishan Singh asked him about Toba Tek Singh. The man laughed raucously. "It is neither in Pakistan nor in Hindustan," he said, "because I haven't given any orders yet."

Bishan Singh pleaded with this "God" to give the orders so that the question of Toba Tek Singh could be settled once and for all. The man said that he was too busy, that there were too many other orders to be taken care of.

Finally Bishan Singh lost his temper. "Oper di gur gur di bay dhania di mung di daal di of wahay guruji, the khalsa and wahay guruji the fathey!" He probably wanted to say that if the man had been a Sikh god instead of a Muslim god, he might have helped Bishan Singh.

A few days prior to the transfer, Bishan Singh was visited by an old Muslim friend. Seeing him, Bishan Singh turned to leave. The guard restrained him. "He's come to see you," the guard said. "This is your friend, Fazal Din." Bishan Singh glanced at his friend briefly, then began muttering his customary nonsense. Fazal Din came forward and placed a hand on his shoulder.

"I wanted to come and see you earlier. I've just been so busy. Your family has left for Hindustan, and everyone is fine…I helped them in whatever way I could. Your daughter Roop Kaur?…" He paused in mid-sentence.

"Roop Kaur?" Bishan Singh looked thoughtful.

"Yes…she…she's fine too," Fazal Din said haltingly. "She also left with the others."

Bishan Singh remained silent.

"They requested me to check on you every once in a while," Fazal Din continued. "Now I hear you're being taken to Hindustan. Give my regards to Bhai Baleer Singh and Bhai Vadhwa Singh…and sister Amrit Kaur. Tell Bhai Baleer I am all right. One of the two cows he left behind has calved, had two calves…One died six days after the birth…And if there's anything more I can do, tell them I am ready anytime. And here, I brought you some sweets."

Taking the bag of sweets from him, Bishan Singh handed it to the guard who was standing nearby.

"Where is Toba Tek Singh?" he then asked Fazal Din.

"Where is Toba Tek Singh?" Fazal Din repeated in amazement, adding, "Where it was before?"

"Is it in Pakistan or in Hindustan?" Bishan Singh asked.

"In Hindustan…well, no, no, in Pakistan, I think." Fazal Din became flustered.

Bishan Singh was muttering again. "Oper di gur gur di annexe di bay dhania di mung di daal di of Pakistan and Hindustan of di dur fitay moonh!" And with that he walked away.

All preparations for the transfer had been completed. Lists of patients had been exchanged, and the day of the transfer had been set.

On an extremely cold day, lorries filled with Hindu and Sikh lunatics left the asylum in Lahore, accompanied by the police and some higher officials. At Wagah, the superintendents from both sides met, and after the initial formalities were out of the way, the actual transfer began, continuing all night.

Getting the lunatics out of the lorries and handing them over to the Indian officials proved to be an arduous task. Many of them refused to leave the lorries, and those who did ran about wildly, making it difficult for the guards and other officials to keep them under control; those who were naked tore off any clothing that was forced on them, many swore and cursed, one or two sang, some fought with each other, and others cried or wailed. Confusion was rampant. The women were also a problem, and the cold weather made everyone's teeth chatter.

Most of the lunatics were not in favour of the transfer because they could not comprehend the reasons for being uprooted from one place and thrown into another. One or two people, not completely mad, shouted, "Pakistan Zindabad!" and "Pakistan Murdabad!" This infuriated both the Muslims and Sikhs, and altercations between them were avoided with great difficulty.

When Bishan Singh's turn came to cross the border, he asked the official who was entering his name in a register, "Where is Toba Tek Singh? In Pakistan or in India?"

The official laughed and said, "In Pakistan."

On hearing this, Bishan Singh leaped back and ran towards the remaining group of men who awaited their turn. The Pakistani soldiers caught him and tried to force him back to the checkpoint. He resisted vigorously.

"Toba Tek Singh is here!" he yelled. "Oper di gur gur di annexe di bay dhania di mung daal di of Toba Tek Singh and Pakistan!"

The authorities attempted to reason with him. "Look, Toba Tek Singh is in Hindustan now—and if he's not there yet, we'll send him there immediately." But he was adamant and would not budge from the spot where he stood. When the guards threatened to use force, he installed himself in a place between the borders and stood there as if no power in the world could move him.

Because he was a harmless man, he was allowed to remain there while the transfer continued.

Before the sun rose, a piercing cry arose from Bishan Singh, who had been quiet and still all this time. Several officers and the guards ran towards him; they saw that the man who had stood on his legs day and night for fifteen years now lay on the ground, prostrate. Beyond a wired fence on one side of him was Hindustan, and beyond a wired fence on the other side was Pakistan. In the middle, on a stretch of land that had no name, lay Toba Tek Singh.

Translation from Urdu by Tahira Naqvi

Cyril and Sophie Vas,
Teresa's parents
Karachi, circa 1915

Lajwanti _____

Do not touch lajwanti, for she will curl up and die.   Punjabi folk song

The carnage of the Partition was at last over. Thousands of people joined hands, washed the blood off their bodies, and turned their attention to those who had not been physically mutilated, but whose lives had been shattered and souls had been scarred.

In every lane, in every locality, "Rehabilitation" committees were set up, and in the beginning there was a lot of enthusiasm for programmes like Trade for the Displaced, Land for the Refugees, and Homes for the Dispossessed. There was, however, one that was neglected by everyone. That was the programme for the rehabilitation of women who had been abducted and raped. Its slogan was "Honour them. Give them a place in your hearts." This programme was opposed by the priests of Narain Baba's temple and by all those good and orthodox people who lived in its vicinity.

A committee was formed to campaign for the implementation of the programme by the residents of Mohalla Shakoor, a locality near Narain Baba's temple. Babu Sunderlal was elected its secretary by a majority of eleven votes. According to Sardar Sahib, the lawyer, the old petitioner of Chauki Kalan, and other well-respected people of the locality, no one could be trusted to do the job with greater zeal and commitment than Sunderlal because his own wife had been abducted. Her name was Lajo—Lajwanti.

Every morning Sunderlal, Rasalu, Neki Ram, and others led a procession through the streets of the city. They sang hymns and folk songs. But whenever they started singing, "Do not touch lajwanti/for she will curl up/and die," Sunderlal's voice would begin to choke with tears. He would continue to follow the procession in silence and wonder about Lajwanti's fate: "Where is she now, how is she, does she ever think of me, will I ever see her again?…" As he walked on the hard and stony streets, his steps would falter.

But soon there came a time when he ceased to think about Lajwanti with so much sorrow. To ease his pain, he began to sympathize with the sufferings of others and immersed himself in service to them. But even though he devoted himself to giving solace to those who needed it, he could not help wondering how fragile human beings really were. A careless word could hurt them. They were delicate like the lajwanti plant; the mere shadow of a hand could make them tremble and wither...And how often had he mistreated Lajwanti himself. How frequently had he thrashed her because he didn't like the way she sat or looked, or the way she served his food!

His poor Lajo was a slender, naive village girl—supple and tender and fresh, like a young mulberry bush! Tanned by the sun, she was full of joyous vitality and restless energy. She moved with the mercurial grace of a drop of dew on a large leaf. When Sunderlal first saw her, he thought that she wouldn't be able to endure hardships. He himself was tough and well built. But he soon realized that she could lift all kinds of heavy weights, bear a lot of suffering, and even tolerate the beatings he gave her. He began to treat her even more cruelly and lost sight of the limit, beyond which the patience of any human being breaks. Lajwanti herself was, perhaps, responsible for the blurring of these limits; for even after the severest of beatings, she would begin to laugh happily if she saw a faint smile on Sunderlal's face. She would run up to him, put her arms around his neck, and say, "If you beat me again, I shall never speak to you..." It would be obvious that she had left the thrashing behind. Like the other girls of the village, she knew that all husbands beat their wives. Indeed, if some men let their wives show independence and spirit, the other women would turn up their noses in contempt and say, "What kind of man is he! He can't even control a woman!" The fact that husbands were expected to beat their wives was also in their folk songs. Lajo herself used to sing, "I shall never marry a city boy/He wears boots and my back is slender..."

Nevertheless, when Lajwanti saw a city boy, she fell in love with him. His name was Sunderlal. He had come to her village with the bridegroom's party to attend Lajwanti's sister's wedding. When he saw Lajwanti, he had whispered in the bridegroom's ear, "If your sister-in-law is so spicy, yar, your wife must be really hot!" Lajwanti had overheard Sunderlal. She did not notice that his boots were large and ugly, and she forgot that her back was slender.

Whenever the processionists sang the song about lajwanti in the morning, Sunderlal would feel tormented by memories of his wife, and he would swear to himself, "If I ever find her again, if I ever again do...I shall honour her and give her a place in my heart...I shall tell everyone that the women who were abducted are innocent. They are victims of the brutality and the rapacity of the rioters...A society that refuses to accept them back, that does not rehabilitate them...is a rotten, foul society, which should be destroyed..." He would spend long hours pleading with people to take such women back into their homes, to give them the respect due a mother, daughter, sister, or wife. He would exhort people, "Never remind them, either by word or gesture, of the humiliations they have suffered; don't ever reopen their wounds. They are gentle and fragile like the leaves of the lajwanti…If you touch them, they will curl up and die…"

In order to make the work of the Committee for the Rehabilitation of Women more generously and widely accepted, Sunderlal had organized many processions through the city streets. The processionists sang hymns and folk songs. The best time for such processions was around four or five in the morning, when there was neither the chatter of people nor the noise of traffic. Even the watchful street dogs slept quietly near the warm tandoors. When people, wrapped in their quilts and sleeping comfortably, heard the singers, they would mutter drowsily, "Oh, those singers again." Children would open their eyes, listen to the chorus chanting, "Honour them, give them a place in your hearts," and be lulled back to sleep.

People listened to Sunderlal's sermons and pleas, sometimes with patience and sometimes with barely concealed irritation. The most intolerant, however, were those women who had come safely across from Pakistan and were now as complacent as large cauliflowers. Their husbands, who stood around them like stiff and proud sentinels, often turned away from Sunderlal and the processionists with a curse.

But words heard in the morning are not easily forgotten. Even if one doesn't understand them, one repeats them like a futile argument, collides with them, hums them as one goes about the tasks of the day. It is because such words had left their mark on some people that, when Miss Mridula Sarabhai arranged for the exchange of abducted women between India and Pakistan, some families from Mohalla Shakoor agreed to take them back into their homes. Their relatives went to the outskirts of the town near Chauki Kalan to receive them. For some time, the rescued women and their relatives stared at each other like awkward strangers. Then, with their heads hanging in shame and sorrow, they went back to their ruined homes to try to rebuild their lives. Rasalu, Neki Ram, and Sunderlal encouraged them with slogans: "Long live Mahinder Singh," "Sohanlal Zindabad"… They shouted slogans till their voices became hoarse.

There were some amongst these abducted women whose husbands, parents, brothers, and sisters refused to recognize them. "Why didn't they die? Why didn't they take poison to preserve their virtue and honour? Why didn't they jump into a well? Cowards, clinging to life! Thousands of women in the past killed themselves to save their chastity!…" Little did these people understand the courage of the women, the awesome strength with which they had faced death and chosen to go on living in such a world—a world in which even their husbands refused to acknowledge them.

One woman, whose husband turned away from her, sadly repeated her name again and again, "Suhagwati…Suhagwati…"

Another, when she saw her brother in the crowd, cried, "Oh, Bihari, even you refuse to recognize me? You played in my lap as a baby!" Bihari wanted to reach out to her, but stood rooted in his place, paralyzed by the look in the eyes of his parents. His hard-hearted parents turned for instruction to Narain Baba, who stared up at the sky as if searching for an answer from the heavens—but the heavens are no more than an illusion created by our fearful imagination, and the sky is merely the furthest thing to which our eyes can see.

Sunderlal watched the last woman step down from the trucks Miss Sarabhai had brought from Pakistan. Lajo was not in any of them. With patience and quiet dignity, Sunderlal again immersed himself in the work of the committee. The committee members began to lead processions in the evening as well. They had also started organizing small meetings. At these sessions, the old and asthmatic lawyer, Kalka Prashad, would first make a speech full of Sufi sayings, while Rasalu would stand dutifully beside him with a spittoon. During Kalka Prashad's speech, the loudspeaker would hiss and sputter with strange sounds. Then Neki Ram, the pleader, would get up to say something. But the longer he talked and the more he quoted from the Shastras and the Puranas, the more he ended up making a case against the cause he meant to plead for. Watching him make a mess of the argument and lose ground, Babu Sunderlal would intervene to say something. But after only a few sentences, he would stop. His voice would choke. Tears would begin to flow down his face, and overcome with emotion, he would be forced to sit down. A strange hush would descend upon the audience. The few broken sentences spoken by Sunderlal from the depth of his sorrowing soul always made a far greater impression than the Sufi sermons of Kalka Prashad. But the effect would never last long. People would shed a few tears, feel morally cleansed and uplifted, and then return to their homes, as unconcerned as ever about the fate of the abducted women…

One evening, the processionists found themselves in the vicinity of a temple located in the stronghold of the traditional and the orthodox. Sitting on a cement platform under a peepal tree was a crowd of the faithful and the devoted, listening to the Ramayana. Narain Baba was reciting that section in which a washerman, having thrown his wife out of his house, said that he wasn't Raja Ramchandra, who took Sita back even after she had lived with Ravana for years. Stung by the rebuke, Ramchandra had ordered Sita, who was virtuous and faithful, out of his palace even though she was pregnant. Commenting on this situation, Narain Baba said, "That was Ram Rajya! In it even the word of a washerman was respected."

The processionists stood and listened to the recitation of the Ramayana and the commentary. The last sentence provoked Sunderlal, and he said, "We don't want such a Ram Rajya, Baba!"

"Shut up!…Who are you?…Quiet!…," the people in the audience shouted at Sunderlal.

Sunderlal stepped forward and said, "No one can stop me from speaking."

There was another chorus of angry protests. "Silence…We will not let you speak!" From one corner of the crowd, someone even shouted, "We will kill you!"

Gently, Narain Baba said, "Sunderlal, you don't understand the sacred traditions of the Shastras!"

Sunderlal retorted, "But I do understand that in Ram Rajya, a washerman's voice can be heard, but not the voice of Sunderlal."

The same people who had threatened to kill him a moment ago now made space for him under the peepal tree and said, "Let him speak…let him speak…"

As Rasalu and Neki Ram urged him on, Sunderlal said, "Shri Ram was our God. But tell me, Baba, was it just that Ram accepted the word of a washerman as the truth, and doubted the word of his great and honourable Queen?"

Playing with his beard, Narain Baba answered, "Sita was his wife, Sunderlal! You don't understand the importance of that fact!"

"Yes, Baba," Babu Sunderlal replied. "There are many things in this world which are beyond my comprehension. Yet, I believe that in Ram Rajya, a man cannot commit a crime against his own self. To inflict pain on oneself is as unjust as hurting someone else…Even today, Lord Ram has thrown Sita out of his home because she was forced to live with Ravana… Did Sita commit any sin? Wasn't she, like our mothers and sisters today, a victim of violence and deceit?…Is it a question of Sita's truthfulness, faithfulness, or is it a question of Ravana's wickedness? Ravana was a demon… He had ten human heads, but his largest head was that of a donkey!…Once again, our innocent Sitas have been thrown out of their homes…Sita… Lajwanti…"

Sunderlal broke down and wept. Rasalu and Neki Ram picked up their red banners, pasted with slogans that morning by schoolchildren, and started yelling, "Sunderlal Zindabad!" Somebody from the procession shouted, "Mahasati Sita, Zindabad!" And someone else cried, "Shri Ramchandra!"

There was pandemonium. Many voices shouted, "Silence! Silence!" But it was too late. What Narain Baba had achieved, after months of careful teaching, had been undone in a few moments. Many people who had been with him joined the procession led by Kalka Prashad and Hukum Singh, the writer of petitions from Chauki Kalan. These two old people tapped their sticks hard on the ground and raised their banners…Sunderlal walked along with them. There were tears in his eyes. Today he felt his loss even more deeply…The processionists sang with great enthusiasm:

Do not touch lajwanti,
for she will curl up
and die.

Cyril Vas (standing behind cart)

Mattie Vas (second from left),
Teresa's aunt
Goa

The people sang lustily; their song filled the air. The sun had not yet risen. The widow in house number 414 of Mohalla Shakoor stretched her limbs and shifted uneasily in her bed. At that moment Lal Chand, who was from Sunderlal's village and whom Sunderlal and Khalifa Kalka Prashad had helped to set up a ration shop, came running up to Sunderlal. Excited, he cried out breathlessly, "Congratulations, Sunderlal!"

Sunderlal put some tobacco in his chillum and said, "Congratulations for what, Lal Chand?"

"I just saw Lajo Bhabhi!"

The chillum fell from Sunderlal's hand, and the tobacco scattered on the floor. "Where did you see her?" He took Lal Chand by the shoulder and, when he didn't answer quickly enough, shook him hard.

"At the Wagah border."

Sunderlal let go of Lal Chand and said despondently, "It must have been someone else."

"No, Bhai," Lal Chand said, trying to convince him, "I did see her…I saw Lajo."

"How could you recognize her?" Sunderlal asked as he gathered the tobacco scattered on the floor and rubbed it on his palm. "All right, tell me: what are her identifying marks?" he asked as he filled Rasalu's chillum with tobacco.

"A tattoo mark on her chin…another on her cheek…"

"Yes…yes…yes…" Sunderlal cried excitedly, "And a third one on her forehead!" He didn't want to have any doubts.

Suddenly he recalled all the tattoo marks on Lajwanti's body; she had had them painted on her body when she was a child. They were like the soft green spots on a lajwanti plant that disappear when its leaves curl up. Whenever he tried to touch them with his fingers, Lajwanti would curl up with shyness…would try to hide the tattoo marks on her body as if they were some secret and hidden treasure, which could be despoiled by a predator and a thief…Sunderlal trembled with fear and hope; his body began to burn with a strange longing and a pure love.

He again put his hand on Lal Chand's shoulder and asked, "How did Lajo reach Wagah?"

Lal Chand replied, "There was an exchange of abducted women between India and Pakistan."

"What happened then?" Sunderlal asked as he kneeled on the floor. "Tell me, what happened after that?"

Rasalu got up from his cot and, wheezing like a tobacco smoker, asked, "Is it true that Lajo Bhabhi has come back?"

Sticking by his story, Lal Chand said, "At the Wagah border, Pakistan returned sixteen of our women in exchange for sixteen of theirs…But there was some argument…Our volunteers objected that most of the women the Pakistanis had sent back were old, middle-aged, and utterly useless. A large crowd gathered, and heated words were exchanged. Then one of their volunteers pointed at Lajo Bhabhi and said, 'Is this one old? Look at her...Look...Have you returned any woman who is as beautiful as she is?' Lajo Bhabhi stood there trying to hide her tattoo marks from the curious gaze of people. The argument got more heated. Both sides threatened to take back their 'goods.' I cried out, 'Lajo...Lajo Bhabhi!' But our own policemen beat us with their canes and drove us away."

Lal Chand bared his elbow to show the mark of a lathi blow. Rasalu and Neki Ram continued to sit in silence, and Sunderlal stared vacantly into space. Perhaps he was thinking about Lajo, who had returned and yet was so far away...He seemed like a man who had undergone an ordeal and no longer had the strength to ask for help. The violence of the Partition, he felt, still continued. It had merely taken a new form. The only difference was that now people felt no sympathy for those who had suffered. These days if you asked someone about Lahna Singh and his Bhabhi, Banto, who used to live in Sambharwal, the person would curtly answer, "They are dead," and walk away as if nothing serious had happened, nothing out of the ordinary.

There were even more cold-blooded people around now: people who traded in flesh, in living and suffering human beings. They treated women like cows at a cattle fair. At least the slave traders in the past had some conventions and courtesies, and they settled their terms of sale in private. Now the buyers and the sellers had given up the formalities of the old slave traders. They bargained for the women in the open marketplace. The Uzbek buyer stood before rows of naked women and prodded them with his fingers...The women he rejected stood before him sobbing helplessly, clutching their garments and hiding their faces in shame.

Sunderlal was getting ready to go to the Wagah border when he heard about Lajo's return. The news was so sudden that at first he was confused. He couldn't decide what to do. He wanted to go to her at once and yet was afraid to meet her. He was so bewildered that he wanted to spread out all the committee's banners and placards on the floor, sit in their midst, and weep. But then he pulled himself together, and slowly, with measured steps, he made his way to Chauki Kalan, where the abducted women were being exchanged.

Suddenly Lajo was standing in front of him and was trembling with fear. She knew Sunderlal as no one else knew him. He had always mistreated her, and now that she had lived with another man, she dared not imagine what he would do to her.

Sunderlal looked at Lajo. Her head was covered with a red dupatta like a typical Muslim woman, and one end of it was thrown over her left shoulder. She had learned to imitate the women she had lived with in the hope of evading her captors someday. But recently, events had moved so fast—and she had thought of Sunderlal so desperately—that she had the time to neither change her clothes nor think about the way she had worn her dupatta. She was in no state of mind to think about the basic differences between Hindu and Muslim culture or worry about whether her dupatta had to be thrown over her left shoulder or her right. She stood before Sunderlal, trembling with hope and despair...

Sunderlal was shocked. Lajo looked healthier than before. Her complexion seemed clearer and her eyes brighter, and she had put on weight... She looked different from what he had imagined. He had thought that suffering and sorrow would have reduced her to a mere skeleton, that she wouldn't have the strength to utter even a few words. He was startled to see that she had been well treated in Pakistan. He was puzzled. "If she had been comfortable and happy there, why did she agree to return?" he wondered. "Perhaps she has been forced to return by the Indian government..." He didn't, however, say anything to her because he had sworn not to chastise her. It was clear to her that he had failed to read the signs of pain and humiliation in her face. He didn't notice that the brightness of her face was feverish and that her body had lost its youthful tautness. For Sunderlal, the thought of confronting his wife, who had been abducted and raped, was strangely disturbing. But he did not flinch from doing his duty, and he behaved in a manly and courageous manner.

There were many other men at the police station with him. One of them even shouted, "We don't want these sluts! They were defiled by Muslims." But that voice was drowned out by slogans shouted by Rasalu, Neki Ram, and the old lawyer of Chauki Kalan. Cutting through all the noise was the harsh and grating voice of Kalka Prashad. He was coughing and shrieking into the loudspeaker about the need for a new Shastra and a new Veda, which would help people understand the new world confronting them... While people continued to shout slogans, make speeches, and scream abuses, Sunderlal took Lajo by her hand and began walking back towards his home. The scene was a reenactment of the old story about Ramchandra leading Sita back to Ayodhya after years of exile. As in the past, there were rejoicing and sadness, celebrations welcoming the couple home, and a sense of shame at the sufferings they had endured.

Even after Lajwanti's return, Sunderlal continued to work with devotion for the Rehabilitation Committee. He fulfilled his pledge in both word and deed, and those who had earlier mocked him as a sentimental idealist were now convinced of his sincerity. Many people were happy that his wife had returned. There were some, however, who were annoyed at the turn of events. The widow who lived in house number 414 wasn't the only woman who kept her distance from the house of Babu Sunderlal, the social worker.

But Sunderlal ignored all those who either praised him or abused him. The queen of his home had returned and had filled the emptiness of his soul again. He enshrined Lajo like a golden idol in the temple of his heart and guarded her like a jealous devotee. Lajo, who had once trembled before him, was touched by his unexpected kindness and generosity and slowly began to flourish and blossom.

Sunderlal no longer called her Lajo. He addressed her as "Devi." Lajo was deliriously happy. She had never known such joy before. So that she could feel clean again, she wanted to tell Sunderlal, with tears in her eyes, all that she had suffered. But he always shrank away from hearing her story, and Lajo felt apprehensive about her new life of love and kindness. Sometimes at night, when he slept, she would lean over him and gaze at his face. Whenever he caught her doing so and asked her for an explanation, she would merely mumble a vague reply, and he would fall back into exhausted sleep…

Of course, soon after her return, Sunderlal had asked Lajwanti about those "dark days."

"Who was he?"

Lajwanti had lowered her eyes and said, "Jamal." Then she had raised her eyes apprehensively and looked at Sunderlal. She had wanted to say something more, but the look in his eyes was so strange that she had lowered her eyes in silence once more.

"Did he treat you well?" he had asked as he played with her hair.

"Yes."

"He didn't beat you, did he?"

Lajwanti had leaned back, rested her head against his chest, and replied, "No." After a pause, she had added, "He didn't beat me, but I was terrified of him. You used to beat me, but I was never afraid of you…You will never beat me again, will you?"

Sunderlal's eyes had filled with tears, and in a voice full of shame and remorse, he had said, "No, Devi…I shall never beat you again…never…"

"Devi!" Lajwanti had softly echoed the word and begun to sob.

At that moment, she had wanted to tell him everything, but Sunderlal had said, "Let us forget the past! You didn't do anything sinful, did you? Our society is guilty because it refuses to honour women like you as goddesses. It ought to be ashamed of itself. You shouldn't feel dishonoured."

And so Lajwanti's sorrow remained locked up in her breast. Helplessly, she gazed at her body and realized that, since the Partition, it was no longer hers, but the body of a goddess. She was happy, ecstatically happy. But she was also apprehensive. She was afraid that her dream world would suddenly be shattered one day, that she would hear the sound of the footsteps of a stranger…

Slowly, happiness was replaced by suspicion. This was not because Sunderlal had begun to mistreat her again, but because he continued to treat her with excessive kindness. Lajo didn't expect him to be so gentle…She wanted to be Lajo again, the woman who could quarrel with her husband over something trivial and then be caressed. The question of a fight didn't even arise. Sunderlal made her feel as if she was precious and fragile like glass, that she would shatter at the slightest touch…She began to gaze at herself in the mirror and came to the conclusion that she would never be Lajo again. She had returned home, but she had lost everything…Sunderlal had neither the eyes to see her tears nor the ears to hear her sobs… Every morning he went out with the procession through Mohalla Shakoor and joined Rasalu and Neki Ram in singing:

Do not touch lajwanti,
for she will curl up
and die!

Translation from Urdu by Alok Bhalla

Incognita _____

When Mohammad Raees of our village came to ask if he could make a telephone call from the office, I merely pushed the phone towards him with my left hand, without raising my eyes from the file. I didn't hear the name of the person Raees asked for on the telephone; however, when he repeated, "But this was the number she gave me," some unknown reason prompted me to note down the number on the paper lying before me. Replacing the receiver, Raees looked at me guiltily. Amused by his comical expression, I said, "Try dialing again."

I watched Raees's face as he started dialing again after opening his diary to confirm the number. Meanwhile, the guilty expression had vanished from his face. A moment later, he said, in embarrassment, "Sorry, I'm very sorry. The call has been diverted to you again."

When Raees began to wring his hands after replacing the receiver, it was I who said, to save him from awkwardness, "The person who gave you the number must have made a mistake, or you have noted it wrongly. So, who are you trying to call?"

"You wouldn't know the person."

"Who answered the call?"

"A lady."

Though slightly embarrassed at mentioning the "lady," Raees informed me in good humor that her voice was extremely sweet. Rather like Tripti Mitra's.

I laughed out loud. "You are well acquainted with Tripti Mitra's voice on the telephone, it seems?"

Raees guffawed, too. He said, "No, why would that be? Haven't I heard her plays on Kolkata radio?"

I agreed with Raees. Once heard, the voice of Tripti or Shaoli Mitra cannot be forgotten. Observing that Raees had let slip the opportunity to converse with a lady with such a voice, I said, "It's hopeless; you can't accomplish anything at all."

Raees was embarrassed. Eventually, he said, "I'll take your leave, brother."

Alec Vas, Teresa's uncle,
in British Indian Army uniform
circa 1915

I, too, had been hoping that Raees would leave soon. The telephone number was staring me in the eye. I didn't know if Raees had seen me writing the number on a piece of paper; even if he had, he wouldn't tease me too much about it. He was much younger than I was, but would address me as "brother" because we hailed from the same village. He taught now at a college in Comilla. When he visited Dhaka, he would see me at least once and call me every now and then.

After Raees had left, I felt quite amused. I'm quick to avail myself of any opportunity to chat with women on the telephone. Although I can't quite offer a detailed explanation for this, I can say that the thought of whispering into the ear of someone who is somewhere far away, through this inanimate instrument, produces an extraordinary thrill. When old Dr. Muhammad Enamul Haq named the telephone a dur-alapani, or "long-distance communicator," in his attempt to popularize Bengali definitions of English words, I think nobody was happier than I. When he was young, he certainly did not have the opportunity to converse on the telephone. If he had, this incomparable name would have become ours earlier.

Let us return to what I was saying. While I was thinking of a couple of points with which to engage Tripti in an interesting conversation on the telephone, my senior officer sent across an urgent file. I received two telephone calls as well. Neither call was for me. One was for my peon, the other for a colleague from a different section. The peon could not take the call because I had sent him downstairs, but the colleague chattered for a full fifteen, perhaps twenty, minutes in a pure Barisal accent, on subjects such as the sale and purchase of land, his niece's wedding, and his son's job interview. Trying to concentrate on the file marked URGENT, I found my colleague's Barisal vocabulary excessively jarring to the ears. I put down my pen and sat in silence. When the conversation was over, I opened the file again, only to find that it was necessary to discuss the matter with my senior officer before presenting my conclusions. By then, Tripti-or-Shaoli had vanished from my consciousness; when she reappeared, it was almost two o'clock.

Glancing again at the number I had got from Raees, I smiled to myself as I dialed one digit at a time. I think I have an inborn affinity with this instrument. And yet I am an utterly rustic person, far from being accustomed to the sight of a telephone from birth. The first time I ever saw one was when I was a student of Class Eight or Nine. And I actually used a telephone only after completing college. That, too, after I arrived in Dhaka. How my hands would tremble at first, and even my throat would feel parched. I would speak in a very loud voice. Lest I hold the receiver upside down, I would remind myself that one must keep one's mouth close to the end of the receiver attached to the wire. When I consider why the telephone should cast such a deep shadow over the life of one such as myself, I feel it's because of this congenital affinity. If I tell an anecdote, you will understand what I mean. Since my wife will not read this, I state fearlessly in writing that, before marriage, we used to engage in many telephone conversations. Even after marriage, I have engaged in a few long-distance talks that have come close and then floated away like flotsam in a tide. I have no regrets about them. One of my tele-mates called me a few days back to ask how my chats with beautiful strangers were going. Without pausing to think, I said, "Wonderful. I can't leave the throne vacant after all." I think she was upset to hear my answer.

Long live the telephone, known in refined language as the long-distance communicator. Dear departed Dr. Muhammad Enamul Haq, you might seem fearsome to students of the Bengali department on account of your grammar textbook and your history of literature. But you are a man after my own heart for coining this term. I shall now use your long-distance communicator to speak to Tripti Mitra or Shaoli Mitra. Please grant me your blessings.

The phone rang just twice before Raees's Tripti-or-Shaoli-Mitra answered it. "Hello."

"Is this 654321?"

"Yes."

I suddenly couldn't remember what topic of conversation I had planned to raise after Tripti-or-Shaoli said yes. As I groped for words—groped all around the receiver, all around the room, in all the leaves of the deodar tree beside the window—the voice at the other end asked in considerable surprise, "Who are you—whom do you want to speak with?"

"No, I mean, no woman could be expected to answer the phone at the number I have dialed."

Exactly, exactly as in the play *Aparajita,* Tripti-or-Shaoli laughed in a husky voice. "But the number you mentioned is correct."

Summoning up a catch in my throat, as if I had never been so surprised in my life, I said, "That's what I think, too, but how is it possible?"

"Quite a while ago, a gentleman had also called, asking for this number. Was it you who made that call?"

I hastily replied, "No, no, why would it be me?"

"Oh-oh-oh."

From Tripti-or-Shaoli's expression of surprise as she said "Oh-oh-oh," I struggled for a while to assess her age; finally, I blurted out, "The sound of your voice is exquisite, I must say."

I thought my comment would have pleased her. But I could not understand what she felt; I only heard her say, "Is that so?"

"I'm merely speaking the truth."

Tripti-or-Shaoli gave a small laugh, followed by an even smaller reply, "How would I know?"

I was looking for just such a cue, one I could build on to extend the conversation. As soon as I heard her say, "How would I know?" I replied, "Perhaps you are not meant to know, but we listeners can tell."

This time she laughed rather loudly. I sensed that my words had struck home. I have seen that when words are appealing, both parties can effortlessly carry on chatting for twenty to thirty minutes even while asserting that there is nothing to be said. I immediately began to prepare myself. And just then, the voice at the other end said, "I'll ring off today."

"Will you?"

"Can you tell me the time?"

"Twelve past two."

Tripti-or-Shaoli let out what sounded like a scream of pain. Before I could ask what had happened so suddenly, or why she had cried out, I heard her say, simply, "Goodbye."

She had barely pronounced the word when I heard the click of the receiver being replaced. It suggested that somebody had turned up or that she was almost caught out, or that at around two o'clock, she had some urgent task she had forgotten or become confused about in the course of our conversation.

I knew the number, of course. Should I call her again? There was no hope of her calling me back. She didn't know my number!

No, I made no other calls that day. Not the next day, nor the day after. The root of the matter lay elsewhere. After I left the office, I don't know whether the peon, while arranging the things on my table, had tucked Tripti-or-Shaoli's phone number away under some papers or thrown it in the wastebasket; but I did not see it when I came to work the next day. I remembered that I was to make a call that day, but not finding the number within easy reach, I couldn't, nor under the pressure of work did I find time to hunt for the number. At the end of the day, I asked the peon, "Where have you thrown the slip of paper on which I had noted a phone number yesterday?"

The peon simply could not recall the paper I was referring to. In a very calm voice, I just said, "Before discarding papers and other such things, you must show them to me."

Coming out of the office, I felt it was better that I had not called that day. It was very simple: if my words had moved Tripti-or-Shaoli's heart, she would surely have awaited my phone call today; and if they had not moved her, she would have forgotten them. Perhaps she had spoken to me civilly because it was the first occasion, but there was no guarantee that she would do so on the second day as well. In this situation, it was necessary to let a few days pass for me to gain greater worth in her eyes.

On the third day, when Tripti-or-Shaoli's phone number peeped out from amidst a pile of assorted papers, the urge for communication sky-rocketed. I had not yet decided how to begin the conversation, but I had decided to disconnect the call if she did indeed speak harshly to me. Replacing the receiver would not harm me in any way. She knew nothing about me: neither my name, place of work, nor my telephone number. Hence, if she were to swear at telephone pests—labeling them bastards or swines, demanding to know if they didn't have mothers and sisters of their own—I would digest the insults myself, with not a soul in the world to bear witness. I would remain respectable in the eyes of my wife and children. But how extraordinary! Tripti-or-Shaoli was not at all annoyed at receiving my call. When I reminded her of our previous conversation, she answered, with the same theatrical laugh, "Yes, I remember."

"How amazing, you have a very sharp memory, I must say!"

"Is that so?"

"Certainly. Otherwise, how would you remember all the things we had said the other day?"

"Yes, that is true!"

Immediately, a way of pleasing Tripti-or-Shaoli occurred to me. I said, "You must have been a very bright student, but I don't know whether you still are."

"Your assumption is correct, but that was ages ago."

Before I could ask what "ages ago" implied or what she used to study at the time, she asked, in a very natural manner, "Why did you call today?"

I was not ready for such a question. When I laughed to hide my discomfort, she asked, "What is it that makes you laugh?"

Whether this was a reproach or wounded pride, I could not comprehend. How could I tell her, or explain to her, that speaking to women on the telephone was one of my few pleasures, that I had been rather eager to speak to her? Finally, I blurted out the truth.

"There's quite a resemblance between the sound of your voice and the voices of Tripti Mitra and Shaoli Mitra."

"What? Did you say Tripti Mitra and Shaoli Mitra?"

"Yes, the two renowned theatre personalities of Bengal! The mother-daughter duo."

"I know, I know. Tripti Mitra is the wife of Shambu Mitra; she hails from Thakurgaon in Dinajpur. What an extraordinary artiste, and my voice is supposed to resemble hers? What nonsense!"

"I speak the truth."

"No, no."

"Yes, yes."

From "no-no" and "yes-yes," we slipped into an exchange of no and yes until the entire matter struck us as extreme. It was I who broke the spell. "I think we are behaving like children."

Startled, Tripti-or-Shaoli paused abruptly. But only for an instant. After that, when she burst into laughter—people of eminence would describe her laugh in formal language as bursting the floodgates of mirth—I shouted to stop her, saying, "What's this—what's the matter with you?"

She stopped laughing and replied, "There is a child in every human being."

My mind failed to grasp her meaning. I thought that I might as well ask her, but before I could pose the question, she asked anxiously, "What is the time?"

"It is quarter to one."

"Oh, OK."

From her answer, it was clear that there was no cause for anxiety. I was about to initiate a new line of conversation by simply asking, "On the last occasion, too, why did you disconnect the line after asking the time?" But just then, I saw the chairman's special peon, Mannan, standing before me.

"What is it, Mannan?"

"Sir sends you his greetings."

Signaling with my hand that I would be coming shortly, I told Tripti-or-Shaoli about Sir's message and put the phone down. When I returned to my room after a discussion with the chairman, it was almost two o'clock. Immediately, I called Tripti-or-Shaoli again. But this time the voice that answered seemed to belong to a maidservant, who informed me that Begum sahib was in the outer room and would not take the call.

I was not offended by the maidservant's response. A person might be busy, I thought, or at such a time a guest might need to be entertained in the outer room, and so on. Deciding that I would call her the following day and ask about her eagerness to know the time, I wound up my office work for the day and went home. Nobody could tell how much turmoil that question was causing in my mind. I was affectionate to my children, amorous to my wife; and through my entire period of wakefulness, as I fondly cherished Tripti-or-Shaoli's words, I saw beauty in all things in the world, the entire universe brimming over with sweetness, and in the kite stuck in a tree branch, I saw the supreme beauty of the universe. The sorrow of it belonged to the person who had lost the kite; but I couldn't be certain that the joy of it belonged to me. Today, I would adorn Tripti-or-Shaoli with a new name. What name might that be, what name would render this unseen woman romantic to my imagination? As I thought about these things, suddenly a name—"Anamika," the Nameless One—presented itself to me, concentrating within itself all the minutest joys of the universe, an image of complete bliss.

Today when I called, not at twelve or one in the afternoon but at around ten o'clock, joy choked my throat when Tripti-or-Shaoli answered upon the very first ring. But at the very outset, she wanted to know, "Who is speaking?"

"Me. It's me."

"But who are you?"

I was utterly baffled. Counting today, I had called four times; I had not needed to mention my name on the other two occasions besides the first. At that moment, the fact that I couldn't ask for Mrs. So-and-so or say that I wanted to speak to her seemed to me the most dangerous situation I had encountered in the course of my extensive perambulations on the path of long-distance communication. In a hesitant tone, I answered, "You see, I don't know her name, but I have spoken to her several times before this."

"Oh, I understand."

Tripti-or-Shaoli let out a long sigh. Then there was silence. Unable to guess if she had rung off, I said, "Hello?"

"Ji, you had been speaking to my mother."

"Your mother?"

Amazement had rendered me speechless. Mother and daughter had identical voices, just like Tripti and Shaoli Mitra!

"Yes, my mother. Because our voices are similar, many people mistake us for each other."

"Yes, Kolkata's Tripti Mitra and her daughter Shaoli Mitra's voices are also impossible to distinguish unless one is told who it is."

"I know that."

With extreme deference, I asked, "Is your mother not in?"

"She is."

"Is it possible to call her to the phone?"

"No. Ma does not speak to anyone today."

I was caught in a dilemma, not sure if I should ask why she didn't speak to anyone that day or if I should put the receiver down. I could sense that a strange sound was coming from my throat. Understanding the situation, Shaoli came to my rescue. She informed me, "It's because my father went missing on this day, that's why."

"When, when did he go missing?"

"In 1971. Baba went to work, never to return. As Baba would go off duty at two o'clock, Ma waits in the outer room from two o'clock onwards."

Translation from Bengali by Radha Chakravarty

from *The Other Side of Silence*

The political partition of India caused one of the great human convulsions of history. Never before or since have so many people exchanged their homes and countries so quickly. In the space of a few months, about twelve million people moved between the new, truncated India and the two wings, East and West, of the newly created Pakistan. By far, the largest proportion of these refugees—more than ten million of them—crossed the western border that divided the historic state of Punjab, Muslims travelling west to Pakistan, Hindus and Sikhs east to India. Slaughter sometimes accompanied and sometimes prompted these movements; many people died from malnutrition and contagious disease. Estimates of the dead vary from 200,000 (the contemporary British figure) to two million (a later Indian estimate), but that somewhere around a million people died is now widely accepted. As always, there was widespread sexual savagery: about 75,000 women are thought to have been abducted and raped by men of religions different from their own (and indeed, sometimes by men of their own religion). Thousands of families were divided, homes destroyed, crops left to rot, villages abandoned. Astonishingly, and despite many warnings, the new governments of India and Pakistan were unprepared for the convulsion: they had not anticipated that the fear and uncertainty created by the drawing of borders based on headcounts of religious identity—so many Hindus versus so many Muslims—would force people to flee to what they considered "safer" places, where they would be surrounded by their own kind. People travelled in buses, in cars, by train, but mostly on foot. Called kafilas, the great columns of people could stretch for dozens of miles. The longest of them, said to comprise nearly 400,000 refugees travelling east to India from western Punjab, took as many as eight days to pass any given spot on its route.

From Chapter One

This is the generality of Partition: it exists publicly in history books. The particular is harder to discover; it exists privately in the stories told and retold inside so many households in India and Pakistan. I grew up with them: like many Punjabis of my generation, I am from a family of Partition refugees. Memories of Partition, the horror and brutality of the time, the harking back to an often mythical past in which Hindus and Muslims and Sikhs lived together in relative peace and harmony—these have formed the

Sophie Vas, with Ken, Teresa, and Eric
circa 1925

staple of stories I have lived with. My mother and father come from Lahore, a city that is loved and sentimentalized by its inhabitants and that lies only twenty miles inside the Pakistan border. My mother tells of the dangerous journeys she twice made back there to bring her younger brother and sister to India. My father remembers fleeing Lahore to the sound of guns and crackling fire. I would listen to these stories with my brothers and sister and barely take them in. We were middle-class Indians who had grown up in a period of relative calm and prosperity, when tolerance and "secularism" seemed to be winning the argument. These stories—of looting, arson, rape, murder—came out of a different time. They meant little to me.

Then, in October 1984, Prime Minister Indira Gandhi was assassinated by her security guards, both Sikhs. For days afterwards, Sikhs all over India were attacked in an orgy of violence and revenge. Many homes were destroyed, and thousands died. In the outlying suburbs of Delhi, more than three thousand were killed, often by being doused in kerosene and then set alight. They died horrible, macabre deaths. Black burn marks on the ground showed where their bodies had lain. The government—after Mrs. Gandhi's death, headed by her son Rajiv—remained indifferent, but several citizens' groups came together to provide relief, food, and shelter. I was among the hundreds of people who worked in these groups. Every day, while we were distributing food and blankets, compiling lists of the dead and missing, and helping with compensation claims, we listened to the stories of the people who had suffered. Often, older people who had come to Delhi as refugees in 1947 would tell us that they had been through a similar terror before. "We didn't think it could happen to us in our own country," they would say. "This is like Partition again."

Here, across the River Jamuna, just a few miles from where I lived, ordinary and peaceable people had driven their neighbours from their homes and murdered them for no readily apparent reason except their belonging to a different religious community. The stories of Partition no longer seemed quite so remote: people from the same country, the same town, the same village could still be divided by the politics of their religious differences and, once divided, could do terrible things to each other. Two years later, working on a film about Partition for a British television channel, I began to collect stories from its survivors. Many of these accounts were horrific and of a kind that, when I was younger and heard them second or third hand, I had found hard to believe: women jumping into wells to drown themselves so as to avoid rape or forced religious conversion; fathers beheading their own sons and daughters so the children would avoid the same dishonourable fate. Now I was hearing them from witnesses whose bitterness, rage, and hatred—which, once uncovered, could be frightening—told me they were speaking the truth.

Their stories affected me deeply. Nothing as cruel and bloody had happened in my own family so far as I knew, but I began to realize that Partition was not, even in my family, a closed chapter of history—that its simple, brutal political geography infused and divided us still. The divisions were there in everyday life, as were their contradictions: how many times have I heard my parents, my grandmother speak with affection and longing of their Muslim friends in Lahore, and how many times with irrational prejudice about "those Muslims"; how many times had I heard my mother speak, with a sense of betrayal, about her brother who had married a Muslim…It took 1984 to make me understand how ever present Partition was in our lives too, to recognize that it could not be so easily put away inside the covers of history books. I could no longer pretend that this was a history that belonged to another time, to someone else.

From Chapter Four Part I

Hidden Histories

I cannot now pinpoint exactly when I became aware of the histories of women. I say "became aware" because the process was a sort of cumulative one in which stories began to seep into my consciousness until one day when it became clear that there was something I should be actively seeking.

Even as I say this, it sounds strange to me. As a feminist, I have been only too aware, sometimes painfully so, of the need to fold back several layers of history (or of what we see as fact) before one can begin to arrive at a different, more complex "truth." Why then, I have often asked myself, should the "discovery" of women have come as such a surprise? But it did. Perhaps it was because the initial assumption I brought to my search was a simple one: the history of Partition, as I knew it, made no mention of women. As a woman and as a feminist, I would set out to "find" women in Partition, and once I did, I would attempt to make them visible. That would, in a sense, "complete" an incomplete picture.

There are, of course, no complete pictures. This I know now: everyone who makes one draws it afresh. Each time, retrospectively, the picture changes: who you are, where you come from, who you're talking to, when you talk, where you talk, what you listen to, what people choose to tell you—all of these affect the picture you draw.

I realized, for example, that if it had been difficult for [a man] to talk about his story, how much more difficult it must have been for women to do so. To whom would they have spoken? Who would have listened? I realized too that something I had not taken into account was that, in order to be able to "hear" women's voices, I had to pose different questions, to talk in different situations, and to be prepared to do that most important of things, to listen: to their speech, their silences, the half-said things, the nuances. The men seldom spoke about women. Women almost never spoke about themselves; indeed, they denied they had anything "worthwhile" to say, a stance that was often corroborated by their men. Or, quite often, they simply weren't there to speak to. And what right did I, a stranger, an outsider, have to go around digging into their lives, forcing them to look back to a time that was perhaps better forgotten? Especially when I knew that the histories I wanted to know about were ones of violence, rape, murder.

For a while, then, I held back from speaking to women: there were so many layers of silence encoded into these histories, I told myself, that perhaps I could make my exploration by looking elsewhere—surely I would still be uncovering some of the silences. I turned therefore to some of the very "documents" that I had so often found wanting. Newspaper accounts, a memoir, and other sources helped me to piece together a story: a story of love and of hate, a story of four lives and two nations, a story that brought me back to the histories of women—the story of Zainab and Buta Singh.

Zainab was said to have been abducted as a young Muslim girl while her family was on the move to Pakistan in a kafila. No one knows who her abductors were or how many hands she passed through, but eventually she was sold to a Jat from Amritsar district, Buta Singh. Like many men who either abducted women themselves or bought them, Buta Singh performed the "chaddar" ceremony and "married" Zainab. The story goes that, in time, the two came to love each other. They had a family: two young girls. Several years after Partition, a search party on the lookout for abducted women traced Zainab to Amritsar, where she was living with Buta Singh. It was suspected that Buta Singh's brother—or his nephews—had informed the search party of Zainab's whereabouts. Apparently, their concern was that Buta Singh's children would deprive them of the family property, that their share would be reduced. Like many women who were thus "rescued," Zainab had no choice in the matter. She was forced to leave. Newspaper reports describe the scene as a poignant one: the entire village had assembled to see her off. She came slowly out of her house, carrying her child and clutching a small bundle of clothes. Her belongings were stowed in a jeep, and as she boarded it, she turned to Buta Singh and, pointing to her elder daughter, is reported to have said, "Take care of this girl, and don't worry. I'll be back soon."

Not surprisingly, property figured in Zainab's recovery as well. Her parents had been killed, but the family had received grants of land in Lyallpur as compensation for property they had left behind in Indian Punjab. Zainab and her sister had received their father's share, and an uncle had been allotted the adjoining piece. Rumour had it that it was he who had been the moving spirit behind Zainab's rescue: he was keen the land remain in his family, and he wanted that Zainab, when found, should marry his son, which would then ensure the property would remain with them. The son had no interest in marrying Zainab, and as the story is told, he was reluctant in part because she had lived for many years with a Sikh. Discussion on this issue went on in the family for some time, and Buta Singh occasionally received snippets of news from neighbours and others who kept him informed.

Meanwhile, Buta Singh pleaded his case wherever possible—but to no avail. He tried to go to Pakistan, but this was difficult. One day he received a letter from Pakistan— ostensibly from one of Zainab's neighbours, although no one quite knows—which asked him to go there as soon as possible. Zainab's family, it seemed, was pressing her to marry. Buta Singh sold off his land and put together some money, but he had not bargained for the difficulties of travel between the two countries. He needed a passport and a visa, for which he travelled to Delhi. Here, he first took the step of converting to Islam, thinking perhaps that it would be easier to get to Pakistan as a Muslim. Buta Singh thus became Jamil Ahmed.

And he applied for a passport and a nationality: Pakistani. If that was what would get him to Zainab, that was what he would do. But acquiring a new country, especially in a situation of the kind that obtained at the time, was not easy. The High Commission of Pakistan accepted Buta Singh's application for Pakistani nationality and fed it into the machinery. The question was not a simple one of changing nationality—if such questions can ever be simple. The two countries were virtually at war; deep-rooted suspicion of each other's motives was the order of the day; people could no longer move freely across borders. How then could the appeal of a man who says he's in love with the nationality of the "enemy" be accepted at face value? After many months, the application was rejected. (Interestingly, according to newspaper accounts of the same period, a high-profile actress, Meena, wished to become a Pakistani citizen and applied for citizenship; this was immediately granted, and her "defection" made much of in the press.)

Buta Singh did not, however, give up easily. He applied for a short-term visa, and because people in the Pakistan High Commission were familiar with him by then, he was granted it. Now Buta Singh, alias Jamil Ahmed, made his way to Pakistan—and arrived to find that Zainab had already been married to her cousin. This could well have been the end of the world for him, but by a strange quirk of circumstance, he was given another chance to fight for her. In his rush to find out about her, he had forgotten to report his arrival to the police. (To this day, Indians and Pakistanis are required to report their arrival within twenty-four hours of crossing the border.) For this oversight, Buta Singh had to appear before a magistrate, and apparently he told the magistrate that he had been so distracted by Zainab's situation that he had neglected to report his arrival. The magistrate then ordered Zainab to be produced before the court, and she was asked to give a statement. It was at this point that all Buta Singh's hopes were dashed. Closely guarded by a ring of relatives, Zainab rejected him, saying, "I am a married woman. Now I have nothing to do with this man. He can take his second child, whom I brought from his house…"

The next day Buta Singh put himself under a train and committed suicide. A suicide note in his pocket asked that he be buried in Zainab's village. This wish, however, was to remain unfulfilled. It is said that when Buta Singh's body was brought to Lahore for an autopsy, large crowds gathered outside; some people wept; a filmmaker announced he would make a film based on the story. Later, a police party took Buta Singh's body to Zainab's village but was stopped from burying it there by people of her community. They did not want a permanent reminder of this incident, and Buta Singh, or Jamil Ahmed, was taken back to Lahore and buried there.

In death Buta Singh became a hero. The subject of a legend, fittingly situated in the land of other star-crossed lovers: Heer and Ranjha, Sohni and Mahiwal. Zainab, meanwhile, continued to live, her silence surrounding her. Unable to grieve and to mourn her lover and, in all likelihood, unable to talk. She was one among thousands of such women.

Zainab and Buta Singh's story stayed with me: it was a moving story, but more, I kept returning to it out of a nagging, persistent sense of dissatisfaction. As it was told, this was the story of a hero and a "victim." We learnt something about the hero: his impulsive nature, his honesty and steadfastness, his willingness to give up everything for the woman he loved, the strength of his love. But nothing about the victim. Try as I might, I could not recover *her* voice. What had Zainab felt? Had she really cared for Buta Singh, or was she indifferent to both the men in her life? How had the experience of abduction, almost certainly of rape, marked her? It was said that Zainab and Buta Singh were happy, that they were even in love. Yet the man had actually bought her, purchased her like chattel: how then could she have loved him? I realized I had to go back to talking. If any women were still alive, this was perhaps the one way in which I could learn about their experiences, their feelings.

The decision wasn't an easy one. There is a point at which research becomes an end in itself. The human subject you are researching becomes simply a provider of information, the "informant," devoid of feelings of her own, but important for your work. I did not want to be in this kind of violative—and exploitative—position. I decided that I would impose my own silences on this search. I knew by now that the history of Partition was a history of deep violation—physical and mental—for women. I would then talk to only those who wanted to talk about it. And I would continue to explore other sources to help me recover the histories of women. Providentially—or so it seemed at the time, for I realize now that once there is an involvement in something, you begin to take notice of related things—the next step offered itself.

A Tradition of Martyrdom

The violence that women faced in the aftermath of Partition is shrouded in many layers of silence. If in historical accounts we hear little about the rape and abduction of women, what we do know about violence in general relates only to men of the "other" community. There is seldom, if ever, any acknowledgment (except perhaps in fiction) that Hindu and Sikh women could have become the targets of Hindu and Sikh men. Yet in the upheaval and the disruption of everyday life, Hindu

From Chapter Five Part II

men could hardly have become miraculously innocent. One of the myths that survivors increasingly—and tenaciously—hold on to is how communities and families stayed together in this time of crisis: how then can they admit to such disruption from the inside, and by their own members?

It was in 1986 that I first came across stories of family and community violence. At the time, I had no idea of its scale, and only gradually did I learn exactly how widespread it had been. Mangal Singh was one of the first people I spoke to when I began to collect stories about Partition. In Amritsar Bazaar where he lived, Mangal Singh was considered something of a legend. The last surviving brother of three, he had made his way over to Amritsar in August 1947 with nothing but the "three clothes on my back." Once over the border, Mangal Singh occupied a piece of vacant land left behind by Muslims who had moved to Pakistan. "My heart was heavy," he said, "and this space was open, large, empty. I thought, Let me stay here, this emptiness is good for me, this emptiness and clear space." Here, he set up home and began the painful process of scratching together a living and starting again. With small amounts of money borrowed from relatives and friends—he told me, "If you needed a few hundreds or even thousands of rupees for anything, you were able to get them because people helped out"—he started a shop that sold fans and electrical spare parts. In time, he married and started a family. When I met him, he was in his seventies, a grandfather surrounded by a large, extended family. His sons ran the business while he spent most of his time with his grandchildren.

Many people had urged me to talk to Mangal Singh, and I was curious about him. His legendary status in his neighbourhood came from the fact that, at Partition, he and his two brothers were said to have killed the women and children of their family—seventeen of them—before setting off across the border. I found this story difficult to believe: how could you kill your own children, your own family? And why would you? At first Mangal Singh was reluctant to speak to me: "What is the use of raking all this up again?" he asked. But then, after talking to his family, he changed his mind. They had, apparently, urged him to speak. They felt he had carried this particular burden for too long. I asked him about the family that was gone. He described them thus: "We were people of substance. In those days people had a lot of children—so we had many women and they had many children…There were children, there were girls…nephews and others. What a wonderful family it was, whole and happy."

Why, then, had he and his brothers thought it fit to kill them? Mangal Singh refused to accept that the seventeen women and children had been killed. Instead, he used the word "martyred":

> After leaving home we had to cross the surrounding boundary of water. And we were many family members, several women and children who would not have been able to cross the water, to survive the flight. So we killed—they became martyrs—seventeen of our family members, seventeen lives…Our

hearts were heavy with grief for them, grief and sorrow, their grief, our own grief. So we travelled, laden with sorrow, not a paisa to call our own, not a bite of food to eat…but we had to leave. Had we not done so, we would have been killed, the times were such…

But why kill the women and children? I asked him. Did they not deserve a chance to live? Could they not have got away? He insisted that the women and children had "offered" themselves up for death because death was preferable to what would almost certainly have happened: conversion and rape. But could they really have offered themselves? Did they not feel any fear? I asked him. Angrily, he said,

Fear? Let me tell you one thing. You know this race of Sikhs? There's no fear in them, no fear in the face of adversity. Those people [the ones who had been killed] had no fear. They came down the stairs into the big courtyard of our house that day, and they all sat down and they said, You can make martyrs of—we are willing to become martyrs, and they did. Small children too…what was there to fear? *The real fear was one of dishonour. If they had been caught by the Muslims, our honour, their honour would have been sacrificed, lost. It's a question of one's honour…if you have pride you do not fear.* [My italics.]

But who had the pride, and who the fear? This is a question Mangal Singh was unwilling to address. If accounts such as his were to be believed, the greatest danger that families, and indeed entire communities, perceived was the loss of honour through conversion to the other religion. Violence could be countered, but conversion was somehow seen as different. In many ways, their concern was not unfounded: mass and forcible conversions had taken place on both sides. Among the Sikhs particularly, the men felt they could protect themselves, but they were convinced that the women would be unable to do so. Their logic was that men could fight, die if necessary, escape by using their wits and their strength, but the women had no such strength at hand. They were therefore particularly vulnerable to conversion. Moreover, women could be raped, impregnated with the seed of the other religion, and in this way, not only would they be rendered impure individually, but through them, the entire community could be polluted, for they would give birth to "impure" children. While the men could save themselves, it was imperative that the women—and through them, the entire race—be "saved" by the men.

A few years after I had spoken to Mangal Singh, I began to look at newspaper reports on Partition, searching for similar accounts of family violence. On 15 April 1947, *The Statesman*, an English daily newspaper, had carried the following story:

The story of 90 women of the little village of Thoa Khalsa, Rawalpindi district…who drowned themselves by jumping into a well during the recent disturbances has stirred the imagination of the people of the Punjab. They revived the Rajput tradition of self-immolation when their menfolk were no longer able to defend them. They also followed Mr Gandhi's advice to Indian women that in certain circumstances, even suicide was morally preferable to submission.

About a month ago, a communal army armed with sticks, tommy guns and hand grenades, surrounded the village. The villagers defended themselves as best they could…but in the end they had to raise the white flag. Negotiations followed. A sum of Rs 10,000 was demanded…it was promptly paid. The intruders gave solemn assurances that they would not come back.

The promise was broken the next day. They returned to demand more money and in the process hacked to death 40 of the defenders. Heavily outnumbered, they were unable to resist the onslaught. Their women held a hurried meeting and concluded that all was lost but their honour. Ninety women jumped into the small well. Only three were saved: there was not enough water in the well to drown them all.

The story referred to incidents of communal violence in Punjab that had actually begun some months before Partition, in March 1947. Early in this month, a number of Sikh villages in Rawalpindi district were attacked over a period of nine days (6 to 13 March, although in some places sporadic attacks continued up to 15 March). The attacks themselves were said to be in retaliation for Hindu attacks on Muslims in Bihar; also, the Sikh political leader, Tara Singh, is said to have made provocative statements in Lahore to which Muslim political leaders had reacted. It is futile to speculate whose was the primary responsibility: the reality is that once it became clear that Partition would take place, both communities, Muslim and Hindu, started to attack each other. In Rawalpindi district, in the villages of Thamali, Thoa Khalsa, Mator, Nara, and many others, the attacks ended on 13 March, when the army moved in and rescued what survivors were left. In many villages the entire population was wiped out; in others, there were a few survivors.

A small community of survivors from these villages lives in Jangpura and Bhogal, two middle-class areas in Delhi. It was from them that I learnt a little more about the "mass suicide" in Thoa Khalsa described above. Because they could lay claim to this history, survivors from Thoa Khalsa—and this is true even today—seemed to have a high standing in the Rawalpindi community. People spoke of them—as they had done of Mangal Singh—in tones of awe and respect. Conversely, the two brothers from a neighbouring village who had lost their sisters to abductors were spoken of as if they were the ones who were somehow at fault. Clearly the women's "sacrifice" had elevated their families, and their communities, to a higher plane. The first person from whom we heard the story of Thoa Khalsa was Basant Kaur, a tall, upright woman in her seventies. According to her, she was one of the women who had jumped into the well; because it was too full, she did not drown. I reproduce below a long excerpt from her interview.

Basant Kaur
"I keep telling them these stories…"

My name is Basant Kaur. My husband's name was Sant Raja Singh. We came away from our houses on March 12, and on the 13th we stayed out, in the village. At first, we tried to show our strength, and then we realized that this would not work, so we joined the morcha to go away. We left our home in Thoa Khalsa on the 12th. For three or four days we were trapped inside our houses, we couldn't get out, though we used to move across the roofs of houses and that way we could get out a bit. One of our people had a gun, we used that, and two or three of their people died. I lost a brother-in-law. He died from a bullet they fired. It hit him and he died. So we kept the gun handy. Then there were fires all around, raging fires, and we were no match for them. I had a jeth, my older brother-in-law, he had a son, he kept asking give me afim [opium], mix it in water and I will take it. My jeth killed his mother, his sister, his wife, his daughter, and his uncle. My daughter was also killed. We went into the morcha inside the village, we all left our houses and collected together in the centre of the village, inside the sardaran di haveli, where there was also a well. It was Lajjawanti's house. The sardar, her husband, had died some-time ago, but his wife and other women of the house were there. Some children also. They all came out. Then we all talked and said we don't want to become Musalmaan, we would rather die. So everyone was given a bit of afim, they were told, you keep this with you…I went upstairs, and when I came down there was my husband, my jeth's son, my jethani, her daugh-ters, my jeth, my grandsons, three granddaughters. They were all killed so that they would not fall into the hands of Musalmaans. One girl from our village, she had gone off with the Musalmaans. She was quite beautiful, and everyone got worried that if one has gone, they will take all our girls away…so it was then that they decided to kill the girls. My jeth, his name is Harbans Singh, he killed his wife, his daughter, his son…he was small, only eight days old. Then my sister-in-law was killed, her son and her daughter, and then on the 14th of March we came to Jhelum. The vehicles came and took us, and we stayed there for about a month and then we came to Delhi.

In Delhi there were four of my brothers, they read about this—the camp—in the papers and they came and found us. Then, gradually, over a period of time the children grew up and became older and things sorted themselves out. My parents were from Thamali. Hardly anyone survived from there. You know that family of Gurmeet's, they had two sisters, the Musalmaans took them away. Whether they died or were taken away, but they, their bodies were never found…Someone died this way, someone that, someone died here and someone there, and no one got to know. My parents were burnt alive.

That whole area was like jungle, it was village area. One of my brothers survived and came away, one sister. They too were helped by a Musalmaan, there were some good ones, and they helped them—he hid them away in his house—and then put them into the vehicles that came, the military ones. The vehicles went to Mator and other places. In Mator, Shah Nawaz made sure no harm came to them. People from Nara managed to get away, but on the way they were all killed. Then my brothers read the papers and got to know. My husband, he killed his daughter, his niece, his sister, and a grandson. He killed them with a kirpan. My jeth's son killed his mother, his wife, his daughter, and a grandson and granddaughter, all with a pistol. And then, my jeth, he doused himself with kerosene and jumped into a fire.

Many girls were killed. Then Mata Lajjawanti, she had a well near her house, in a sort of garden. Then all of us jumped into that, some hundred…eighty-four…girls and boys. All of us. Even boys, not only children, but grown-up boys. I also went in, I took my two children, and then we jumped in—I had some jewellery on me, things in my ears, on my wrists, and I had fourteen rupees on me. I took all that and threw it into the well, and then I jumped in, but…it's like when you put goyas, rotis into a tandoor, and if it is too full, the ones near the top, they don't cook, they have to be taken out. So the well filled up, and we could not drown…the children survived. Later, Nehru went to see the well, and the English then closed it up, the well that was full of bodies. The Pathans took out those people who were at the top of the well—those who died, died, and those who were alive, they pulled out. Then they went away—and what was left of our village was saved, except for that one girl who went away.

I was frightened. Of course, I was, but there was also…we were also frightened that we would be taken away by the Musalmaans. In our village, already, in the well that was inside the village, girls had jumped in. In the middle of the night they had jumped in. This happened where the morcha was. The hundred…eighty-four women who jumped in they were just outside, some two hundred yards away from Lajjawanti's house. In the morcha, the crowd had collected in Lajjawanti's house. She was some seventy, seventy-five years old. A tall, strapping woman. She did a lot of seva of all the women, she herself jumped into the well. Many people were killed in the morcha, and the Musalmaans climbed on top to kill the others, and then many came and tried to kill people with guns, one of them put a gun to my jeth's chest and…and we began to jump in. The others had died earlier, and we were in the morcha, the well was some distance away from Lajjawanti's house, in a garden. My nanan and her daughter, they were both lying there…close by there was a ladle, I mixed afim in it, and gave it to them, and she put it in her mouth…she died, and I think the village dogs must have eaten her. We had no time to perform any last rites. An hour or so later, the trucks came…just an hour.

She did path, and said don't throw me away, let me have this afim, she took God's name and then she died. We had afim because my jeth's son used to eat it, and had it with him and he got more and gave it to everyone.

My jeth's son, his daughter-in-law and his daughter, they died in Jhelum later, when we were going to the Dinia camp, on March 15 or so. The camp was close to the Jhelum. Four days we fought, and we remained strong, then around the 12th we got into the morcha, on the 13th our people were killed, and then the trucks came in the evening and took us to Rawat, a village.

They brought us there [to the well]. From there...you know there was no place...nothing to eat, some people were eating close by, but where could I give the children anything from...I had barely a few paise...my elder son had a duvanni [two annas] with him, we thought we could use that...my brother's children were also hungry...but then they said the duvanni was khoti, damaged, unusable...[*weeping*] such difficulties... nothing to eat...we had to fill their stomachs...today they would have been ranis...so many of them, jethanis, children...I was the youngest...now I sit at home and my children are out working and I keep telling them these stories...they are stories after all...and you tell them and tell them until you lose consciousness...

Teresa (right) and her ayah
Depot Lines, Karachi, circa 1930

Family servants with their children
at the home of Gilomena Dias,
Teresa's aunt
Cincinnatus Town, Karachi, circa 1930

Pali

Life goes on and on. Its ends never meet. Neither in the mundane world of realities, nor in fiction. We drag on drearily in the hope that someday these ends may meet. And sometimes we have the illusion that the ends have really joined.

Manohar Lal and his wife had also once lived under a similar illusion. They believed that a great calamity had at last passed over their heads. That the knots that had formed in their lives had been untied. But knots of life never get fully resolved even in stories, much less in one's life. No sooner is one knot untied than another knot forms in its place. The story thus never comes to an end.

One end of Manohar Lal and his family's life was left behind in a small town distantly situated across the border of Pakistan, a country newly carved out at the time of the Partition. With their meagre belongings, the little that they could carry, Manohar Lal and his family had joined the caravan of the countless uprooted people heading for India. The dust raised by their feet hung like a haze in the atmosphere. Like a big river forming into many channels on its onward sweep towards the sea, this vast concourse of unfortunate humanity also proceeded towards the boundary line demarcating the two countries.

Manohar Lal, his wife, and their two children—a little girl in her mother's arms, and Pali, a boy of four, holding his father's finger—trudged along, carrying their bundles on their heads, their weary eyes searching their way through the haze, their ears pricked for any stray remark that might guide them onto the correct path. They were anxious to know the lay of the land and, more than that, what was in store for them.

On the last day, the refugee camp had started emptying out. Carrying their belongings on their heads, the refugees left the camp and proceeded towards the convoy of lorries, ranged one after the other along the road, which would carry them to the border. Holding his son's finger and carrying a heavy bundle on his head, Manohar Lal walked towards the lorries, his wife, Kaushalya, following close on his heels, her baby daughter nestled in her arms. Like her husband, she carried a big bundle on her head. The refugees were frantically throwing their things into the lorries and storming their way into the vehicles, some of them wriggling in through the windows. Manohar Lal was struggling to push his way towards the entrance when he suddenly realized that his son, Pali, was not holding his finger. Kaushalya had already managed to enter the lorry. Manohar Lal felt no alarm, thinking that the child must be around somewhere. The sensation of the child's grip still lingered on his hand. Everybody was madly pushing from behind. There was a babble of sounds, and the crowd got more frantic with the passing of every moment. The camp managers shouted at the top of their voices, urging the passengers to hurry up and get into the lorries. They had to cross the border before nightfall.

When Manohar Lal failed to find Pali, he became very anxious. He rushed back crying, "Pali! Pali!" but failed to get any response. Becoming alarmed, he raised his voice. His son's name rang in the air above the pervading din. Then he started running frantically alongside the lorries, which had started leaving one by one. The lorry in which his wife was standing with their suckling child was jam-packed, and its horn was blowing insistently, warning the people that it was ready to start. Manohar Lal's throat had gone dry shouting "Pali! Pali!" His legs shook and his head reeled. Such was the irony of the situation for this homeless man: he was shouting for his son on a road crowded with people, and yet he appeared to be shouting in a desert.

He was still searching for Pali when the lorry started moving. His wife's anxious eyes were fixed on her husband in the crowd, and to her horror, he suddenly disappeared from her view. Alarmed, she started wailing. Locks of her hair tumbled over her face, blinding her for a moment, and her child nearly slipped from her arms. She breathed heavily, her chest working like bellows.

"Stop! Stop! Hai, stop the lorry!"

But nobody listened to her. All of them had their own worries to contend with. They were all shouting and crying. Hers was not the only family being driven from its home. There were many of those who had only half of their luggage on the lorry; the other half lay scattered on the road. An old woman, apparently a grandmother, was having difficulty climbing into the moving lorry. She was pushed from all sides and struggled to keep her foot on the footboard. As the lorry moved forward, Kaushalya's eyes went wide with horror. In a daze, she searched for only one image in the crowd: her husband. Then she burst out crying, her plight like that of a bird whose nest was being destroyed before its very eyes.

She heard someone shouting, "Stop the lorry! Stop the lorry!" Other voices joined the cry. The lorry slowed down.

Kaushalya had thrown out one of her bundles and was going to hand her wailing child to a man standing on the road when she saw Manohar Lal running up. But their son was not with him. God only knew which whirlpool had sucked in poor Pali!

Manohar Lal heard some voices being directed towards his wife. "The child must be somewhere here." The people gestured to Manohar Lal to hurry. "Get in, get in!" they advised him. "He must have got on some other lorry." There were other voices, loaded with venom and irritation. "Will the lorry keep waiting for your child? If you want to search for your child, you'd better get down from the lorry." The people had suddenly become callous. If they had not seen Manohar Lal running up, perhaps Kaushalya would have got down from the lorry, wailing, and they would have thrown out her luggage after her. They were right. They had to get across the border before nightfall. So many lives were at stake. Surely, the lorry could not keep waiting for one child.

The refugees' hearts had dried of all sentiments. Pali had once gotten lost before, and the whole mohalla had gone out in search of him. And now someone kept crying, "Get down, you! If you want to search for your child, get down, and let us proceed!"

The husband and wife could not decide whether to get down from the lorry or stay in it. Having failed to find any trace of Pali, Manohar Lal and Kaushalya kept looking out on the road. Slowly, the town was left behind, and the noise abated. Only Kaushalya kept wailing. The trees, the fields full of greenery swept past their gaze. Pali, lost somewhere in the crowded small town, receded from his parents. Kaushalya's wailing gradually changed into a whimper. The mental anguish of the passengers expressed itself in the moans of the insane, and then changed into heart-rending cries before petering out into an anguished silence. The lorries moved on, lurching from side to side. Slowly, the morning haze cleared up. Looking up at the vast expanse of the impassive sky where one or two stars were still winking at him, Manohar Lal tried to console his wife. "We may yet find him," he said. "He can't get lost like this. Some kindly soul must have taken charge of him and pushed him into some other lorry." He looked at Kaushalya's abstracted gaze, and seeing the grief on her face, he said in utter desperation, "What can we do if we don't find him? God had been benign enough to spare a child for us. We must be thankful to him for that. You know Lekhraj's three children were killed before his very eyes. It's God's will. We must resign ourselves to it."

Kaushalya's empty eyes were still glued on the road. There was nothing strange about losing a child under these circumstances. There was no sense in creating so much hubbub over it. As time passed, the uprooted passengers fell to talking with one another, the women following their men's example. Here and there was the sound of laughter.

The evening shadows lengthened as they neared the border. The convoy stopped for a short while at one point. Manohar Lal promptly got down and ran past the lined-up lorries, shouting, "Pali! Pali!" He peeped into all the lorries through their windows, but he got no response from any lorry. His voice seemed to be echoing back from the wilderness. He could not find Pali anywhere.

On reaching the border, the refugees were transferred to other lorries, which had been parked there to receive them. The lorries raced through the darkness towards Amritsar. The sky, studded with myriad stars, looked so mysterious! Overwhelmed by the immensity of the situation, the refugees had become very quiet, and some of them had started dozing to the rhythmic jolts of the lorries. There were others who just sat there, staring at nothing. Manohar Lal's wife had again started crying. Her incoherent loudness made people think that she was going mad. Then her crying changed into moans, and the onlookers felt reassured that she was not mad yet. She must indeed be missing her child very much. At last, she rested her head against Manohar Lal's shoulder and fell asleep. Manohar Lal silently resolved that if he failed to find Pali when they arrived, he would go back to his old town in Pakistan and, following up certain clues, try to locate him and bring him back home.

The convoy tore through the darkness on its way to Amritsar. People were too absorbed in themselves to think of what lay in store for them. Perhaps their minds had stopped thinking. Fate had thrown a black curtain across their eyes, and they could discern no ray of hope through it. There were only the joltings of the lorries and weariness. Their eyes had become glazed and their throats were parched, and above them were myriad twinkling stars that seemed to mock them.

That night after crying for hours, Pali fell asleep at last, his head resting against Zenab's bosom and his sobs slowly dissolved in a sea of affection. A woman's bosom is the greatest shield against man's afflictions, and the greatest source of love and affection. Zenab had, so to say, caught the child firmly within her citadel of love. For the first time in her life, she was overwhelmed by a sense of joy that only a woman bereft of a child can experience. A tiny, delicate body was clinging to her, as if the child was specially made to fit into the contours of her body.

Her heart swelled up with maternal feeling. "Why don't you speak?" she asked the child.

Shakur, who had been lying in the courtyard in a cot adjacent to Zenab's, kept gazing at the sky sprinkled with millions of stars. It reminded him of Zenab's deep-blue chunri, in which she had first come to his house as a bride. Her chunri had glittered like stars. As he looked at her face glowing behind her chunri, Shakur had felt as if the sun had descended into his courtyard.

Shakur made a living by selling chinaware. Carrying a big basket loaded with cups, saucers, plates, and pots on his head, he would go from lane to lane and from street to street hawking his wares, waving a thin cane stick over his basket. He had been doing it for years. That late afternoon, as the evening came down upon the small town, he had chanced upon a small boy who had been thrown to one side by the ebb and tide of the crowd. He was standing at the corner of the lane crying, "Pitaji! Pitaji!"

Shakur stopped on seeing the small boy. Then he sat down by the boy's side, uttering soothing words to him. He wiped the child's tears with the end of his kurta, and the child stopped crying. "Come, I'll take you to your father," Shakur had said. "But where's your father?" Holding the child's hand, Shakur had taken him to the place from where the convoy of lorries had departed carrying the refugees. The lorries had left long before, and even the dust raised by them had long since settled down. The refugee camp was lying deserted. In the darkness of the night, when Shakur climbed the steps to his house, Pali was fast asleep, his head resting against Shakur's shoulder.

Shakur was a god-fearing man, timidly taking every step in life. When rioting started in the town, he kept himself aloof from the troublemakers. When the grain market was set on fire and there were stray cases of stabbing in the streets, Shakur had remarked, "It is God's anger visiting us." He would repeat this remark every time there was a violent occurrence.

"Why are you silent?" Shakur asked his wife.

"What's there to say?" Zenab replied in a lazy voice, which trailed into silence. She was enjoying the feel of the child's small body. She felt for a moment as if all the obstructions in her path had crumbled and her body was getting lighter. But she did not want to tell her husband that she had come upon a precious boon. Even the touch of that small unknown child clinging to her had sent a thrill through her body.

"All the Hindus and Sikhs left their houses," Shakur said. "They have gone for good. The camp has emptied. Now nobody would dare venture this way."

Zenab gave no reply. The child mumbled in his sleep, heaved a deep sigh, and, resting his head upon Zenab's bosom, fell asleep again.

Zenab looked up at the sky. It was resplendent, as if reflecting her good fortune. As if echoing Shakur's thoughts, she said, "Leave him at the place from where you picked him up, lest some unfortunate curse should befall us."

"Why should any curse befall us? We are giving the child shelter," Shakur mumbled. "If we deliver him to the Police Station, they can't restore him to his parents."

They were trying to read each other's mind.

"What's his name?" Zenab asked, rubbing her cheek against the child's cheek.

"How do I know? When I asked him, he said Pali. Pali."

"These Hindus have such queer names. What a funny name! Pali! If I had a son, I would have named him Altaf."

They lay silent for a long time, lost in their own thoughts. If nobody came to claim the child, he would become hers. A child prancing about in the courtyard! She hoped nobody would turn up to enquire. The tailor, Mahmud, had kept a Hindu woman in his house, and no one had bothered to investigate. Mir Zaman had ransacked the Hindu tailoring shop next to his and had kept the stolen things in his shop for all to see. Nobody had taken him to task for it. And as for her, she was only giving refuge to a child—a lost child whom her husband had found crying in the street. What was wrong with that? But Shakur's mind was sometimes filled with fear.

On waking up the next morning, the child found himself among strangers and started crying and repeating, "Pitaji, Pitaji!" Zenab put a bowl of milk against his lips and kept fondling his head and caressing his back. But little Pali would not stop crying and soon broke into hiccups. Zenab's eyes went to the door, worried that someone would hear the child crying and force his way into her house. Yes, the child was there all right, and all said and done, it was a stolen child. What if someone got wind of it? She must keep the child hidden from prying eyes for some days.

Pali stopped crying at last. He sat in a corner, maintaining a grim silence and emptily staring this way and that. He kept sighing, and Zenab sometimes felt that with the coming of the child, she had herself become rootless.

Shakur had thought that within a day or two, after becoming familiar with his environment, the child would start feeling at home. But he still had misgivings. One never knew. His parents might be searching for him and might track him down to Shakur's house. A large number of refugees still had to migrate. Shakur feared the police might come to know about the lost child and create serious trouble for him.

The first two days were nothing short of an ordeal. On the third day, the child became a little communicative. He saw a white cat sitting on the wall of the courtyard and beamed at it. The cat jumped down and sat on the floor. The child ran towards it, crying, "A cat! A cat!" Zenab felt so happy.

There was a knock on the door. It sounded loud and ominous. Zenab and Shakur looked towards the door in alarm, their hearts pounding hard.

"They have come," Zenab said apprehensively. "The people to whom the child belongs!" Fear streaked across her eyes.

"Could be the people from the Police Station!" Shakur said, his fear mounting moment by moment.

Another powerful blow. It sounded like a heavy lathi crashing against the door. "Open the door!" A voice invaded the house from the other side of the door.

As Shakur proceeded to open the door, Zenab hurriedly moved into the inner room with the child.

It was neither the police havildar on the other side of the door, nor the child's parents. It was the bearded maulvi of the neighbouring mosque standing there, holding a thick lathi. There were two men standing behind him, both armed with lathis.

"Is there a kafir's child in here?" the maulvi barked, stepping into the courtyard. "Who has brought him here?" The two men wielding lathis followed the maulvi into the courtyard.

"Are you hiding another kafir in your house too?"

Shakur ran in and hurriedly returned, carrying a murha.

"I swear by the Holy Quran that we are not hiding any kafir in our house," Shakur said. "We have only given shelter to an orphan boy."

"Where's that orphan?"

"Ji, he's sleeping inside."

The maulvi cast a suspicious look at Shakur and then tapped the floor sharply with his lathi.

"Produce him before me! I want to see him."

Zenab came out carrying Pali in her arms.

"So you are giving refuge to a kafir child?"

"I've adopted the child, Maulvi sahab. It's no sin to adopt a child," Zenab said in a firm, steady voice.

"Have you had him circumcised? Has he read the kalma?"

New life surged back into Zenab. The maulvi had not come to snatch the child from her. He had come only to make him a Mussalman. Zenab stood silent before the maulvi.

"Why don't you speak? You give a kafir's polluted child a place in your lap. You give him your breast to suckle. Do you want to nurture a snake?"

The maulvi's argument had driven Zenab against the wall. No, she couldn't refute his argument. Why hadn't she thought of it before? But she had found nothing polluted about the boy, nor did he look like the young one of a serpent. She was going to speak when the maulvi banged his lathi on the ground and said, "Bring this kafir's son to the holy mosque. Early tomorrow morning. Or you must be prepared to face serious consequences!"

The maulvi dramatically took a full turn and walked out. As soon as he had gone, Zenab tossed her head happily and smiled. All that the maulvi wanted was that the boy should say the kalma and be circumcised. Why wait till tomorrow? She was prepared to do it right now. What was there to fear? The maulvi had not threatened to take the child from her. He had not even hinted at it.

The circumcision was performed the very next morning. Little Pali was terrified at the sight of the razor and clung to Zenab's legs.

The circumcision done, the maulvi petted and consoled little Pali, ignoring the fact that all the time the child had kept uttering "Pitaji! Pitaji!" in great agony. The maulvi did not mind it at all. He just smiled indulgently. The neighbours came and felicitated Shakur and Zenab.

The maulvi gave the boy the gift of a red Rumi cap with a black tassel and placed it on the boy's head himself. Zenab gave him a brand-new white muslin kurta to wear and helped him to put it on then and there. The maulvi then lifted the boy and placed him in Zenab's arms.

"Take him!" the maulvi said happily. "He's your own child, not a kafir's. He belongs to the whole community."

The child was renamed Altaf—from Pali to Altaf. Carrying Altaf in her arms, Zenab went around distributing sweets in the mohalla.

Gradually, the child took to his new ways. Within a year, little Pali, now crockery seller Shakur Ahmed's son, Altaf Husain, became a familiar figure in the area. He played in his courtyard, hawking chinaware and aping his father's drawn out, lusty cry. He would collect all the utensils from the kitchen and put them in a basket, which he carried on his head and trotted round the courtyard announcing, like his father, the articles he had for sale.

When the month of Ramzan came, he would plant himself in the middle of his courtyard and proclaim to the beat of an empty tin canister, "Get up, you pious Muslims! Wake up from your sleep! Keep your holy fast!"

Shakur and Zenab lost no time in putting Altaf in the school attached to the local mosque. Sitting on the brick platform outside the mosque, he memorized the Quran along with other boys, swaying his head rhythmically in consonance with the lines from the holy book.

Zenab and Shakur's lives started revolving in a new orbit around Altaf. They wove their dreams around him. One day, Shakur would stop hawking his wares from door to door. Instead, he would set up a shop where father and son would sit together, conducting sales. They would not be at the mercy of others. They would be their own masters and sleep peacefully, with not a care in the world. Zenab eagerly looked forward to the day when Altaf's bride would set foot in her house, wearing ceremonial anklets.

Two years passed happily in this manner. One day, the chinaware seller had gone on his rounds, and little Altaf was at school. Only Zenab was at home. Sitting behind the tarpaulin curtain, she was grinding wheat.

There was a knock at the door. "My man is not at home," she responded from where she was sitting. "Come back in the evening."

After a pause, a voice said, "There's a court summons in Shakur Ahmed's name. He has been asked to report to the Police Station."

Zenab stopped grinding the wheat. Adjusting her palla over her head, she got up and stood behind the tarpaulin curtain. A tremor of fear ran through her spine. "What's the matter, ji?" she asked.

"Send him to the Police Station tomorrow morning. It's urgent."

"What for, ji?" She asked in a tremulous voice.

"They have come from Hindustan to claim the child. There is a letter to that effect."

Zenab shook from head to foot.

"Send him to the Police Station tomorrow morning," the man repeated. "Don't forget."

Zenab heard the man's retreating steps from behind the curtain.

There are some wounds that heal with the passage of time, leaving a mark on the mind. But there are certain griefs that slowly eat into the heart like termites, completely ravaging the body. There is nothing a man can do about it. When Kaushalya reached India with her husband, her lap was bereft of a child.

That day, if the convoy of lorries had safely reached the border and Manohar Lal had gone across it with his wife and child, they would have forgotten about Pali's separation from them as time passed. Unfortunately, it did not happen like that. They had just crossed the city limits when something happened. The convoy was passing along the road when a mob suddenly emerged from the fields flanking the road and raised war cries. Rushing up, they blocked the road. They wore masks, brandished swords and spears, and shouted filthy abuses. Most of the lorries had already passed, but the last three could not escape. Those in the lorries heard the same heart-chilling sounds of brandished swords and spears that Manohar Lal and Kaushalya had heard in the town from which they were escaping. Kaushalya did not even know at what point a heavy jolt knocked her down. She only heard Manohar Lal's voice, "Here, give me the child." Then that sound faded as she got another powerful push from behind, which sent her crashing to the floor of the lorry. When she regained her senses, all round her in the darkness she heard whistles blowing to the accompaniment of groans behind her. She felt something clammy on the floor under her hand. It could have been water; it could as well have been blood. The lorry suddenly started, and as she looked out, she felt as if the stars were moving with the lorry. Her throat was parched, and she desperately needed water. Then the stars started revolving, and she passed out.

Even on reaching Delhi, Manohar Lal could not get over the sensation of being crushed under a heap of dead bodies. He feared that if he could not extricate himself, he would die under their weight. While slogging along on the roads of Delhi with his wife and bemoaning the loss of their children, he realized that if he did not turn his back on the calamitous past, he would perish on those very roads. He hired a pushcart and set up shop in one of the bazaars of Delhi. When he returned home late at night, tired and weary, he would find his wife moaning as if she was on the verge of insanity, and his courage would desert him. What if she really went mad? How would he take care of her with so many other problems to handle? The small spark of life that was left in him would be extinguished too.

Taking her hand in his own, Manohar Lal assured Kaushalya that it was not too late for them to have another child. But at the mention of children, her condition would worsen. She would start trembling, and sometimes she wailed in such a heart-rending manner that even he became jittery.

The government had set up large organizations to trace abducted women and lost children and to retrieve stolen goods. Government officials made frequent trips to Pakistan for this purpose. Manohar Lal took time from his work to visit these government offices and meet influential people in order to seek their help in tracing his child. But he was too unimportant for anyone to take much notice of him. Month after month passed, but he obtained no leads. It was not easy to trace a lost child in a town swarming with people. When he had started looking, he had hoped that he had only to visit the town and identify the particular spot where Pali had been separated from him. He might find Pali at the entrance of some lane, eagerly looking for his father. He would immediately pick up the child in his arms and, on returning to Delhi, put him in Kaushalya's lap.

What vain hopes! Things were just the reverse of what he had hoped. It was as if his way were like a single thread hidden in a tangled mass: he did not even know where to start. For two full years, no progress was made on his case. Then he was allowed to accompany rescue parties of government officials and social workers who visited Pakistan from time to time. He would pack his small tin trunk and join them. But each time he returned, plucking his hair in despair.

After another two years, he at last had a lead. He learnt that the boy was living in his erstwhile hometown with a man named Shakur Ahmed, who owned a chinaware shop. This time Manohar Lal was quite sanguine that his trip would not prove fruitless.

The first time the police havildar came with the summons for Shakur, Zenab was greatly upset, her condition like that of a fish that has been thrown out of water. She felt that her dreams were crumbling before her very eyes.

Shakur returned in the evening, and his face turned pale on hearing the news. The news soon went round the mohalla, and many sympathizers dropped in to console him. The maulvi also came, tapping his lathi on the ground.

"You need have no fears," the maulvi said. "How dare they touch the child! Now that he has accepted Islam, we won't let him fall in the hands of kafirs."

Maulvi sahab's words revived Zenab's drooping spirits. He was right. Pali was not the same child who had slept in Zenab's arms on his first night in their house. If someone had come to claim him then, she wouldn't have stood in the person's way. But things were different now.

The elders of the town went into a huddle, and it was decided that Maulvi sahab would himself deal with the police. Maulvi sahab had an ingenious scheme up his sleeve. The police havildar would be tutored to report that he had not found Shakur at home, and hence the summons could not be served on him. If the havildar persisted in making calls, Shakur and his wife would leave the town for a few months and stay somewhere else with the child.

"The havildar be damned!" Maulvi sahab said. "I know how to cut him down to size!" He went away tapping his lathi and feeling very important.

A strange game of hide-and-seek started thereafter. The high-ups in government make agreements, but it is the petty government functionaries who execute these agreements. The orders would come from above to produce the boy before the authorities. Walking straight in line with his nose, a police constable from the Police Station would go to the right house. He would bang on the door, make threatening noises, pocket a rupee, and write on the summons papers that he had found the house locked and, on enquiry, had learnt that the residents had gone away and there was no knowing when they would return.

This was not a question of a small bribe, or one of returning an adopted child. The matter was taking on a religious cast. By not sending away the child, the police were doing a service to religion—something considered to be a pious act.

Months passed and merged into years.

On one occasion, the entire rescue party descended upon Shakur Ahmed's house, but found it locked. The family had been notified in advance and had disappeared before the arrival of the party. Shakur Ahmed, it transpired, had gone to Shekhupura to meet his brother, and no one had any information as to when he would return. When the party reached Shekhupura, it learnt that Shakur Ahmed had left for Lyallpur only a day earlier with his wife and child. "Yes, there was a child with them. But we do not know the man's address. He didn't leave any address behind before going away."

During this game of hide-and-seek, three years passed. Manohar Lal's face had started turning dark. His cheeks became deeply lined, and his hair showed streaks of gray. All the time, the dust of despair kept blowing before his eyes. He could not even distinguish between a truth and a lie. Life was mauling Manohar Lal with the same ferocity that a hawk tears a bird apart with its beak.

Whether it was the result of Manohar Lal's determination or the effect of Kaushalya's sighs, after seven years Manohar Lal found himself sitting in Shakur Ahmed's courtyard. He had gone there with a government rescue party and a woman representative of a social-service organization. Representing the Pakistani side were two police officers and a magistrate to conduct the proceedings. The meeting had been made possible by the intervention of a high Government of India official who had persuaded his counterpart in Pakistan.

At the meeting, Manohar Lal was required to prove that the child was really his. There was a legal angle to it, and he had to conform to a set procedure and convince the officials of his right to the child.

There was tension in the courtyard. The Maulvi sahab was sitting a little apart from the officials. Many people had gathered outside Shakur Ahmed's house. Zenab was sitting behind a tarpaulin curtain on the verandah. Her face looked pale, but her eyes were sharp and watchful, like the eyes of an eagle guarding its nest. Altaf Husain sat leaning against her, looking tense and bewildered. Zenab squeezed his shoulder frequently.

Before the proceedings started, Maulvi sahab issued all sorts of threats, perhaps to intimidate Manohar Lal.

"Nobody can take away the child. No kafir can touch him," he kept muttering.

The head of the Indian party asked the magistrate several times to order the maulvi to be quiet and reminded the magistrate that if the maulvi did not stop interfering, tension would increase.

Since Partition, the blood on the roads and streets had dried, but its stains were still visible here and there. The fire that had engulfed the houses had died out long since, but the charred frames were still standing. The mad frenzy of Partition had abated, but its effects still lingered in the minds of the people.

"Call the child!" the magistrate said, starting the proceedings.

"We have not stolen anybody's child," Zenab's agitated voice said from behind the curtain. "Why should I send him out?"

"Produce the child before me." The magistrate repeated his order. Shakur Ahmed went behind the curtain to fetch the child.

Manohar Lal's heart was pounding hard. The most decisive moment of his life had come. He was eager to have a look at his long-lost child. At the same time, his mind was assailed by doubts and fears.

The boy was made to stand before the magistrate. Seeing the crowd in the courtyard, he became nervous and clung to Shakur's legs. Putting his finger in his mouth, he looked around at the people as if stupefied.

"Son, come here," the magistrate said. "Look at who is here. Do you know any of them?"

"Nobody should prompt the boy," the police officer said in a warning tone. "Let the child decide for himself."

Manohar Lal failed to recognize his own son: an eleven-year-old boy with a Rumi cap perched on his head and wearing a muslin kurta and salwar. Manohar Lal's eyes were beginning to deceive him. He stared at the boy for a long time. Then the image of his own child flashed through his mind, and his throat choked with emotion. *Pali!* he cried. *Pali, my son!* But his voice died in his throat. He was not supposed to draw the boy's attention to himself.

The boy surveyed the people sitting in the courtyard. His expression recorded no change at the sight of Manohar Lal. He was looking as scared as before—only a little more so. Manohar Lal watched him intently. He had grown quite tall and fair and handsome and healthy. Manohar Lal felt that the time of decision had come and gone. The dice seemed to be loaded against him. Shorn of all joys, his life would remain bare and empty like a sandy waste.

Breaking the silence, the maulvi said, "So you have seen it. The child has failed to recognize him. Had he been this man's child, he would have dashed forward to him. And look at this man's audacity—he has come to demand another's child!"

The lady social worker was greatly annoyed. "Come here, son," she said. "Look, who's the man sitting in front of you?"

"No prompting please!" the police officer warned the social worker. "Leave the child alone. Let him find out for himself."

Zenab was sitting inside, holding her breath and feeling uncertain.

Addressing Shakur, the social worker said, "You've yourself admitted that he is not your child—that you've adopted him."

Before Shakur Ahmed could reply, the maulvi banged his lathi on the floor and said, "We don't deny that he is an adopted child. But how can one accept this man's contention that the boy is a Hindu child and belongs to him?"

The magistrate nodded his head as if he was in agreement with what the maulvi had said. He looked at the child, then at Manohar Lal. Manohar Lal felt more and more hopeless. His own child was standing before him, and all he could do was watch him listlessly. The opportunity to get him back seemed to have slipped through his fingers.

"The child has become nervous," the social worker said.

"Please keep quiet!"

"What more do you want?" the maulvi asked. "It's already decided. You people may go."

The social worker turned to Manohar Lal. "Yes, now I remember," she said. "Where's the photograph you showed me the other day?"

As proof, Manohar Lal had not been able to bring anything except a small photograph. Once at Kaushalya's request, he had had himself photographed with her at the Baisakhi fair. In the picture, little Pali was sitting in his lap. But it could serve no useful purpose at the moment. Pali had grown quite big and bore no resemblance to the little boy of the photograph. Manohar Lal took it out of his pocket and passed it on to the magistrate.

"My son is in this photograph. It's the same child. You can see for yourself."

Shakur Ahmed flared up. "Janab, this photograph proves nothing," he said to the magistrate. "I too have a photograph."

He went in his house and came back with a framed photograph. Wiping it with his sleeve, he handed it to the magistrate.

"It's the same child whom you see standing in front of you," he said, pointing towards the boy in the photograph. "You can verify for yourself."

"Come here, child." The magistrate placed Manohar Lal's photograph in front of the boy without making any comment, convinced that he would not be able to recognize anybody in it.

The boy looked intently at the picture for some time. Then, lifting his hand, he placed his forefinger on Manohar Lal's image and cried, "Pitaji!" Then his finger slowly moved towards the woman in the photograph. "Mataji!" he exclaimed.

The child's eyes remained fixed on the photograph. A strange restlessness seemed to seize him.

Manohar Lal burst out crying. He thrust the end of his turban into his mouth to suppress his sobs.

The magistrate placed the other photograph in front of the child. The child beamed. "Abbaji! Ammi!" he exclaimed.

A wave of joy surged through Shakur Ahmed. Zenab peeped out from behind the curtain. Her eyes were brimming with tears.

The maulvi's face had remained taut all this time. Then his expression suddenly mellowed.

"Now he is a Mussalman's son, not a Hindu's. He has read the kalma," the maulvi said with an air of finality.

"Please be quiet!" the social worker cried.

"Why should I remain quiet? This man had thrown him away and disappeared. We brought him up!" The maulvi's voice rose.

Hearing the maulvi's loud and threatening voice, the boy ran to Shakur and clung to his legs. Then he ran towards the veranda and hid behind the curtain.

The people outside must have heard what was going on in the courtyard, for suddenly voices resounded. "Allah ho Akbar!"

The lady social worker and the two Indian officials stoutly put forward the plea that, since the child had recognized his father, he should be restored to him without further ado. But things seemed to be taking an ugly turn. The tension was mounting. While the child was sitting in Zenab's lap with his arms around her neck, the complexion of the problem was undergoing a change. It had become a Hindu-Muslim matter. Questions like "Whose child is he?" and "Who brought him up?" seemed to have become irrelevant.

Finding himself at the end of his tether, Manohar Lal had an idea. Getting up, he went and stood near the curtain. Folding his hands, he said, "Bahen, I'm not begging you for my child. I'm begging you for my wife's life. She has lost both her children. She is missing Pali very much. His absence is driving her insane. Day and night she keeps thinking of him. Please have pity on her."

The area behind the tarpaulin curtain remained steeped in silence. The officials of both countries watched the curtain intently. The maulvi rose to his feet. He had no doubt that Zenab would hurl the choicest abuses at Manohar Lal. Instead, they heard the sound of sobbing. "Take away the child. I do not want an unfortunate woman's curse to fall upon me. How could I know you had lost both your children?"

Manohar Lal felt like going behind the curtain and falling at the woman's feet.

An hour later the child was given a send-off. Amidst tears, Zenab and Shakur helped him put on new clothes, which had been specially made for the forthcoming Id. They put a new Rumi cap on his head. Then Zenab said, "I will part with the child on one condition. You must send him to us every year on the occasion of Id to stay with us for a month. Do you agree? Then give me your word."

Manohar Lal's body tingled. His hands still folded in supplication, he said, "He is your wealth, bahen. I give you my word. I'll remain indebted to you all my life."

The wheel of life started moving again. The same meandering paths, the same turnings, the same ups and downs. If things had ended there, this narration would have assumed the form of a story, possessing something of interest for everybody. But nothing ever ends, nothing ever comes to finality. The powers that be struck out one more name from the long list of the abducted, and transferred that name to the list of the found.

The government jeep was travelling at great speed. By the side of the driver sat an armed guard and next to him the police officer. At the back of the jeep sat father and son, tightly set against each other, and opposite them the lady social worker. The child looked lost and forlorn. In contact with the boy's body, Manohar Lal's body had again started tingling warmly. The cords of affection that had snapped were slowly reconnecting.

They crossed the border in the afternoon. Getting down from the Pakistani jeep, they submitted their papers to the scrutiny of the Indian authorities stationed on the other side of the boundary line. Manohar Lal, his son, and the others then drove off in another jeep towards Amritsar.

The jeep had not gone far when the lady social worker, as if acting on sudden impulse, extended her right hand, whisked the Rumi cap off the boy's head, and flung it out of the jeep. The red cap with the black tassel flew in the air and landed in the dust at the edge of the road.

"My cap!" the boy's hand went to his head. "Hai, my cap!"

The lady social worker leaned towards the boy. "You are a Hindu boy. Why should you wear a Muslim cap?"

Manohar Lal did not appreciate the brusque manner in which the cap had been removed from the boy's head and thrown away. "That must have hurt the boy's feelings. He doesn't know that it is a Muslim cap," Manohar Lal said to the social worker. "Why did you throw it away? Stop the jeep. I must retrieve the cap."

The boy had pulled a long face and was on the verge of tears. His hand resting over his head, he kept moaning over the loss of his cap. "Oh, my cap!" he cried again and again.

"He is still a child, ignorant of these things," Manohar Lal explained patiently. "See, he's still crying."

"Let him cry," the woman said. "Crying is not going to do him any harm. You're not going to give him a Rumi cap to wear, are you? He'll stop crying in a short while."

The jeep raced on, raising clouds of dust behind it.

Far away from the border, in a small town where many refugees had settled down, the news spread at the speed of lightning that Manohar Lal and Kaushalya's son had returned. The impossible had happened. God's mill, they said, grinds slow, but it grinds fine. The boy was returning after seven years. A lucky child indeed! The women kissed the child's head and bowed their heads in gratitude to God. "See, bahen, one who is ordained to live lives long…See, bahen, the child you were holding against your bosom was snatched away by death right from your arms, and the one who had stayed away from you and was lost and forlorn has come back hale and hearty. Nobody can harm a person who has God's benign protection."

Back home, the child kept whimpering as he had done during the first two or three days of his arrival in Shakur's house. On the first day, he kept watching his mother, Kaushalya, from a distance. He saw nothing of those traits in her that he hazily remembered. The loss of her children seemed to have wreaked havoc on her youth. Dim memories of the past were slowly reviving in the child's mind: hazy, nebulous, incoherent. He vaguely remembered his small sister lying in his mother's lap. And the buffalo that stood tethered outside their door and on whose back he used to enjoy riding. Also the wooden bed that was a permanent fixture outside their house. He could hear a babble of sounds rising higher and higher every moment. The identity of his mother had gradually started returning to his mind. But sometimes he still wondered if the boy who was standing before her, finger in mouth and brazenly staring at her, was really Pali. He would feel more and more confused.

Three or four days passed in this manner.

Then came Sunday. The dholak began beating in Manohar Lal's courtyard from early morning. The women of the mohalla gathered in the courtyard and sang in tune to the rhythmic beat of the drum. Two small cotton carpets had been spread in the courtyard, and a few cane seats were lined against the walls. There were also some cots to sit on in case too many guests arrived. Kaushalya was looking her normal self. She was not silent or withdrawn as before. She even laughed a little. That morning she wore a red chunri hemmed with threads of gold—a red chunri, the traditional Hindu symbol of matrimonial bliss and good fortune.

Manohar Lal was all attention to the guests. He was not tired of telling his friends that the people back in Pakistan had taken great care of his son. He could not match the attention and affection they had showered on him. He would indeed remain indebted to them all his life.

The narrow courtyard was filled with guests. Holding a big platter of laddoos, Manohar Lal was about to go round to distribute the sweets when Pali did something strange. He had been sitting by the side of his mother, listening to the women playing the dholak and singing, when he abruptly got up and fetched a mat from inside the house. He spread it on the floor, sat down on it, folding his legs under his thighs, and started saying his namaz.

The people sitting in the courtyard watched him with curiosity. But their curiosity soon changed into dismay.

"What's going on, Kaushalya?" a woman asked. "What's your son doing?"

Manohar Lal was feeling embarrassed by his son's behavior in front of his guests. He should have anticipated this and done something to prevent it from happening. He apologetically said to the man standing by his side, "Every afternoon right at this hour he sits down to say his namaz. He instinctively knows that it's time for namaz."

"Don't you stop him?" a voice asked.

"He's still a child. He'll learn soon enough."

A man who was regarded as a big shot in the mohalla said in a loud voice for all to hear, "He must at once get rid of this nasty habit. We don't want to have a Muslim among us."

The boy continued with his namaz while the people around him watched with feelings of disgust.

Manohar Lal said as if in self-defence, "You know, those people didn't have a child of their own. And—"

"Manohar Lal!" The big shot who was regarded as the Chaudhri of the mohalla cut him short. "You must know those people have foisted a Muslim convert on you and yet you have nothing but praise for them."

The boy was still sitting on his folded legs and, with his palms raised upwards, repeating his namaz prayers. The Chaudhri went and stood by the boy's side.

His namaz finished, the boy was wiping his face with both hands when the Chaudhri caught him by the wrist and dragged him to the middle of the courtyard.

"What were you doing?" he asked the boy.

Pali was unnerved. "I was saying namaz," he said in a faint voice.

"We won't allow you to do such silly things in this house," the Chaudhri barked at Pali. "No namaz hereafter. Do you understand?" Turning round to the people watching, he remarked, "Those Muslas have planted the poison of fanaticism in his mind. And at such a tender age!"

He stood thinking for a while. "Better call a pandit," he said in a decisive tone to a friend. "And also a barber. We must perform the boy's mundan. And let him keep a proper tuft. Those rascals! They have planted a Musla among us."

Pali stood there looking utterly confused.

"What's your name, boy?"

Pali looked timidly at the massive bulk of the Chaudhri and mumbled in a subdued voice, "Altaf, Altaf Husain, son of Shakur Ahmed."

The Chaudhri glared at the boy. With great difficulty, he restrained himself from slapping him. The boy felt that the pressure of the man's grip on his wrist had increased. He gave the man a terrified look.

"No, your name is Pali—Yashpal!"

The boy stood silent and then mumbled, "Altaf."

"Repeat that name again and see what happens. I'll pull out your tongue!"

"Have you seen these Musla doings?" the Chaudhri said, turning to the people around him. "They call it conversion: religious conversion. Reform!"

The barber arrived, followed by the pandit. Accompanying the pandit was a man carrying ghee and other ingredients for performing a havan.

The boy was again made to sit on a mat. The barber sharpened the razor on his palm and, according to the directions given by the pandit, started shaving the boy's head. As long as the ceremony lasted, the boy kept sobbing with bowed head. Once he got up in fright, and crying "Ammi, Ammi, Abbaji!" he ran towards the wall of the courtyard. Standing with his back against the wall, he looked at the Chaudhri like a deer at bay, watching a hunter. At the suggestion of the Chaudhri, Manohar Lal went to fetch the boy. He held the boy's hand and gently brought him back to the mat.

A tuft of hair was left in the middle of his cropped head. Pali was bathed, then given a brand-new dhoti and kurta to wear. To the chanting of mantras, he was given a sacred thread.

"Child, what's your name? Say five times, Pali, Pali, Pali…"

Sometime later, looking every inch a brahmachari, Yashpal, Pali, stood at the door with folded hands, seeing off the guests. The relatives and guests caressed his head and blessed him while departing. Manohar Lal distributed laddoos.

At that time, sitting in their lonely courtyard hundreds of miles away, Zenab and Shakur were conjecturing. Zenab said, "He is gone, and with him is gone all the gaiety of this house. At this time I used to go out into the street in search of him. He would try to hide from me, running into nooks and corners. I would never know where to find him. Oh, it was such joy! Well, what do you think? Will he come to visit us for Id? Will those people send him here? I think they will."

"Oh yes, you once told me you had a cousin living in Bareilly. We shall go and stay with him and meet our son. What do you think of that?"

Zenab wiped her eyes again and again.

Translation from Hindi by the author

The Claim _____

There were just three passengers in the tonga when it left the stand. If the bus had not appeared in the distance, Sadhu Singh would have waited a bit longer for a fourth. For as soon as the bus pulled up, his passengers would invariably climb out of the tonga and board it. Thus the necessity of departing just before the bus arrived. Until then, though, he would not leave the stand without a fourth passenger, however impatient his other passengers were. The bus cost five paise for a ride from Kachari to Model Town, so the tonga also travelled that route for five paise apiece. If there were four passengers, he could make five annas. Otherwise, by driving his horse one and a quarter miles he would gain just ten to fifteen paise. He had made three trips since morning to Model Town, but had collected barely seventeen annas. His horse panted so heavily in the scorching June sun that it was hardly prudent to work him so hard for a mere ten paise. But without it, Sadhu Singh could not even buy feed. Very few people travelled in summer, and he was, moreover, in competition with the bus, which took barely five minutes to go from Kachari to Model Town.

"Go, Afsar, go! Make a sacrifice! Go!" Standing up, he turned the reins and began to employ his whip. Till he had crossed the washermen's sector, he hoped he might meet some passenger on the road. But the whole sector was empty, with the exception of a few washerwomen dozing in the doorways. Emerging from the area, he loosened up on the reins and moved out a bit on the pole in order to better distribute the tonga's weight.

As the bus came up from behind, the woman seated at the back began to yell, "You coaxed us into your tonga and now you're clopping along as if you've come out to do a tour of the streets! If it was to take this long, you might have said so and we could have taken the bus. If we didn't have something important to do, do you think we would have come out in such heat?"

Leaping up, Sadhu Singh moved farther out onto the pole and started cracking his whip. "Go! Test your mettle, sacrifice your youth! Run with the speed of a bullet! Memsahib is getting angry. May your speed be blessed, Afsar! Strike up a gallop!"

But even under the crack of the whip, Afsar did not increase his speed. He shook his head back and forth a few times and continued on at his own pace. The bus came up from behind, blowing its horn, and passed on ahead, leaving the tonga in a cloud of dust.

"Look at that! The bus has gone on ahead! And you claimed we'd get there first!" the woman said again.

Without bothering to reply, Sadhu Singh kept on cracking his whip. And Afsar, disregarding the whip completely, continued to trot.

The road was no more than a mile and a quarter long. After the sun went down, it could be crossed in a snap. But in the full heat of the afternoon, there was no shade and the whole vicinity seemed shrivelled and desolate. In certain spots, the tar of the street had melted. And the neighbouring ponds, usually of a depth of nine feet, had completely dried up. Sadhu Singh began to wonder how hot it would get if this was just the beginning of summer.

"Go, Raja! Go, boy! May your life be blessed. Be generous and go like a bullet! May your mother's milk be blessed!"

The tonga's three passengers were headed for the Claims Office. Sitting towards the front, the Sikh was saying that his claim for 60,000 rupees had been accepted: he was getting half in cash and the other half in some form of property. Sitting at the back, the woman was cursing those officials who were processing her claim of just 18,000 rupees. In Gujaranwala, her family had had four houses and an orchard of three and a half acres. If it had been four acres, she said, they would have got more money. Had they known that beforehand, they would have filed a claim for four acres. They had therefore perished due to their own honesty! At home, she had two young girls whom she had to leave alone while making the daily rounds from Batala to Jullunder. Her husband had died making such trips, and she herself was constantly ill.

"I don't know whether or not I'll get to see the money from these butchers during my lifetime! I guess I'll die in torment and leave my children behind, in mourning." Her tone was more like that of someone lodging a complaint than of someone conversing with others. From the expression on her face, it appeared as if she had just suffered a terrible shock.

The man beside her was sitting silently, his forehead wrinkled in deep thought.

"Madam, have you got anything from your claim?" the Sikh asked sympathetically.

"As of now, I've got 6,000 in all," she said. "But I have children at home. What can I do with 6,000? My children are used to eating and wearing the best. I could spend that much on them in a month! And people tell me I got that money quickly only because I'm a widow. They did me a favour giving me so much!" And she began to wipe her eyes with the hem of her sari.

The man who had been sitting silently turned towards the Sikh and said somewhat scornfully in a guttural voice, "It's true when they say the intellect of woman is enchained!"

"How have I angered you that you should insult me?" Wiping her tears, the woman flared up. "I didn't ask for your property. I'm lamenting all that I have left behind."

"You're not alone there. We've all come here, leaving our ancestral homes behind. Thank God, you got 6,000! There are some among us who've not got even a paisa. Our problem is that both I and my wife are alive and well. If I were to perish, my children might get a few pieces of bread! I'm going blind, my joints ache—by living, am I any better than the dead? But there's such blindness in the government office that they don't see what a man needs—they just keep their accounts of the living and the dying. If I were to be given a thousand rupees today, I could open a little shop. My children don't even have a torn shirt to wear!"

"That's really a question of one's personal fortune! Can someone's sorrow in any way console someone else?" the Sikh asked, interjecting. "Both you and I have experienced sorrow, as has this lady here—which one of us is not unhappy? Some are less, some are more."

"You're getting 60,000 rupees! What do you have to be unhappy about?" The man became even more fretful.

"And that I am getting it is also a matter of luck," the Sikh replied. "I used my head when I filed the claim, and look at the result! If I hadn't, we would have been sent away with 10,000 or 20,000."

"You filed a claim for more than you were worth?"

"Our property was worth 150,000 rupees. But we found out that if we filed an accurate claim, we wouldn't get nearly that much. So, praying to Waheguru, we filled out a claim that might realize for us, more or less, the true worth of our property. But those crooks nonetheless accepted a claim for only 60,000. There are six of us brothers—so we'll have to be satisfied with 10,000 apiece."

"I said as much to him, but he just wouldn't listen!" The woman began to rub her hands despondently.

Both men looked at her inquiringly.

"I kept telling him that no matter how much we left behind, we should file a claim for double. But he was such a fool that he insisted on claiming only what we were worth. 'Why should we be dishonest now, no matter what suffering we have had to undergo!' If he were here, I'd ask him who was happier—us or all the crooks in this business. Some people have collected two or three times what they left behind. And I sit here with 6,000! God, these people are slowly starving my children to death!"

The man sitting next to her turned his face away and put his hand on his forehead. The Sikh again expressed his sympathy. "Nothing comes of crying, madam. Whatever is fated is precisely one's lot. The Creator has already determined all of this. Be satisfied with what you get."

"Am I the only one who should remain content? The whole world might enjoy itself, and I ought to rest content with my lot!" She went on crying.

"Get there as fast as you can, driver! Why are you going so slowly?" the man beside her asked impatiently.

Irritated, Sadhu Singh cracked his whip time and again, but there was no change in the horse's pace. Then he began to crack the whip across the horse's back. "To hell with you, Afsar! May a wasp sting your tail! Go quickly, boy!" But despite his fear of the wasp, Afsar did not quicken his speed.

Having deposited his passengers outside the Claims Office, Sadhu Singh did not meet a single passenger on his return. He stopped for a while by the turning towards the market, but no pedestrian appeared on any of the three roads that converged there. A few rickshaw pullers were sleeping in the shade of Shop 13. Sadhu Singh felt like having the shopkeeper make him a glass of lime juice and then perhaps lying in the shade for a while. But there was no shady place to tie the tonga nor any drainpipe at which to water the horse, which was alternately neighing and hanging its tongue out, almost prostrate with heat. Even the seventeen annas in his pocket were not really his own. To buy feed for the horse, he needed at least two rupees. So he wet his lips with his tongue and turned the horse's face in the direction of the city.

He drove the tonga along the straight, desolate road, where even the trees stood with their branches drooping, oppressed by the heat. Nearby, birds were chirping in the bushes.

Sadhu Singh slackened the reins, half reclining on the backseat and letting his mind hover among the branches of a mango tree he had planted with such pleasure in the courtyard of his home in Pattoki. Through nine years of familiarity, that nine-rupee-a-month house had come to seem like his own. How many times had Hiran said that if you plant and tend a tree in someone else's yard, one day you'll leave it for others to enjoy! But who would have thought then that he would leave the house, never to be lucky enough to even pass by it again!

These days, the mango tree should be producing good fruit. And Hiran?

Fruit had appeared on the tree for the first time that year. And in his happiness, who knows how many unripe mangoes he had eaten!

"Why are you intentionally ruining your teeth?" Hiran would ask him, irritated.

"It's the fruit of my own tree, darling! My teeth wouldn't spoil, eating it." And he enfolded Hiran's half-bloomed youth in his wide embrace.

The mangoes had turned from green to yellow and from yellow to red when the riots began. Blood flowed in every street of Pattoki. At midnight, the rioters entered their sector of the town. When their door was broken down, he was lying close to Hiran on the charpoy. Quickly, he decided to spring towards the backyard. But Hiran, standing a few times on tiptoe, was unable to make the jump. And before she could summon the courage to try again, a hand from behind yanked her back.

Darkness, fields, and railway tracks—lifeless hands and feet and hunger—ticket, coupon, card, and number.

NAME: SADHU SINGH

FATHER'S NAME: MILKHA SINGH

CASTE: KHATRI

PROPERTY: NONE

MONEY: NONE

CLAIM: ?

What claim could he make?

That mango tree of his, for whose maturity he had waited impatiently—eating whose green fruit, he had been spoiling his teeth—the years of the future to be spent in the shade of that tree?

The house's own special smell, which, emanating from a bundle of clothes, enveloped everything right up to the walls of the courtyard. That smell?

And the evenings spent lying in the courtyard, staring at the sky?

And all the plans of the coming life that rose up in the mind while going in and out of his house?

"Tell me, Hiran, will your first child be a boy or a girl?"

"Shame on you. What are you saying?"

"OK, shall I tell you? Your first will be a girl. Then two boys. Then another girl."

"Be quiet! Why are you jabbering so?"

"The second girl will be more beautiful than the first. She'll have hair as soft as yours, the same huge eyes, and right here by the chin, a mole—"

"What are you doing?"

"I'll give her a pinch like this, and she'll screech like this—"

That feeling? That thrill? That imagination? That future?

NAME: SADHU SINGH

FATHER'S NAME: MILKHA SINGH

CASTE: KHATRI

NUMBER: ?

CLAIM: ?

The mango tree would have grown big by now. The smell of the walls of the house must have changed. And Hiran—who knows whose children are in her lap today?

Sadhu Singh straightened and sat up as the tonga again reached the washermen's sector. Everyone seemed to be dozing by now. He jerked continuously at the reins. The horse's neck lifted a bit, then bent again as usual.

Reaching the stand, Sadhu Singh watered the horse at the drainpipe and, taking the feed from under the seat, put it before him. The horse thrust his mouth into the feed as Sadhu Singh stroked his back. "If God keeps you well, Afsar, the old days will return. Eat! Fill your belly! Your claims must be filled. May your life be blessed!"

And Afsar, stretching long his neck, silently continued to eat.

Translation from Hindi by Richard Williams

The Dog of Tetwal

The two sides had not budged from their positions for several days now. Occasional bursts of fire—about ten or twelve rounds in a day—were to be heard, but never the sound of human shrieks.

The weather was pleasant; the wind wafted across, spreading the scent of wildflowers. Oblivious to the battle on the peaks and slopes, nature was immersed in its necessary work—the birds chirped as before, the flowers continued to bloom, and lazy honey-bearing bees sleepily sipped nectar in the old, time-honoured way.

Each time a shot echoed in the hills, the chirping birds would cry out in alarm and fly up, as though someone had struck a wrong note on an instrument and shocked their hearing.

September-end was meeting the beginning of October in roseate hue. It seemed that winter and summer were negotiating peace with one another. Thin, light clouds like fluffed-up cotton sailed in the blue sky, as if out on an excursion in their white shikaras.

For several days now, the soldiers on both sides of the mountain had been restless, as no decisive action was taking place. Lying in their positions, they would get bored and then attempt to recite sh'ers to one another. If no one listened, they would hum to themselves. They remained lying on their stomachs or backs on the rocky ground, and when the order came, let off a round or two.

The two sides were entrenched in rather safe positions. The high-velocity bullets crashed against the shields of stone and fell to the ground. The two mountains on which the forces were ranged were of about the same height. Between them was a green valley—a rivulet wriggling like a fat snake on its chest.

There was no danger of air raids. Neither side possessed artillery. Therefore, fires would be lit without fear or danger, and smoke from fires on each side would rise and mingle in the air. At night, it was absolutely quiet. The soldiers on each side could hear bursts of laughter from the other. Once in a while, entering into this spirit, a soldier would begin to sing, and his voice would awaken the silence of the night. The echoes would then reverberate, and it would seem that the mountains were repeating what they had just heard.

One round of tea had just been taken. The pine coals in the stone chulhas had grown cold. The sky was clear. There was a chill in the air. The wind had ceased to carry the scent of flowers, as though they had shut up their vial of perfume for the night. However, the sweat of the pines, their resin, left an odour in the air that was not wholly unpleasant.

The soldiers slept wrapped in their blankets, but in such a way that in a single movement they could arise, ready for battle.

Jamadar Harnam Singh was on guard. When his Rascope watch showed that it was two o'clock, he woke Ganda Singh and told him to take station. He wanted to sleep, but when he lay down, he found sleep a distant proposition, as distant as the stars in the sky. Jamadar Harnam Singh lay on his back and, gazing up at the stars, began to hum:

> *Bring me a pair of shoes, studded with stars*
> *Studded with stars*
> *O Harnam Singh*
> *O Yaara*
> *Even if you have to sell your buffalo.*

Harnam Singh saw star-studded shoes scattered all over the sky, all a-twinkle.

> *I will bring you shoes, studded with stars*
> *Studded with stars*
> *O Harnam Kaur*
> *O Lady, even if I have to sell my buffalo.*

He smiled as the song came to an end, and realizing that he would not be able to sleep, he rose and woke up everybody else. The thought of his beloved had made him restless. He wished for some nonsensical chatter that would recreate the mood of the beloved in the song.

The soldiers did begin to talk, but in a desultory fashion. Banta Singh, the youngest and the one with the best voice, went and sat on one side. The rest, though yawning all the while, kept gossiping about trivial but entertaining matters. After a while, Banta Singh suddenly began singing "Heer" in a melancholic voice.

> *Heer said, The jogi lied; no one placates a hurt lover.*
> *I have found no one—grown weary, looking*
> *for the one who calls back the departed lover.*
> *A falcon has lost the crane to the crow—see, does it remain silent or weep?*
> *Happy talk and stories to entertain the world are not for the suffering one.*

After a pause, he began singing Ranjha's reply to Heer's words:

The falcon that lost the crane to the crow has, thank God, been annihilated.
His condition is like the fakir who gave away his all, and was left with nothing.
Be contented, feel the pain less and God will be your witness.
Renouncing the world and donning the garb of sorrow, Saiyed Waris has
  become Waris Shah.

Just as abruptly as Banta Singh had begun to sing, he fell silent. It appeared as if the soil-tinted mountains also had taken on the mantle of grief.

After a while, Jamadar Harnam Singh let out a mighty oath at an imaginary object, then lay down. Suddenly, in the melancholy stillness of the last quarter of the night, the barking of a dog began to resound. Everyone was startled. The sound did not come from too far off. Jamadar Harnam Singh sat up and said, "From where has this barking one come?"

The dog barked again. Now the sound was much closer. After a few moments, there was a rustling in the bushes.

Banta Singh rose and moved towards the bushes. When he returned, he had with him a stray dog, its tail wagging.

He smiled. "Jamadar sahab, when I asked him, he said, I am Chapad Jhunjhun."

Everyone laughed. Jamadar Harnam Singh addressed the dog affectionately. "Come here, Chapad Jhunjhun."

The dog approached Harnam Singh, wagging its tail. It began sniffing the stones on the ground in the belief that some food had been thrown there.

Jamadar Harnam Singh reached into his bag, took out a biscuit, and threw it in the dog's direction. The dog sniffed at the biscuit and opened its mouth. But Harnam Singh leapt at it and picked it up. "Wait…He could be a Pakistani."

Everybody laughed at this. Banta Singh came forward, stroked the dog on its back, and said to Jamadar Harnam Singh, "No, Jamadar sahab, Chapad Jhunjhun is a Hindustani."

Jamadar Harnam Singh laughed and, looking at the dog, said, "Oye, show me the identification!"

The dog wagged its tail.

Harnam Singh laughed heartily. "This is no identification…All dogs wag their tails."

Banta Singh caught the dog by its trembling tail. "The poor thing is a refugee!"

Jamadar Harnam Singh threw down the biscuit, and the dog immediately pounced on it.

Digging up the ground with the heel of his boot, one of the soldiers said, "Now, even dogs will have to be either Hindustani or Pakistani!"

The Jamadar took out another biscuit from his bag and threw it towards the dog. "Like the Pakistanis, Pakistani dogs will be shot."

"Hindustan Zindabad!" Another soldier loudly raised the slogan.

The dog, which had just begun to move forward to pick up the biscuit, suddenly grew frightened and backed off with its tail between its legs.

Harnam Singh laughed. "Why do you fear our slogan, Chapad Jhun-jhun?...Eat...Here, take another biscuit!" And so saying, he took another biscuit out and threw it.

The soldiers talked on, and soon it was morning.

In the blink of an eye, just as when one presses a button and the electricity generates light, the sun's rays flooded the mountainous region of Tetwal.

The battle had been raging in that area for some time. Dozens of lives of soldiers would be lost for each mountain, and even then the hold of either side was tenuous. If they held the area today, tomorrow their enemies did; the following day, they recaptured it, and the day after that, their enemies did so.

Jamadar Harnam Singh picked up his binoculars and surveyed the surrounding area. Smoke was rising from the mountain in front. This meant that a fire was being stoked there too, tea was being readied, and the thought of breakfast was on the mind; undoubtedly, the other side could see smoke rising from Jamadar Harnam Singh's camp.

At breakfast, each soldier gave a little to the dog, which ate it with gusto. Everyone was taking a keen interest in the dog, as if all wanted to make it a friend. Its arrival had brought with it an element of cheerfulness. From time to time, each one would affectionately address it as Chapad Jhunjhun and cuddle it.

On the other side, in the Pakistani camp, Subedar Himmat Khan was twirling his impressive moustache—which had many a story in its past—and was carefully studying the map of Tetwal. With him sat the wireless operator, who was taking orders from the Platoon Commander for Subedar Himmat Khan. At some distance, Bashir, leaning against a rock, was holding his gun and softly humming:

Where did you spend the night,
my love. Where did you spend...

As Bashir swung into the mood and raised his pitch, he heard Subedar Himmat Khan's stern admonition. "Oye, where were you last night?"

When Bashir's inquiring gaze shifted towards Himmat Khan, he saw him looking elsewhere.

"Tell me, oye!..."

Bashir turned to see what Himmat was looking at.

The same stray dog, which, a few days earlier, had come to their camp like an uninvited guest and stayed on, was back, sitting a little distance away.

Bashir smiled and, turning to the dog, began:

> *Where did you spend the night,*
> *my love. Where did you…*

The dog began wagging its tail vigorously, sweeping the rocky ground around him.

Subedar Himmat Khan picked up a pebble and threw it at the dog. "Saala knows nothing except how to wag his tail."

All of a sudden Bashir looked carefully at the dog. "What's this around his neck?" He started walking towards the dog, but even before he reached it, another soldier took off the rope tied around its neck. A piece of cardboard with something written on it was strung to it. Subedar Himmat Khan took the piece of cardboard and asked the soldiers, "Does any one of you know how to read this?"

Bashir came forward, picked up the cardboard piece, and said, "Yes, I can read a bit." With great difficulty he spelled out "Cha-p-Chapad-Jhun-Jhun…Chapad Jhunjhun…What's this?"

Subedar Himmat Khan twirled his legendary long moustache vigorously. "It must be some word, some…" Then he asked, "Bashir, is there anything else written there?…"

Bashir, immersed in deciphering the writing, replied, "Yes, there is. This is a Hindustani dog."

Subedar Himmat Khan began thinking aloud. "What does this mean? What was it you read?…Chapad?…"

Bashir then answered, "Chapad Jhunjhun!"

One soldier said as if with great knowledge, "Whatever the matter is, it lies here."

Subedar Himmat Khan thought this appropriate. "Yes, it does seem so!"

Bashir read the text inscribed on the cardboard once more. "Chapad Jhunjhun. This is a Hindustani dog."

Subedar Himmat Khan took up the wireless set and, placing the headphones firmly over his ears, personally spoke to the Platoon Commander about the dog—that it had first come to them and stayed for several days, and then one night, it disappeared from their midst. Now that it had returned, there was a rope tied around its neck with a cardboard piece strung on it, on which was written—and this message he repeated three or four times to the Platoon Commander—"Chapad Jhunjhun. This is a Hindustani dog." But they too could not come to any conclusion.

Bashir sat on one side with the dog, speaking lovingly and harshly by turns, and asked it where it had disappeared for the night and who had tied the rope and the cardboard around its neck. But he did not get the answer he desired. When questioned, the dog would just wag its tail in response. Finally, in anger, Bashir caught it and gave it a violent shake. The dog whined in pain.

Having spoken on the wireless set, Subedar Himmat Khan contemplated the map of Tetwal for some time. He then rose in a decisive manner. Tearing off the top of a cigarette packet, he handed it to Bashir. "Here, Bashir, scribble on this in the same creepy-crawly Gurmukhi as they have."

Bashir took the piece of the cigarette packet and asked, "What should I write, Subedar sahab?"

Subedar Himmat Khan twirled his moustache and reflected. "Write... Just write." He took out a pencil from his pocket. Giving it to Bashir, he asked, "What should we write?"

Bashir passed the pencil tip between his lips and began thinking. Suddenly, in a contemplative, questioning tone he asked, "Sapar Sunsun?..." Then, satisfied, he said in a determined way, "OK, the answer to 'Chapad Jhunjhun' can only be 'Sapar Sunsun.' They will remember their mothers, these Sikhras!" Bashir put the pencil to the top of the cigarette pack. "Sapar Sunsun."

"One hundred percent...Write Sa-pa-r-Sunsun!" Subedar Khan laughed loudly. "And write further, 'This is a Pakistani dog!'"

Subedar Himmat Khan took the cardboard piece from Bashir's hand, made a hole in it with the pencil, and, after stringing the rope through it, moved towards the dog. "Take this to your offspring!"

All the soldiers laughed at this.

Subedar Himmat Khan tied the rope around the dog's neck. The dog kept wagging its tail all the while. The Subedar then gave it something to eat and, in a didactic manner, said, "Look, friend, don't commit treachery...Remember, the punishment for a traitor is death."

The dog kept wagging its tail...After it had eaten its fill, Subedar Himmat Khan picked up the rope, led it towards the sole trail on the hill, and said, "Go, deliver our letter to our enemies...But make sure you come back. This is the command of your officer, understand?"

The dog, still wagging its tail, began walking ever so slowly along the trail that took a winding route into the lap of the mountains.

Subedar Himmat Khan took up his gun and fired once into the air.

The shot and its echo were heard on the other side, at the Hindustani camp, but they could not fathom its meaning.

For some reason, Jamadar Harnam Singh had been grumpy that day, and the sound of the shot made him even more irritable. He gave the order to fire. Consequently, for the next half hour a futile rain of bullets poured from each side. Eventually sated by the diversion, Jamadar Harnam Singh called a halt to the firing and began combing his beard with greater ferocity. Having done that, he methodically bundled his hair into a net and asked Banta Singh, "Oye, Banta Singh, tell me: where has Chapad Jhunjhun gone? The ghee didn't go down well with the dog."

Banta Singh missed the implication of the idiom and said, "But we didn't feed him any ghee."

Jamadar Harnam Singh laughed boisterously. "Oye, ill-read lout, there is no use talking to you."

Meanwhile, the soldier on watch, who was scanning the horizon with his binoculars, suddenly shouted, "There, he's coming!"

Everybody looked up.

Jamadar Harnam Singh asked, "What was the name again?"

The soldier on duty said, "Chapad Jhunjhun…Who else!"

"Chapad Jhunjhun?" Jamadar Harnam Singh got up. "What is he doing?"

The soldier answered, "He's coming."

Jamadar Harnam Singh took the binoculars from the soldier and began looking around. "He's coming our way. The rope is tied around his neck… but he's coming from there…the enemy camp…" He let out a great oath at the dog's mother, raised the gun, aimed, and fired.

The shot was off its mark. The bullet hit a short distance away from the dog, causing stones to fly up, and buried itself in the ground. The dog, fearful, stopped.

On the other side, Subedar Himmat Khan saw through the binoculars that the dog was standing on the path. Another shot, and the dog started running the opposite way. It ran with its tail between its legs towards Subedar Himmat Khan's camp.

Himmat Khan called out loudly, "The brave are never afraid…Go back!" And he fired a shot to scare the dog.

The dog stopped again.

From the other side, Jamadar Harnam Singh fired his gun. The bullet whizzed by, past the dog's ear.

The dog jumped and flapped its ears violently.

From his position, Subedar Himmat Khan fired his second shot, which buried itself near the front paws of the dog.

Frightened out of its wits, it ran about—sometimes in one direction, sometimes the other.

Its fear gave both Subedar Himmat Khan and Jamadar Harnam Singh a great deal of pleasure, and they began guffawing.

When the dog began running in his direction, Jamadar Harnam Singh, in a state of great fury, uttered a terrible oath, took careful aim, and fired.

The bullet struck the dog in the leg, and its cry pierced the sky.

The dog changed its direction and, limping, began running towards Subedar Himmat Khan's camp.

Now the shot came from this side—just to scare it. While firing, Himmat Khan shouted, "The brave pay no attention to wounds! Put your life on the line…Go back!"

Terrified, the dog turned the other way. One of its legs had become useless. On three legs it had just about managed to drag itself a few steps in the other direction when Jamadar Harnam Singh aimed and fired. The dog fell dead on the spot.

Subedar Himmat Khan expressed regret. "Tch tch…the poor thing became a martyr!"

Jamadar Harnam Singh took the warm barrel of the gun in his hand and said, "He died a dog's death."

Translation from Urdu by Ravikant and Tarun K. Saint

Whose Story?

It was only after his story was published in the school magazine that I learnt Annu had an important-sounding name: Anil Kumar Chattopadhaya. Class Six.

Annu had always wanted to become a story-writer. He could always spin out stories. I was convinced that he would become a poet or a writer. Not everyone can be a poet; poetic inspiration is a divine gift. Annu had the rare quality that only a genius has.

Even when we played gilli-danda, Annu would sit apart, either lost in thought or busy scribbling in his notebook. I was always curious to know what was going on in his head, how he made his characters come alive, how he wrote about them on the piece of paper before him—how they lived and breathed. Annu sent them wherever he wanted to, made them do whatever he wanted them to, and as they moved from place to place, the plot of a story got created—wonderful! Story-writers are marvelous; they can kill whom they want, give life to whom they want. Aren't they like gods?

Annu laughed. We were in college by then, and he said, "No, that's not true. My characters are not imaginary; they are not under my control. In fact, I am under their control."

Annu even talked like a writer. I always liked that. I felt very proud when his stories were published in the Sunday editions of *Pratap*, *Milap*, and *Jung*.

I showed the newspaper to my mother and said, "See, a story by Annu—Anil Kumar Chattopadhaya. That's his name."

"Really? Read it to me."

I read the story to her. It was about a poor cobbler. My mother had tears in her eyes.

"Arrey, that is the story of Bhiku, the cobbler in our lane. The same thing happened to his mother."

I didn't know that, but I immediately repeated what Annu had told me. "His stories are not imaginary, Ma. He doesn't create characters, but finds them in real life. To do that, one must not only keep one's eyes and ears open, but also keep the windows of one's mind and intellect open."

My mother was very impressed by my speech, which was really Annu's.

There was a large jamun tree in the lane. Bhiku, the cobbler, used to sit under it and repair the shoes of the entire neighbourhood. It was Annu's favourite haunt. Annu's clothes might have been dirty and unwashed, but his shoes were always well polished.

Bhiku was teaching his son, Ghasita, how to stitch the toe strap of a chappal. When I read the story out to Bhiku, his voice choked and he said, "Son, only people like you can understand our pain. Now if you people don't tell our story, who will?"

My respect for Annu increased that day. He was truly a born writer.

After finishing college, I left Delhi and went to Bombay, where I got a job. Annu started helping his elder brother run the baithak from where he distributed Ayurvedic and homeopathic medicines. His elder brother worked in some government office. He used to run the dispensary for two hours every morning and evening. He had recommended Annu for many jobs, but had been unsuccessful in getting him one.

Once, when I went back to Delhi to attend my sister's wedding, I met Annu's elder brother. He was very ill. He said to me, "Why don't you make him see sense? Ask him to do some work. What's the use of writing stories?"

I kept quiet. He coughed and wheezed for a long time. Then he said, "If only that bitch would leave him alone—he would come to his senses."

I asked Annu who the bitch was.

He replied, "Fiction. Bhai Sahib always curses it. He doesn't understand that just as he treats physical illnesses, I treat social and mental illnesses. I lance the pus-filled boils of society, light the path of people who are lost in darkness. I give them weapons to break the chains of their mental slavery."

I felt like applauding him. He talked for a long time and told me that his first book was ready for publication. Many of his stories had appeared in some of the country's leading magazines. He often got requests for stories from journals, but he couldn't write for all of them. He had even begun writing a novel, but he hadn't finished it because he hadn't been able to get enough time away from the baithak. His elder brother, who had two children, had been ill for some years. Poor souls! He was thinking of writing a story about the children.

During our conversation, he talked about great writers. I had heard of some of them—Saadat Hasan Manto, Ahmad Nadeem Qasmi, Krishan Chander, Rajinder Singh Bedi—but the ones he mentioned later were new to me: Kafka and Sartre. Some of the things he said, about Kafka's symbolism and Sartre's existentialism, went over my head. I thought that fiction had been left far behind. But Anil Kumar Chattopadhaya, trying to explain things to me, said, "The importance of a story doesn't merely lie in the development of its plot and the characters involved in it, but in its exploration of the consciousness…"

I didn't, of course, understand what he said, but I couldn't help being impressed by its profundity.

Anil once came to Bombay to attend a writers' conference. I took out the autographed copies of his four books to show him. I used to feel very proud whenever I showed them to my friends. They were books by an important writer—and now he was staying with me! I asked him if he had finished the story about his elder brother's children.

He gave me the sad news. "Bhai Sahib died. Relatives got together and persuaded me to marry his widow. Now I am the father to his two children!"

Anil stayed with me for a few days and then left.

I read about him often in the newspapers. Whenever he published a new book, he sent me a copy.

Years later, I had to go to Delhi again. I took my wife with me. I had promised to introduce her to my friend, the writer.

That evening, Annu was sitting under the jamun tree and getting his shoes polished by Ghasita. That was still his favourite place. We began talking about fiction once again.

"The most important thing about the new kind of story being written is its concern with the changing reality. The real is not only that which can be seen. In fact, reality can't be seen with one's eyes alone. A story isn't merely about logical relationships; it is rather an exploration of the subconscious of the characters."

Amazed, I listened as Anil Kumar continued to talk.

"During the last fifty years, there have been many changes in Urdu fiction. Our stories have made so much progress that they can be compared with the best in the world…"

Ghasita said, pushing the polished shoes towards him, "Whose story are you talking about, Bhai Sahib? The people with whom your stories are concerned are still where they were before. I now sit in my father's place, and you run your brother's baithak. What story of progress are you talking about?"

Handing over the shoes, Ghasita became absorbed in stitching the toe strap of a chappal.

Translation from Hindi by Alok Bhalla

The Owner of Rubble

They had returned to Amritsar from Lahore after seven and a half years. The hockey match was only an excuse; they were more keen to see the bazaars and houses that now belonged to strangers. Groups of Muslims could be seen strolling down every street of the city. Everything in it caught their attention. For them Amritsar was not just an ordinary city, but a place of wonder and surprise.

As they walked through its narrow bazaars, they reminded each other of the past. "Look Fatehdina, how very few misri shops are left in Misri Bazaar!...A panwallah now sits at the corner where Sukhi used to light her bhati...Ah, Khan Sahib, this is Namak Mandi! The girls of this lane were really so namkin that..."

It had been a long time since these bazaars had seen red Turkish caps and turbans with well-starched tassels. In the group that had come from Lahore, there were quite a few Muslims who had been forced to leave Amritsar during the Partition. Some of them were surprised at the changes that had taken place during their absence, while others were saddened. "Allah! How did Jayamal Singh acquire so much land? Were the houses on this side burnt down?...Wasn't this Hakim Asim Ali's shop? Has it now been taken over by a cobbler?"

Some of them could be heard exclaiming, "Wali, that masjid is still standing! These people didn't convert it into a gurudwara!"

The people of the city watched these groups of Pakistanis with eagerness and curiosity. There were, of course, some who were still so suspicious of the Muslims that they turned away when they saw them on the road. But there were many others who walked up to them and embraced them. Most people who met the visitors assailed them with a variety of questions. "What is Lahore like these days? Is Anarkali still as bright and gay as it used to be? We hear that the bazaar of Shah Alami Cate has been completely rebuilt. Krishna Nagar couldn't have changed much, could it? Was Rish-watpura really built from money taken in bribes?...They say that the burqa has disappeared from Pakistan—is that really true?" These questions were asked with such sincerity and concern that it seemed as if Lahore wasn't merely a city, but a person who was related to thousands of others who

Ken and Eric, Teresa's brothers
Depot Lines, Karachi

were anxious about its well-being. The visitors from Lahore were treated as the guests of the whole city, and most people were delighted to talk to them.

Bansan Bazaar is a poor, run-down locality of Amritsar where lower-class Muslims lived before the Partition. Most of the shops there had sold bamboo and wood. They had all been burnt down. The fire in Bansan Bazaar had been the worst of the fires in Amritsar, and for some time it had threatened to send the entire city up in flames. Indeed, the fire had burnt down many of the areas in the neighbourhood. Somehow the fire had been brought under control, but for every Muslim house burned down, four or five Hindu homes had also been reduced to ash. Now, seven and a half years later, a few structures had been rebuilt, but there were still piles of rubble everywhere. Standing in the midst of ruins, the new buildings presented a strange sight.

As usual, there wasn't much activity in Bansan Bazaar that day, because most of the people who had once lived there had perished along with their homes, and those who had fled didn't have the courage to return. That day, however, one old and frail Muslim did venture into the deserted bazaar, but when he saw the new buildings standing next to ruins, he felt as if he was lost in a labyrinth. He reached the lane that turned to the left, but instead of entering it, he stood outside, perplexed. He couldn't believe that it was the lane he wanted to take. On one side of the lane a few children were playing hopscotch, and a little further up two women were screaming and cursing each other.

"Everything has changed except the curses!" the old Muslim mumbled to himself as he stood there resting on his cane. His legs were bent, and his pyjamas were a little torn. His sherwani, which didn't reach up to his knees, was patched in several places.

A child came running out of the lane crying. The old man called out to him in a kind voice, "Come here, son! Come, I'll give you something nice—come." He put his hand in his pocket and began searching for something to give to the child. The child stopped crying for a moment, but then pouted and began to weep again. A young girl of about sixteen or seventeen years came running after him, caught him by his arm, and started dragging him back into the lane. The girl then picked him up, put her arms around him, kissed him, and said, "Stop crying, you little devil! If you don't, that Muslim will catch you and take you away! So stop crying!"

The old Muslim put back into his pocket the coin he had taken out for the child. He took off his cap, scratched his head, and then put the cap under his arm. His throat was dry, and his legs were shaking. He supported himself against the porch of a closed shop in the street and then put his cap on again. Across from the entrance to the lane, a three-storey house stood in the open yard where there used to be a shed for logs of wood. Two well-fed kites were sitting absolutely still on the electric wires running past the house. There was a patch of sunlight near the lamppost. The old Muslim stood quietly for a while in the sunlight and watched the dust being raised by the wind. Then, almost involuntarily, he sighed, "Ya Mallik!"

A young man approached the lane swinging a bunch of keys on a chain. Seeing the old man, he asked, "Miyan, why are you standing here?"

The old man felt his heart beat a little faster, and a slight tremor of excitement ran through his body. He moistened his lips, looked at the young man curiously, and asked, "Son, aren't you Manori?"

The young man stopped swinging the key chain around, clutched it in his hand, and asked with surprise, "How do you know my name?"

"Seven and a half years ago, you were only this tall," the old man said as he tried to smile.

"Did you come from Pakistan today?"

"Yes! We used to live in this lane once," the old man said. "My son, Chiragdin, was your tailor. Six months before the Partition, we had built a new house for ourselves here."

"Oh, Gani Miyan!" Manori said, recognizing him.

"Yes, son, I am Gani Miyan! I know that I shall never meet Chirag, his wife, and his children in this life again. But I thought that I should at least see our house once again." The old man took his cap off, scratched his head, and wiped his tears as they flowed down his face.

"You had left this place long before the Partition, hadn't you?" Manori asked with sympathy in his voice.

"Yes, son, it was my misfortune that I escaped alone before the Partition. If I had stayed here, then along with them, I would have..." As he said those words, he felt that he ought to be more discreet. He stopped himself in mid-sentence, but he let the tears flow from his eyes.

"Forget the past, Gani Miyan. What's the use of thinking about it now?" Manori reached out and grasped Gani Miyan's arm. "Come, I'll show you your house."

In the meanwhile, a rumour had spread that a Muslim standing at the entrance to the lane had tried to kidnap Ramdasi's son...Had his sister not rescued him in time, the Muslim would surely have carried him away! As soon as they heard this news, the women sitting on low stools in the lane picked up their stools and shut themselves in their houses. They also called indoors all the children playing in the lane. By the time Manori and Gani walked through, there was hardly anyone to be seen, except for a single street-hawker and Rakkha Pahlwan, who was sleeping comfortably under a peepal tree near the well. Of course, many curious faces peered out into the lane from behind the windows and doors of the houses. When people saw Gani walking with Manori, they began to whisper. Despite the fact that his hair was now completely white, they had no difficulty in recognizing Abdul Gani, the father of Chiragdin.

"Your house was there." Manori pointed to a heap of rubble in the distance. Gani stared in astonishment. He had reconciled himself to the death of Chirag, his wife, and their children a long time ago. But he wasn't prepared for the shock he received when he saw the ruins of his house. His mouth became parched, his knees weak.

"That heap of stone and ash?" he asked in disbelief.

Manori noticed that the colour had drained from the old man's face. He held him a little more firmly and told him, as if he was narrating a distant event, "Your house was burned down during the riots."

Supporting himself on his cane, Gani somehow walked up to the spot where his house had once stood. All that remained was a heap of dust and ash and a few broken, burnt pieces of brick. Things made of iron and wood had been picked out of the rubble a long time before. By some strange chance, the charred frame of a door still stood in the middle of the rubble. Beyond it were two almirahs, which had been blackened by smoke. After gazing at the heap of rubble for some time, Gani whispered to himself, "Is this all...is this all that is left?" He staggered a little and had to hold on to the charred doorframe for support. A moment later, he sat down and rested his head against the doorframe. Then he began to moan quietly, "Oh, my Chiragdin!"

The doorframe, which had stood like a proud relic for seven and a half years in the middle of the heap of rubble, was so badly seared that it began to crumble. The moment Gani leaned his head against it, small bits disintegrated and scattered on the ground around him. A few pieces of wood and ash fell on his cap and his white hair. Along with the cinders, a long worm fell out of the wooden door and landed near his feet. It raised its head a few times, slithered here and there looking for some hole to hide in, and then wriggled desperately towards a brick-lined drain nearby.

By then many more people were staring out of their windows. They were sure that something dramatic was about to happen. "Chiragdin's father, Gani, is here," they whispered. "He will find out what happened seven and a half years ago." They felt that the rubble would reveal the whole story. That evening, Chiragdin had been eating his dinner upstairs when Rakkha Pahlwan shouted for him from the street and asked him to come down for a minute. In those days, Rakkha was the uncrowned king of the lane. Even the Hindus were afraid of him. Chirag, a Muslim, got up without finishing his food and went downstairs to meet Rakkha. Chirag's wife, Zubaida, and his two daughters, Kishwar and Sultana, watched from the windows upstairs. The moment Chirag stepped out of the door, Rakkha grabbed him by his collar, threw him down on the street, and sat on his chest. Chirag caught Rakkha's hand, which held a knife, and screamed, "Rakkha Pahlwan, don't kill me! O God, help...save me!" Zubaida, Kishwar, and Sultana screamed helplessly and ran downstairs wailing. One of Rakkha's disciples pushed Chirag's arm aside while Rakkha pressed his knee down on his thighs and shouted, "Don't scream, you sister-fucker! You want Pakistan, don't you! I only want to send you there! Now go!" By the time

Zubaida, Kishwar, and Sultana reached the front door, Chirag had been dispatched to Pakistan.

By then all the windows in the neighborhood had been shut. Those who had witnessed the murder had shut their doors and refused to intervene. Even behind shut doors, they could hear the screams of Zubaida, Kishwar, and Sultana for a long time. Rakkha and his companions had arranged to have them sent to Pakistan that very night, but by a different and longer route. Their bodies were later discovered—not in Chirag's house, but in the canal nearby.

For two days, the house was raided. After everything had been looted, someone set it on fire. Rakkha Pahlwan swore that if he ever caught the person responsible for the fire, he would bury him alive. Rakkha had killed Chirag because he had wanted the house for himself. He had even bought everything necessary to perform the purification rituals. But he was never able to discover who had burnt the house down.

Over the last seven and a half years, everyone had accepted the fact that Rakkha was the owner of the rubble that had been left behind. He would neither allow anyone to tie a cow or a buffalo there, nor let anyone put up a temporary shed. No one ever dared to take even a small piece of brick from the rubble without his permission.

People looking out of their windows were sure that Gani would discover the entire story—that he would be able to read the history of his family's fate in the pile of rubble. They watched as Gani sat in the middle of the pile, scratched ash from the rubble with his nails, and scattered it over his head. Then he put his arms around the doorframe and wailed, "Speak to me, Chirag! Say something! Tell me where you are. O Kishwar! O Sultana! My children! O God, why is Gani still alive?"

The fragile doorframe crumbled a little more, and pieces of charred wood fell to the ground and scattered.

Rakkha Pahlwan, who had been sleeping under the peepal tree, woke up or was woken up by someone. When he learnt that Abdul Gani had returned from Pakistan and was sitting on the debris of his house, his mouth went dry. He cleared his throat and spat on the ground near the well. When he looked towards the rubble, his heart beat faster and his lower lip became a little more pendulous.

"Gani is sitting in the middle of the ruins of his house," Laccha Pahlwan, one of Rakkha's disciples, said as Rakkha sat down next to him.

"The ruins of his house? That rubble is mine!" Rakkha said in a hoarse voice.

"But he is sitting there," Laccha said and looked at him meaningfully.

"Let him sit there. Go and get my chillum!" Rakkha said as he stretched his legs and massaged his naked thighs.

"Suppose Manori tells him?…," Laccha asked as he got up to fill the chillum.

"Does Manori want to get into trouble?"

Laccha left to get the chillum.

Dry leaves from the peepal tree had scattered around the well. Rakkha picked them up one by one and crushed them with the palms of his hands. After Laccha had wrapped a cloth filter around the chillum and handed it to Rakkha, Rakkha took a long puff and asked, "Has Gani talked to anyone else?"

"No."

"Here, take it," Rakkha said as he coughed and passed the chillum to Laccha.

Manori helped Gani off the pile of rubble and supported him as he walked towards the well. Laccha crouched on the ground and puffed hard on the chillum. He watched Rakkha's face while keeping an eye on Gani.

Manori walked a little ahead of Gani, as if he wanted to make sure that Gani walked past the well without noticing Rakkha. But Gani had already seen Rakkha and recognized him from the way he sat with his legs stretched out on the ground. As soon as Gani neared the well, he stretched his arms out and said, "Rakkha Pahlwan!"

Rakkha looked up, squinted a little, and stared at Gani. Then he grunted, but didn't utter a word.

"Don't you recognize me?" Gani asked as he dropped his arms. "I am Gani, Abdul Gani, Chiragdin's father!"

The people at the windows continued to gossip. "Now that they have come face to face, they are bound to talk about what happened…Maybe they'll abuse each other…Now Rakkha can't touch Gani. The times have changed…He thought that he was the owner of that rubble!…That heap belongs to neither of them. The government owns the ruin!…That bastard doesn't even let anyone tie his cow there!…Manori is a coward. Why didn't he tell Gani that it was Rakkha who had killed Chirag, his wife, and their children?…Rakkha is not a human being; he is a wild bull. He roams the streets all day long like a bull!…Look how thin poor Gani is! His beard is completely white…"

Gani sat down by the side of the well and said, "Look at my fate, Rakkha! When I went away, I had a fine and happy household, and now there is nothing left but that heap of dust! The only sign of a house that was once inhabited! To tell you the truth, I don't want to leave that pile of rubble behind." His eyes filled with tears.

Rakkha pulled his legs in and sat cross-legged. Then he picked up his towel, which had been lying on the parapet of the well, and wrapped it around his shoulders. Laccha pushed the chillum towards him, and he started puffing on it.

"Tell me, Rakkha, how did it happen?" Gani asked as he wiped his eyes. "You were friends. You loved each other like brothers. Couldn't he have hidden in your house? He was bright enough to have thought of that."

"I don't know," Rakkha replied, but he sounded strangely unconvincing. His mouth was dry. There were drops of sweat on his moustache, and they trickled down to his lips. His forehead felt heavy, and his back ached for support.

"What is it like in Pakistan?" Rakkha asked. His voice was tense, and the veins on his neck were throbbing. He used his towel to wipe the sweat under his armpits, and then he cleared his throat and spat into the lane.

"What can I tell you, Rakkha?" Gani said as he leaned with both his hands on his cane. "Only God knows how I live. If Chirag had been with me, the story would be different...I tried to persuade him to go with me. But he was determined not to leave his newly built house...This is our lane, he said obstinately; there is no danger here. Like an innocent dove, he didn't consider the threat from outside. All four of them gave up their lives trying to protect that house!...Rakkha, he depended on you. He used to say that, as long as Rakkha was around, nobody would dare to hurt him. But when death finally came, even Rakkha couldn't help."

Rakkha tried to stretch his back because it had begun to ache badly. His sides too had begun to hurt. He couldn't breathe with ease. He felt as if he had stomach cramps. He was perspiring badly, and his feet seemed to be full of thorns. He saw flashes of bright light burst like fireworks before his eyes. He could neither open his mouth nor utter a word. He wiped his face with one end of his towel. And then, quite involuntarily, he whispered to himself, "O dear God, have mercy on me, have mercy on me!"

Gani noticed that Rakkha's lips had become dry and that deep, dark circles hung under his eyes. He placed his hand on Rakkha's shoulder and said, "What happened was fated, Rakkhiya. There is no use moaning about the past! May God bless the virtuous, and may He forgive those who have sinned! Now that I have met all of you, I feel as if I have seen Chirag again. May Allah keep you in good health." And then, with the help of his cane, he stood up. As he started to leave, he said, "Allow me to take my leave, Rakkha Pahlwan."

Rakkha tried to say something. He folded both his hands. Gani looked around at the neighbourhood once more with regret and longing, then walked slowly out of the lane.

The people at the windows started whispering once again. "Once outside the lane, Manori will tell Gani the entire story...Rakkha didn't dare to say anything to Gani...Now he won't dare to stop us from tying our cows in that area...Poor Zubaida! She was such a fine woman! Rakkha has neither a home nor a family. How can he respect the wives and sisters of others?..."

After some time, the women went out of their houses into the lane. The children began to play gilli-danda. Two teenage girls began to argue with each other about something and then came to blows.

Rakkha continued to sit by the well till late into the evening, smoking his chillum and coughing. People who passed by asked him, "Rakkhey Shah, I hear that Gani came from Pakistan today."

"Yes, he came," Rakkha would answer every time.

"What happened?"

"Nothing happened. He went away."

When night fell, Rakkha went to the shop on the left side of the lane and sat on the porch as usual. Every day, he greeted his acquaintances as they passed by and told them about the secrets of the lottery or gave them remedies for good health. But that day, he told Laccha about the pilgrimage he had made fifteen years before to Vaishno Devi. When he went back into the lane after sending Laccha home, he saw that Loku Pundit had tied his buffalo near the ruins of Gani's house. Instinctively, he picked up his stick and drove it away.

Tat, tat, tat…tat, tat!

Then he sat down to rest for a while near the charred remains of the doorframe in the middle of the rubble. Since there was no streetlight nearby, it was dark. He could hear the soft sound of water running through the drain nearby. The silence of the night was pierced by all sorts of sounds rising from the mound of dust and ash…*chick, chick, chick…kirrr-rrrr-ki-ki-ki…*Suddenly, a crow that had lost its bearings fluttered around, then alighted on the doorframe. The wooden frame crumbled a little more, and pieces of burnt wood fell here and there. As soon as the crow settled down on the doorframe, a dog that had been sleeping in one corner of the rubble got up and started barking at it loudly. *Bow-wow-wow-wow…bow-wow-wow-wow!* At first the crow stayed where it was, but then it flapped its wings rapidly and flew up to the peepal tree near the well. After chasing away the crow, the dog turned towards Rakkha Pahlwan and began to growl at him. In order to chase away the dog, Rakkha shouted at him, "Go away, shoo, shoo!…"

But the dog became more aggressive and began to bark louder. *Bow-wow-wow-wow!*

Hat-hat…durr-durr-durr!

Bow-wow-wow-wow…bow-wow-wow-wow!

Rakkha picked up a stone and threw it at the dog. The dog moved away a little but didn't stop barking. Rakkha called it a son-of-a-bitch, then got up, slowly walked to the well, and lay down on the platform. As soon as he left, the dog followed him, continuing to bark at him. After some time, when the dog saw no one moving about in the lane, it twitched its ears and went back to the rubble. Sitting down in a corner, it continued to growl.

Translation from Hindi by Alok Bhalla

Eric Vas at family home
(after move from Depot Lines)
Cincinnatus Town, Karachi, circa 1930

Father

In the middle of any winter's day, when the sun had risen directly overhead, Shobhana would be carefully arranging the couple of Bengali newspapers, the copies of *Ramayana, Mahabharata,* and *Chandi,* and the spectacle case beside the bed on the red carpet on the long first-floor balcony facing west. In the meantime, her father-in-law, Shekharnath, would have finished his midday meal. Having rinsed his mouth and wiped his face with a towel, he would drag his unsteady, eighty-year-old body onto the balcony.

Reading his religious books and newspapers in the middle of the day had been Shekharnath's cherished habit for a long time, but in recent years he had become severely racked by arthritis. From time to time he had excruciating pain in his shoulders and hips and felt as though someone had thrust a burning hot blade into them. Physiotherapy and strong doses of medicine had had little effect. Nowadays, once his lunch had settled in his stomach, his eyelids would get heavy and any more reading of his books or newspapers would send him off to sleep.

When he went out on the first-floor balcony, the rays of the midday sun shone steadily across his legs, but as the sun tended towards the west, its warmth gradually spread over his entire body, providing a tonic that he badly needed. Today, as on other days, Shekharnath fell asleep almost as soon as he had lain down, and when he woke up, it was well into the afternoon. The sun had gradually moved behind the tall buildings and trees to the west.

Awake, Shekharnath continued to lie there. He took his round bifocal glasses from their velvet case and put them on. His whole body was bathed in the balm of the dim golden sunshine of the late afternoon. He knew that Shobhana would soon come with a cup of saccharine-sweetened tea and that no sooner would he finish it than the last of the day's light would start to fade. The winter evening would fall softly, and the temperature would suddenly drop a few degrees. Then Shobhana would not let her father-in-law stay a moment longer on the open balcony but would hurriedly take him inside. Shekharnath was waiting for that.

It was Sunday.

At the other end of the balcony, a group of yellow-beaked blackbirds scampered about, now and then bursting into a joyous chirping, while from the ground floor came a tremendous racket, which meant that Sandip, Shobhana, Raja, and Ruku were engaged in a lively game of table tennis or carom.

Sandip, an executive of a leading multinational company, was Shekharnath's one and only son, and Raja and Ruku were his grandchildren. Raja was studying first-year English honours at St. Xavier's, and Ruku was in Class Eleven at Calcutta Girls'. Sandip and Shobhana were like friends to their children, spending their spare time with them in conversation, watching good videos, or playing such games as carom. No sound was coming from anywhere other than the frenzy of the blackbirds and the frivolity downstairs.

In front of the house was thirty-foot-wide Abhay Haldar Road, which ran straight to the tramline. On the other side of the road was a middling-size park. In Shekharnath's neighbourhood, most of the houses were of one or two storeys, though there were several of three storeys, while on the other side of the park there was a stretch of high-rise buildings.

There was hardly anyone on Abhay Haldar Road, and on the main road only one or two trams and a truck or a minibus were running, seemingly in no hurry and with no destination. Further on, in the park, countless children wearing various-coloured clothes ran all about, and groups of mothers or nurses watched over them. It was like a scene in a silent movie in Eastman colour.

Shekharnath was sitting up and looking out at the road. The blanket around him had come loose, and as he was slowly readjusting it, he noticed a taxi pull up opposite the tramline and a middle-aged lady get out. She asked something of someone in the street—apparently inquiring about an address—then started walking towards Shekharnath's house, but the taxi remained at the junction. Shekharnath's dull, eighty-year-old eyes could barely make out that there was someone as well as the driver in the taxi.

The lady was about fifty and had a handsome, dignified appearance. A little excess flesh had accumulated on her cheeks and around her neck and waist, but the last vestiges of beauty had not yet disappeared from her face. She was wearing an expensive sari, and her eyes were featured by a fashionable pair of glasses; on her right shoulder she carried a very fine lady's bag, and in her left hand was a large suitcase.

Shekharnath watched without curiosity, but was surprised when the lady, looking at the numbers of the houses, stopped in front of his house, Shanti Niwas. Although she had become a little portly, there were still remnants of one who, thirty years ago, might have been a slender and vivacious young woman: her innocent, oval mouth, her sparkling eyes with their thick lashes, the dimple in her chin, and her smooth, unlined cheeks. Shekharnath muttered to himself, "My God, let it not be her!"

The front door was directly under the first-floor balcony, and when she came to it, she could no longer be seen from above. When she pressed the doorbell, its musical sound rang throughout the house, and a few moments later Shekharnath could hear the door being opened. He guessed that Sandip and the others would be eager to see who the caller was.

Shekharnath remained seated, his nerves on edge. Then he could just make out the lady saying, "Is this the home of Shekharnath Bandyopadhyay?"

He recognised the voice. Although it had become a little rough after all that time, it still sounded like the vibrant, resonating hum of the sitar.

Sandip said, "Yes. Who do you want?"

"I—I have come from Dhaka. Can we sit down and talk?"

"Yes, yes. Of course. Come in." Shekharnath heard the door being shut.

The visitor said she had come from Dhaka. Then it had to be her. Despite the abundance of fresh air on this winter afternoon, it seemed as though his breath had stopped and his lungs would crack.

The excited racket had stopped, and everything downstairs had become quite still. At first Shekharnath could not decide what he would do. But after looking for a few moments down at the street in the dying rays of the sun, he made up his mind. In a few minutes, Sandip or Shobhana, or both of them, would run up to the first floor, but he would not look at the face of the one who had come from Dhaka. After all this time, she had died in his mind. Shekharnath had tried to forget her, praying for her death year after year. Would her coming now to Calcutta after thirty years open up that old wound buried deep in his breast?

Shekharnath hoisted up his worn old body, and a current of pain shot from his waist down to the soles of his feet. On another occasion, he might have uttered a sound of grief, but he no longer had the feeling for it.

His own room was on the left of the balcony. There were two doors to it: one led into the house, the other out onto the balcony. His heart thumping, Shekharnath went into his room and shut both doors.

There was very little furniture in the room. A freshly laundered bed was made up on a thick mattress on an old-style bedstead against one wall. On the other side was a small stand with figures of gods and goddesses ranging from Kali to Ganesh. There was also a clothes rack, a wardrobe, and a couple of antiquated iron trunks. On one wall was a Bengali calendar with a picture of Lakshmi, the goddess of wealth, and above that was a framed photograph of a woman in her midforties. The smiling and beautiful lady was Hemlata, Shekharnath's wife. The photograph had been taken in 1963, the year in which she was burned to death in Mirpur. It was the last picture ever taken of Hemlata.

Shekharnath bolted both doors against whoever might come. Then he got up onto the bed. In a strange reverie, he sat and looked at his wife's photograph.

So many times Shekharnath had resolved not to look back, for in the passing of those thirty years he had been buffeted both inside and out. Who could say how much heartache he had suffered? Sandip had only been a fifteen-year-old boy then. As Shekharnath looked at Hemlata's face, he tried to forget the grief, the sorrow, the distress.

Time's magic hand had healed so much of the pain, and Shekharnath sometimes felt that it had all been forgotten, but the dark side of memory had preserved intact all that he thought had been dispelled—the terror, the panic, the nightmare. He remembered how Hemlata had been so terribly frightened when, in the time after Partition, waves of refugees were rolling out of East Pakistan into West Bengal, Tripura, and Assam. She had said to him, "Come. Let's go and find a place to live in Calcutta." At that time in East Pakistan, it was not such a problem to sell property.

Shekharnath, then thirty-five or thirty-six, was a junior administrative officer in MacKenzie Brothers' jute mill, which was situated beside the Dhaleshwari river at Mirpur, about forty miles from Dhaka. Shekharnath's family had lived in this town for a hundred and fifty years, and his was the seventh generation. In all that time, no one had ever thought of moving anywhere else. For generation after generation, the roots of the Bandyopadhyay family had been set deep in the soil of this old town. It would not have been at all easy to pull them up.

Shekharnath had retorted, "Why should we go to Calcutta? Have we done anything wrong? This is my home, and here I'll stay."

"But don't you see? Every day so many people are leaving—"

"Let them. We are not going."

Hemlata looked worried as she said, "I know in my heart that we won't be able to keep on staying here."

On the one hand, Shekharnath was staunchly orthodox, assiduously observing all the rituals and practices integral to the life of a brahman; on the other, he was infinitely trusting of his non-Hindu neighbours. He said emphatically, "We know everyone in this town. None of them would ever so much as scratch us."

Hemlata said nothing.

Shekharnath went on, "There have been not a few riots in Mirpur, but have we been hurt? Haven't people run to us in time of danger?"

Their neighbours were magnanimous and compassionate and had always stood by them in any time of trouble. At the time of the 1946 riots, when blood flowed throughout undivided India, they allowed no one to lay a finger on Shekharnath. But be that as it might, Hemlata did not have the same faith in people that her husband had—he had maintained a foundation of trust even after Partition—though she did not, of course, openly express whatever suspicions she had about anyone in the town. She asked apprehensively, "But what about Khuku? What will be her future?" Khuku was the pet name of their only child at that time. To the world she was known as Manika, and she would later earn her living in education. Khuku then was five.

Shekharnath had no trouble discerning the implication in Hemlata's question. She was the daughter of a traditional Barisal brahman family, like his, who had come to her father-in-law's house saturated with all the old values and conservatism of her father's house, so the orthodoxy of the Bandyopadhyays was a part of her too. Hemlata's thoughts and ideas, her worries and concerns, were all enclosed by a strong iron frame beyond which it was impossible for her ever to stray.

Secretly Shekharnath felt a little amused. He had said, "You must be mad to be worrying now about the future of a little five-year-old girl!"

"I wouldn't be worrying if the country had remained as it was. Anyhow, Khuku won't be five forever."

"Do you think that everyone around here has become inhuman?"

"Perhaps not. But Khuku's—"

"You want to talk about her marriage?"

Hemlata had said nothing but had looked straight at her husband.

Shekharnath had responded, "The country may be divided, but not everyone is going to shut up their homes and go across the border. From among those who stay, you will certainly find the boy of your choice for Khuku…"

Suddenly, there was a gentle tapping on the closed inside door, and along with it, Shobhana's quiet voice could be heard. "Father…Father…"

Shekharnath was awakened from his memories, but he refrained from giving any answer. He knew why Shobhana had come.

After calling for a little longer, Shobhana went away. A little later there came the familiar sound of a pair of feet running impatiently up the stairs and stopping in front of the door. It was Sandip.

"Father, open the door!" he called urgently. He sounded agitated and excited.

Silent, Shekharnath sat there as though struck dumb.

Sandip went on, "Open the door, open the door! Didi has come from Dhaka."

Shekharnath's heart seemed to stop, then to beat with such force that he could almost hear it. It was as though a thousand drums were being beaten wildly inside his chest.

Sandip was calling anxiously, "Father, won't you come and see Didi?!"

Shekharnath remained seated. Crestfallen, confused, and embarrassed, Sandip stopped calling and went back downstairs.

Instantly Shekharnath was again lost in his memories of those days beside the Dhaleshwari…

Soon after the talk with Hemlata about Khuku, the atmosphere at Mirpur changed. Like the flood of refugees who had gone to India, countless people were now migrating to East Pakistan, having been uprooted from their homes in the states of Bihar and Uttar Pradesh. After the big cities of Dhaka, Chittagong, and Khulna had been filled, many of them went to Mirpur. Like the East Pakistani refugees, these people from India felt angry and resentful for all they had lost and were singularly bent on revenge. The jaws of Mirpur's new arrivals took on a ruthless set, and their eyes blazed with fire.

The poison of the profound hatred and mistrust that were integral to the two-nation theory in no way abated after Partition; indeed, it gradually increased. Relations between India and Pakistan were so complex and sensitive that for the flimsiest of reasons a violent commotion might be ignited on either side of the border. Malice had set its gunpowder to the winds; all it wanted was a spark.

In the meantime, Mirpur too became heated, and from time to time petty riots broke out. However, as before, Shekharnath's neighbours kept him and his family safe.

A number of years passed in what seemed to be no time at all, during which the British directors of MacKenzie Brothers turned the jute mill over to a Dhaka industrialist and left the country. The environment at the mill was no longer the same, and Shekharnath could see that he had become unwanted. He talked about this a lot with Hemlata. By then Khuku had grown, and they also had another two children, the boys Sandip and Sanjay.

It was not only the atmosphere at the factory but also the looks and actions of the neighbours in whom they had placed their hope and trust that began to change. The boundless faith in people that Shekharnath had maintained even after Partition was starting to crack. One minute he would think of going to Calcutta; the next he would decide to hold out a little longer. In actuality, Calcutta was totally unknown to him; he could not imagine where they would live or how Hemlata and the children would survive should they go there.

Eventually, another riot broke out in Mirpur, but before their formerly well-disposed neighbours could run to their aid, their house was set alight, Hemlata was burnt to death, and Khuku was abducted. Shekharnath, who was at the mill, and the boys, who were in school, survived it all.

Now Shekharnath was no longer resolved to stay. Sympathisers advised him, "Go to Calcutta. It's no longer good to stay here." And so the family arranged for the sale of the house, realising no more than an eighth of its true value.

After they got to Calcutta, relations who had gone there straight after Partition bought them the house on Abhay Haldar Road. Sandip and Sanjay were enrolled in a good school, and Shekharnath got a minor position in a mercantile firm. But Sanjay did not live very long, dying of a wrongly diagnosed disease a few years later.

After losing almost everything, Shekharnath hung on tightly to Sandip, in whom his life was now bound up. Sandip was a very peaceable and amenable boy, and he was also an exceptionally talented student. He took a master's degree in commerce with first-class honours and, after graduating, was appointed to a company secretaryship in a multinational firm. Then Shekharnath arranged for his marriage.

Shekharnath had gone to Calcutta with two gaping wounds in his heart: Hemlata and Khuku. Hemlata had been murdered, but Khuku? Every day he prayed to God that Khuku too might be dead. But God had not heard his prayer.

Shekharnath was not aware that evening had fallen until he noticed the small circles of fog that had formed in the cold winter dark under the streetlights outside.

He did not want to get down from the bed and turn on the light in his room, and he was quite oblivious to the cold north wind coming in through the open window. He remained sitting there, unaware, unfeeling. For some time, he thought of nothing, then he noticed the sound of four pairs of feet on the stairs. This time Sandip and Shobhana had come together, and Raja and Ruku had come with them.

Again there was a knock at the door, and they all started calling together, "Father! Father! Grandfather! Grandfather!"

And as before, Shekharnath sat there inert and unresponsive through it all.

Then Sandip's voice rose over all the others'. He said, "Don't worry, Didi has gone. You won't have to see her. Now open the door." There was a mixture of pain and sorrow and worry in his voice.

How amazing! Once Shekharnath heard she had gone, he felt a strange sense of anxiety over the one he had not wanted to see, the one whom he had wanted to be dead for the last thirty years. He dragged himself down from the bed, switched on the light, and opened the door.

For a few moments, his family fixed their eyes on him, then they all came into the room together.

Shekharnath was wearing nothing other than a dhoti and a short-sleeved, homespun shirt. The cold wind continued to blow through the open window from the street, and he was shivering from the cold, though he did not realise it. Shobhana ran to a corner of the room and took a shawl from the clothes rack, wrapped it tight around her father-in-law, and helped him onto the bed.

Sandip, Raja, and Ruku walked up to Shekharnath, but they did not sit down. Sandip said, "What's the matter, Father? Didi has been trying to find us for so many years. At last she got this address from the Indian High Commission in Dhaka and rushed straight here, but you sat in your room with the door locked and didn't call for her at all! She left in tears. She won't come back again." He paused for a moment, then continued, "What do you imagine Harun-da thinks?"

"Who is Harun-da?" Shekharnath choked on the words.

"Didi's husband."

No sooner had Sandip uttered the word than the look on Shekharnath's face changed altogether. He looked extremely distressed, as though he had stopped breathing. Immediately he heard the Muslim name Harun and was thrown completely off balance by all his old brahmanical prejudices. In a broken and indistinct voice, he mumbled, "Husband…Khuku's husband…"

Sandip noted his father's reaction. He had been all the while calm, unperturbed, and forbearing, but now he became a little agitated. "You know, Harun-da has done so much for Didi! If he had not reached out to her, who knows where she might be today!" He then went on to explain that at the time of the riot in Mirpur in 1963, when some of the rabble had abducted Khuku, Harun was a subdivisional officer in that region. Some months later, he rescued Khuku and took her into his own house. Then he tried to find Shekharnath and his family in order to return her to them, but by then they had gone to Calcutta. After a few years of trying and getting no news of Shekharnath, he married the rejected girl for the sake of her respectability. There was no objection of any kind from his parents; rather, they accepted Khuku with open hearts. Harun, the young officer of those days, was now a joint secretary in the Ministry of Education. They had one son, a doctor, and two daughters, who were studying in college.

"Perhaps you will say," said Sandip, "that it would have been right for Didi to have committed suicide. But I say that it was right that she married Harun. There was nothing more honourable she could have done."

Shekharnath was nonplussed. What was Sandip saying—the son of an orthodox, conservative brahman family? Shekharnath stared at him, utterly stunned.

It seemed that something had come over Sandip. Speaking his mind he said, "Could you have found such a boy for Didi in our community? Never." To underscore his feeling, he said in English, "They are happy. Extremely happy."

Shekharnath wanted to say something, but he could not articulate the words.

Sandip went on, "It is terribly wrong, Father, that Didi will never come back here to us."

Shekharnath said nothing.

"Harun-da had come too. He wanted to see how the daughter was received in her father's house, then he would come in himself. But that was the end of it."

There was an element of irony in what his son had said, but Shekharnath was not aware of it. Breathing heavily, he said, "He came too?"

"Yes. He waited in the taxi opposite the tramline."

Shekharnath remembered that he had seen someone sitting in the taxi when Khuku had gotten out. That must have been Harun!

A few moments later, Shekharnath's family left. Shobhana brought dinner for him at half past eight: two whole-meal chapatis, some potato-and-cauliflower curry, a bowl of milk, and a sweet. Having served her father-in-law his meal, she made up his bed, helped him into it, tucked the mosquito net in all around him, and left the room

On any other night, Shekharnath's eyes would have shut as soon as he had lain down, but he could not get to sleep. Time and again, Khuku's face appeared before his eyes. After lying there for a long time, he drew aside the mosquito net, got down from the bed, and walked somewhat unsteadily around the room. He felt that his heart was continually cracking, quite beyond his control.

Towards daybreak, having not slept all night, Shekharnath had made up his mind. He went into the bathroom attached to his room, washed his face, and then went to the other end of the first floor and stood outside Raja's room. He called a few times, and Raja woke up. He was surprised when he opened the door. "Grandfather," he said, "it's you! What's the matter?"

"Nothing," said Shekharnath. "Where is your aunt putting up in Calcutta?"

"At some hotel in Park Street."

"Can you take me there right now?"

Raja could hardly believe his ears. Astonished, he said, "You want to go there?"

Shekharnath nodded his head slowly. "Yes," he said.

"But you won't see her if you do."

"Why not?"

"They're going to Dhaka today on the early-morning flight. They'll have left the hotel by the time we get there."

Shekharnath thought for a moment, then said, "In that case, have a quick wash and get ready. We'll go to the airport. There's no need to say anything about this to anyone now."

He returned to his own room and quickly changed his clothes. Beside him was a small iron trunk; he opened it and took out a small leather bag, then closed the trunk.

When he left the house silently with Raja a few minutes later, none of the others had woken up.

The houses all around, the tramline, and the distant park were clouded in fog that winter morning. No one had turned off the streetlights yet, which were as lustreless as the eyes of dead fish. The sun was still very late in rising.

When Shekharnath and Raja reached the airport by taxi, they saw that Khuku and Harun had got there before them. Khuku—or Manika—caught sight of Shekharnath from a distance. She and Harun stopped in their tracks, as did Raja and Shekharnath. Shekharnath's heart started to thump, and he noticed that Khuku's lips were trembling. On her face were sorrow and joy and pride and accusation—so much was reflected there!

Without realising it, the father had, step by step, gone up to his daughter. Suddenly the fifty-year-old Khuku began to sob like a child. Then, with an extraordinary passion, she threw herself at her father's feet, but did not touch him. With both his hands, he raised his daughter up and held her to his chest for a long time. He felt his chest being bathed in tears.

Harun was standing a little away from them. He had an exceptionally handsome, intelligent, and vivacious face. Shekharnath called to him. He came and touched Shekharnath's feet, and Shekharnath held him too, to his chest.

The announcement came over the public-address system that passengers for Dhaka should board the aircraft, as it was ready for takeoff.

Very slowly Shekharnath released Khuku and Harun and took from the leather bag a gold necklace, a pair of gold bangles, and a diamond ring. Giving his daughter the necklace and the bangles, he said, "I've not given you anything. Your mother had these made for your wedding." Giving the diamond ring to Harun, he said, "Put this on. I don't know if it will fit you. If not, take it to a goldsmith and have it altered."

Nothing was said for a while.

After another announcement from the public-address system, Harun said, "We have to go now."

Shekharnath slowly nodded his head.

Harun said, "Do come to Dhaka sometime. I will arrange it all for you."

"But before that, bring the children," said Shekharnath.

"We will."

Harun and his wife walked towards the security enclosure. As he watched them, Shekharnath thought to himself, "What a fine boy!" And at that moment he was not at all aware of the age-old tradition running in his blood.

Translation from Bengali by John W. Hood

Mozel

Tirlochen was looking at the sky for the first time in four years, and only because he was upset and had gone up to the terrace at Adwani Chambers so that he could think rationally in the open air.

The sky, clear and cloudless, stretched like a taut grey tent over all of Bombay. Scattered lights extended to the horizon. It seemed that the stars had fallen from the sky, alighted on the tops of buildings—which in the darkness of the night looked like large tree trunks—and glimmered on them like glow worms.

Being under the open sky was a new experience for Tirlochen, a new feeling. He realized that in the four years he had spent in his flat, he had been deprived of one of nature's great blessings. It was nearly three o'clock. The air was light and buoyant. Tirlochen was used to the fan's mechanical breeze, which weighed him down. When he awoke in the mornings, he felt as if he had been beaten all night. But now, in the morning air, every pore of his body seemed to be joyously absorbing the freshness. When he came up to the terrace, his mind was burdened with disturbing thoughts, but in half an hour the fever in his brain had abated and he found himself thinking rationally.

Kirpal Kaur and her entire family were in a neighbourhood dominated by staunch Muslims. Several houses had already been burnt down, and a great many lives had been lost. Tirlochen might have taken Kirpal Kaur and her family out of there, but a twenty-four-hour curfew had been imposed, there were Muslims everywhere, and surrounded by these dangerous people, Tirlochen felt helpless. In addition to that, there was news pouring in from Punjab of the widespread killing of Muslims by Sikhs. Any hand, any Muslim hand, could reach out at any time, seize Kirpal Kaur's delicate wrist, and push her towards the well of death.

Kirpal's mother was blind, her father was a cripple, and her only brother was in Devlali overseeing a new contract.

Tirlochen was vexed with Kirpal's brother, Niranjan. Tirlochen read the newspaper every day and had warned Niranjan a week ago about the rapidly spreading disturbances. "Forget about these contracts for the time being," he had told Niranjan, adding candidly, "We're going through a very delicate phase, and although you must stay with your family, it would

Beatrice Fernandes, Teresa's cousin
1931

be even better if you brought them over to my house. It's true there isn't much space, but in times of trouble one can manage." Niranjan ignored the warning. And when Tirlochen finished lecturing him, he smiled under his thick moustache and said, "Yar, you worry needlessly. I've seen many such disturbances here. This is not Amritsar or Lahore; this is Bombay... Bombay. You've been here for four years; I've lived here for twelve years... twelve years."

What did Niranjan think Bombay was? He probably figured this was a city where disturbances, if they did develop, would disappear of their own accord, as if by magic. Or he might have thought this was a storybook castle impervious to catastrophe. But Tirlochen could see very clearly that the mohalla was not safe at all. As a matter of fact, he would not be surprised if he read in the next morning's paper that Kirpal and her parents had been murdered.

He was not concerned about Kirpal's blind mother or her handicapped father. It would be fine, as far as he was concerned, if they died and Kirpal was spared. Better too if her brother also got killed, because then the way would be clear for him. Niranjan was not a stone in Tirlochen's path, but more of a khangar. And thus when Tirlochen talked to him, he called him Khangar Singh instead of Niranjan Singh.

The morning air blew lazily. Without a turban, Tirlochen's head felt pleasantly cooled. But inside his head, innumerable thoughts ran about haphazardly...Kirpal Kaur was a newcomer in his life. Although she was the sister of Khangar Singh, who was a strong, well-built man, she herself was small and delicate. She had been raised in the village, but she did not have any of the hardness, the coarseness and masculinity that characterize most rural Sikh women who engage in a great deal of physical labour.

Her features were diminutive, as if still in an early stage of development; her breasts were small and needed many more layers of fat. She was fairer than most Sikh women: her complexion was like raw cotton, and her skin had the texture of mercerized fabric. She was also extremely shy.

Tirlochen and she were from the same village, but he had not lived there long. After completing his primary education, he had moved to the city to continue his schooling, and eventually he became a city person. He visited his village often, but he had never had the occasion to hear of someone called Kirpal Kaur in all that time. Perhaps that was because he was always in a hurry to get back to the city.

College days were in the past now. There was a distance of ten years between the college building and the terrace of Adwani Chambers, and this distance was filled with the unusual happenings that constituted Tirlochen's life. Burma, Singapore, Hong Kong...and then Bombay again, where he had been living for the last four years.

This was the first time in that period that he had examined the sky at night. The vision was not altogether displeasing: a thousand lights glimmered, and the air was light and buoyant.

As he thought about Kirpal, he suddenly remembered Mozel, the Jewish girl who lived in Adwani Chambers. Tirlochen had fallen deeply in love with her; he was in love up to his knees, as they say, and it was the kind of love he had never experienced in all of his thirty-five years.

He first saw Mozel when he moved into a flat at Adwani Chambers that he had rented with the help of a Christian friend. At first glance, Mozel looked like someone dangerously mad. Short brown hair covered her head; her querulous lips were covered with red lipstick, which was badly chapped and caked and reminded him of dried blood. She was wearing a long, loose white dress with a low neckline, the better part of her large, bluish breasts clearly visible. Her arms, which were bare, had a fine layer of down. She seemed to have just walked out of a hair salon after getting a haircut, tiny hairs covering her bare skin.

Her lips were not full, but the manner in which the dark lipstick had been applied gave them the appearance of being thick and fleshy.

Her flat was directly across from his. Between the two was a very narrow passage. Just as Tirlochen had approached the door of his flat, Mozel came out of hers. The sound of the wooden clogs she was wearing caught his attention, and he paused to look at her. Mozel stared at him through her unruly hair, which hung over her eyes, and laughed; Tirlochen was flustered. Quickly he got out his key and turned towards the door. At about the same time, Mozel's wooden clogs slipped on the cemented floor, and she fell over him.

When Tirlochen attempted to pull himself together, he realized that Mozel was sprawled over him in such a way that her dress was pulled up and her bare legs straddled his body. As he made an effort to extricate himself, he became entangled with her; he was all over her, like soap suds.

Mozel patted her dress in place with a smile when Tirlochen, quite out of breath, offered an apology.

"These clogs are no good," she said, and slipping her feet back into her shoes, she walked off, taking wide strides.

Tirlochen had thought it would be difficult befriending Mozel, but they soon became good friends. However, Mozel was extremely stubborn and caused Tirlochen much heartache. She ate with him, drank with him, went with him to the cinema, spent whole days with him on the beach at Juhu, but when he tried to go beyond kissing and hugging, she spurned him. She did it in a way that caused his fervor and his passion to become entangled in his moustache and beard.

Tirlochen had never been in love before. In Lahore, Burma, and Singapore, he had occasionally bought women for a price for a few hours. He had not, even in his wildest thoughts, imagined that in Bombay he would fall deeply, inextricably in love with a wild Jewish girl. Her thoughtlessness and lack of consideration were strange. At his request, she would immediately get ready to go to the cinema with him. But when they were seated in the theater, she would begin to look around, and as soon as she saw an old acquaintance, she would wave frantically and then go off to sit with him without asking Tirlochen to excuse her first.

Sitting in a hotel, Tirlochen has ordered special food for Mozel, but she suddenly spots an old friend and, dropping everything, goes over to sit by his side. Tirlochen burns with anger.

Tirlochen lost his patience with her often because she frequently left him to be with other friends. Sometimes he did not see her for weeks. She might affect a headache or complain of indigestion, which Tirlochen knew was an impossibility because her stomach was hard as steel and could never be upset.

"You're a Sikh," she would say when they finally got together. "You're not going to understand these delicate matters."

"What delicate matters? Those concerning your old lovers?" Tirlochen would ask, angry and bitter.

With her hands on her broad hips, her strapping legs placed apart, she would retort, "Why are you always taunting me about my lovers? Yes, they're my lovers, and I like them. I don't care if you're jealous."

"How will we ever get along if this continues?" Tirlochen would ask rhetorically.

This made Mozel roar with laughter.

"You're a Sikh after all, you idiot!" she exclaimed. "Who asked you to try and get along with me? If you want to get along with someone, go get yourself a Sikhni from your village and marry her. With me, this is how it will always be."

Tirlochen immediately softened. Mozel was actually his greatest weakness; he wanted to hold on to her at any cost. It was true that he often suffered humiliation at her hands. He was belittled in the presence of ordinary Christian boys who were nothing. But he had decided to withstand anything for love.

Normally, humiliation and degradation produce feelings of vengeance, but this was not so in Tirlochen's case. He had stuffed cotton in his ears and shut his eyes to keep out a great many things. He liked Mozel—not only liked her, as he often told his friends, but was in love with her up to his knees. He felt there was nothing else to do except submerge the rest of his body in the mire and be done with the matter altogether.

For two years, he continued in this wretched manner, remaining loyal to her. And one day, when he found Mozel in a good mood, he drew her into his arms and asked, "Mozel, don't you love me at all?"

Mozel extricated herself from his embrace, sat down on a chair, and stared absently at the hem of her dress. Then she raised her heavy-lidded Jewish eyes, batted her thick eyelashes, and said, "I cannot love a Sikh."

Tirlochen felt as if someone had placed live coals on his kesh, under his turban. His whole body was on fire.

"Mozel!" he shouted. "You are always making fun of me. In fact, you know that you're not just making fun of me, but also attacking my love."

Mozel rose and shook her short brown hair in an appealing way. "If you shave off your beard and let your hair down, you'll have young boys running after you, I promise; you're beautiful."

More live coals seemed to have descended on Tirlochen's kesh. He moved forward, pulled Mozel against himself, and fastened his thickly moustached lips on her dark, pink mouth.

She detached herself from his embrace. "I brushed my teeth this morning. You don't have to bother," she said calmly.

"Mozel!" Tirlochen shouted again.

She withdrew a small mirror from her vanity bag and examined her mouth. The thick layer of lipstick had cracked.

"By God, you don't make proper use of your moustache. I could clean my navy-blue skirt with it; with some petrol, we'll be all set."

His anger, after having reached a climax, was now deflated. He quietly sat down on the sofa. Mozel sat beside him and began unravelling his beard, taking out the pins one by one and holding them between her teeth.

Tirlochen was beautiful. Before he had had any facial hair, he had often been mistaken for a girl when he was seen with his kesh down. But now the heavy bulk of hair concealed his features. He was well aware of this fact. But he was a dutiful young man, there was in his heart a reverence for religion, and he did not want to separate himself from the things that were part of religious observance.

When his hair was completely unravelled and hung loose over his chest, he asked Mozel, "What are you doing?"

The pins still held between her teeth, she smiled. "Your hair is so soft. I was wrong to say you could clean my navy-blue skirt with it. Tirlochen, give it to me. I'll braid it and have a first-class handbag made for myself."

Sparks flew in Tirlochen's beard.

He addressed Mozel seriously. "I've never made fun of your religion. Why do you ridicule mine? Look, it's not nice to make fun of anybody's religious beliefs. I would never have tolerated it, and the only reason I do is because I love you very much. Don't you know that?"

Mozel let go of Tirlochen's beard. "I know that," she said.

"Well, then?" Tirlochen began braiding the hair on his beard and retrieved the pins from Mozel's mouth. "You know very well that my love is not frivolous. I want to marry you."

"I know," she said, shaking her head in her characteristic way, and got up to examine a picture on the wall. "I too have made up my mind to marry you."

"Really?!" Tirlochen jumped up excitedly.

Mozel's pink lips opened in a broad smile, and her healthy white teeth shone for a moment. "Yes."

His beard half-done, Tirlochen clasped her to his breast. "When? When?" he asked her.

Mozel moved away from him. "When you have this hair cut short."

Tirlochen, who could have agreed to do anything at that moment, said, "I'll have it cut tomorrow." He gave little thought to what he was saying.

Mozel tapped her feet on the floor.

"You're talking nonsense, Tirloch—you don't have the courage!"

She succeeded in casting out from Tirlochen's mind and heart any ideas about religion that might have remained. "You'll see," he declared.

"I'll see." She ran to him quickly, kissed him on his moustache, and said, "Phoo…phoo." Then she left.

It is useless to mention what troubled thoughts raided Tirlochen's mind and what agony he underwent that night. The next morning he went to the Fort and had his kesh cut and his beard shaved, keeping his eyes shut through it all. Shorn finally, he opened his eyes and studied his face in the mirror for a long time; it was a face that the prettiest girls in Bombay would be compelled to look at appreciatively.

Tirlochen began to feel the same chill that had engulfed him the moment he left the salon. He hastened his step on the terrace, which was overlaid by a network of pipes and water tanks. He did not want to remember the rest of the story, but escape seemed impossible.

He stayed home for a whole day after he had his hair cut. The following day he sent his servant with a note to Mozel, saying he was sick and wanted to see her. Mozel came. Seeing him without his hair, she froze for a second. Then, with a loud "My darling!" she ran to him and plastered his face with kisses.

She stroked his soft cheeks with her hand and ran her fingers through his hair, which had been trimmed to an English cut, and muttered loud exclamations in Arabic. She shouted so much that her nose began to run, and when she realized what was happening, she lifted the hem of her dress and wiped her nose with it. Tirlochen blushed. He lowered her skirt hastily and admonished her, "You should wear something under this."

Mozel appeared not to care. "I feel comfortable this way," she responded, a smile appearing on her lips. The lipstick had caked and cracked in several places.

Suddenly Tirlochen remembered their meeting: when he had bumped into her in the hall and they had become oddly entangled. He hugged her.

"We'll be married tomorrow."

"Sure." Mozel rubbed the back of her hand against the softness of his chin.

They decided the wedding would take place in Poona. Because it was to be a civil marriage, a ten-day notice was required, and since it would be a court proceeding, Poona was the most logical choice. It was not far away, and many of Tirlochen's friends lived there. The plan was to leave for Poona the following day.

Mozel worked as a salesgirl in one of the shops at the Fort. Not far from there was a taxi stand where she had instructed Tirlochen to wait for her. He arrived at the appointed time and waited two and a half hours. But she did not show up. A day later, he found out that she had left for Devlali with an old friend who had just bought a car and that she would be away for an indeterminate period.

What agony did Tirlochen suffer? That is a long story. To put it briefly, he hardened himself and forgot Mozel. Not too long afterwards he met and fell in love with Kirpal Kaur and came to the conclusion that Mozel was a contemptible woman who had a heart of stone and who, like a bird, flitted from one place to another.

However, once in a while, the memory of Mozel returned, gripping his heart fiercely, then flying off, disappearing. She was shameless, she was callous, she was inconsiderate, and yet he liked her. And for this reason he was forced to think of her sometimes, forced to speculate about her whereabouts and wonder what she was doing in Devlali, if she was still with the man who had bought a car or with someone else. Although he was well acquainted with her character, he was deeply hurt by the thought that she was not with him.

He had spent not hundreds but thousands of rupees, but he had done so voluntarily. Mozel did not have expensive tastes. She was attracted to things that were cheap. Once when Tirlochen wanted to buy her a pair of gold earrings he liked very much, she saw a pair of gaudy and inexpensive earrings, fell in love with them instantly, and begged him to buy them for her.

Tirlochen could not figure out what kind of girl she truly was or what the fabric of her being was. She lay by his side for hours and allowed him to kiss her; like soap he blanketed her entire body, but she never permitted him to go a step further than that, saying in a teasing tone, "You're a Sikh— I hate you."

Tirlochen was certain that she did not hate him. If she had hated him, she would not associate with him at all. She lacked self-control and would never have spent two years with him. She would have told him frankly and openly how she felt. She disliked underwear. It made her feel uncomfortable, and although Tirlochen had, on several occasions, warned her of the necessity of wearing it and had attempted to arouse her sense of modesty and propriety, she had refused to comply.

She became irritated when he talked of modesty.

"Modesty—what nonsense is that? If you're so conscious of it, why don't you close your eyes? Is there any kind of dress in which one may not become immodest, or through which your gaze can't travel? Don't talk nonsense with me. You're a Sikh. I know you wear silly underwear resembling shorts under your pants; this too is part of your religion, like your beard and your hair. You should be ashamed—you're an adult and you still believe that your religion is in your underwear!"

In the beginning, Tirlochen was greatly angered by what she said. But later, after some serious thought, he often gave in and began to see a fragment of truth in her arguments. When he had his beard shaved and got a haircut, he felt, with certainty, that he had been carrying a burden that really had no meaning.

Tirlochen came to a halt when he reached the water tank. He cursed Mozel vehemently and put her out of his mind. Kirpal Kaur, a chaste girl with whom he was in love, was in danger. She was in a neighbourhood populated by staunch Muslim families, and several incidents had already occurred. Who cared about the curfew, though? If the Muslims in the chawl so desired, they could very easily get rid of Kirpal Kaur and her parents.

Lost in thought, Tirlochen walked over to the water pipe and sat down on it. His hair had grown considerably. He was sure that within a year he would have his kesh back again. His beard had grown too, but he did not plan to wear it long. There was a barber at the Fort who trimmed it so well that it was hard to tell it had been trimmed at all.

He brushed his fingers through his long, soft hair, sighed, and was about to rise from the water pipe when he suddenly heard the harsh sound of clogs. Who could it be? There were several Jewish women in the building, and they all wore wooden clogs when they were at home. The sound was closer now. Then he saw Mozel standing beside the other tank, wearing the long, loose dress typically worn by Jewish women. She was stretching lazily and lustily, so lustily that Tirlochen thought the air around them might explode.

He got up from the water pipe and wondered where she had suddenly come from. And what was she doing on the terrace at night?

Mozel stretched again. This time Tirlochen felt his bones rattle.

Her robust breasts heaved within her loose dress. Flat and circular bruises floated before Tirlochen's eyes. He coughed. Mozel turned around and saw him. Her reaction was mild. Dragging her feet noisily, she walked up to him and stared at his diminutive beard.

"You've become a Sikh again, Tirloch?"

The hair on his face began to prickle.

Mozel stepped nearer and rubbed the back of her hand on his chin. "This brush is now ready to clean my navy-blue skirt," she remarked with a smile. "But I left the skirt in Devlali."

Tirlochen remained silent.

Mozel pinched his arm. "Why don't you speak, Sardar Sahib?"

Tirlochen did not wish to repeat his past mistakes, but he gazed at Mozel's face in the foggy, early-morning light. There was no particular change in her, except that she seemed to have lost some weight.

"Have you been sick?" Tirlochen asked her.

"No," Mozel answered, fluffing her hair.

"You look thinner."

"I'm dieting." She sat on the water pipe and tapped her clogs on the ground. "So you—that is, you're becoming a Sikh again?"

"Yes," Tirlochen retorted.

"Congratulations!" Mozel took off one of her clogs and began tapping it on the pipe. "Have you fallen in love with another girl?"

"Yes," Tirlochen admitted quietly.

"Congratulations! Is she someone from this building?"

"No."

"That isn't very nice." Mozel was now twirling her shoe around her finger. "One should always think of one's neighbours."

Tirlochen said nothing. Mozel stood up and, coming closer, touched his beard with her fingers.

"Did the girl ask you to grow your hair?"

Tirlochen was uncomfortable; he felt as if his beard was becoming tangled as it did while being combed.

"No," he said rigidly.

The lipstick on Mozel's mouth reminded him of stale meat. When she smiled, Tirlochen had a vision of the butcher's shop where jhatka meat was sold, and he imagined watching the butcher slice a massive artery in two with his knife.

She smiled again, then laughed. "If you shave this beard now, I swear by anyone that if you ask me to, I'll marry you."

Tirlochen wanted to say that he loved a decent, chaste, and pure-hearted virgin and was going to marry her—that compared to her, Mozel was a harlot, an ugly, stupid, inconsiderate woman. But he was not a mean or petty man. All he said was, "Mozel, I've made up my mind to marry this simple, religious girl from my village. For her, I decided to grow my hair again."

Mozel was not accustomed to prolonged thought, but she did reflect for a few moments. She turned toward Tirlochen and said, "If she's religious, how will she accept you? Doesn't she know you cut your hair once?"

"She doesn't know yet. I started growing my beard soon after you left for Devlali—merely to get even—but then I met Kirpal Kaur, and now I tie my turban in such a way that only one person in a hundred can tell that my kesh has been cut; I'll grow it back soon." Tirlochen began running his fingers through his long, soft hair.

Mozel raised her long, loose dress up to her thighs and scratched a fair, fleshy thigh. "That's great…These bloody mosquitoes, they're here too—just look how they bite!"

Tirlochen looked away. Mozel wet a finger with saliva and rubbed it over the spot where she had been bitten. Then she lowered her dress and stood up.

"When are you getting married?"

"Nothing is certain yet," Tirlochen replied, becoming pensive.

They were silent for the next few minutes. Then, sensing his anxiety, Mozel started laughing.

Tirlochen needed a sympathetic ear even if it were Mozel's. He told her the whole story. Mozel started laughing again.

"You're an idiot of the first order! Go and get her—what is the problem?"

"Problem? Mozel, you'll never understand the intricacies of this matter, of any matter. You're a careless sort of girl—that is why you and I haven't been able to keep our relationship going, and for this I'll be sorry for the rest of my life."

Mozel struck the pipe angrily with her foot.

"Sorry be damned…You silly idiot—you have to think about how you are going to save your, what's her name, from being killed…You're sitting here, shedding tears of regret about relationships…We could never have had a permanent relationship because you're a silly man, a coward. I want someone courageous…but let's not talk about that now. Come, let's go and get that Kaur of yours."

She grasped Tirlochen's arm.

"Get her from where?" Tirlochen was confused.

"From where she lives. I know the neighborhood well—come with me."

"But wait, they have a curfew."

"Not for Mozel—come."

She dragged him by the arm to the door, which opened on to the stairs leading down. She was about to open the door when she stopped and looked at his beard.

"What is it?" Tirlochen asked.

"Your beard," Mozel said. "Well…it's OK, it's not too big…If you walk bareheaded, no one will know you're a Sikh."

"Bareheaded? I'm not going there bareheaded," Tirlochen declared in bewilderment.

"Why?" Mozel asked.

Tirlochen pushed back a lock of hair from his forehead.

"You don't understand—she has never seen me without a turban before…She thinks I have a kesh, and I don't want to reveal my secret."

Mozel stamped her feet angrily on the threshold. "You really are an idiot! You stupid ass, it's a question of her life, what's her name, that Kaur of yours with whom you're in love."

Tirlochen tried to explain, "Mozel, she's a very religious girl. If she sees me without a turban, she'll begin to hate me."

Mozel became infuriated. "Oh, your love be damned! I ask you: are all Sikhs stupid like you? It's a question of her life, and you insist on wearing your turban—perhaps that underwear too which looks like a pair of shorts."

"That I wear all the time," Tirlochen confessed.

"That's just great! But think: the problem now is that the mohalla is full of Miyan bhais who are mean and ruthless. If you go there wearing your turban, you will be slaughtered."

"I don't care," Tirlochen declared. "If I go there with you, I'll go with my turban on; I don't want to jeopardize my love."

Teresa (fourth row, far left) and Iris Dias,
Teresa's cousin (top row, far right),
on Jufelhurst High School excursion
Clifton Beach, Karachi

Mozel was exasperated, and as she seethed with anger, her breasts pressed against each other. "You ass, where will your love be when you're not there—your, what's the name of that fool—when she's not there, her family is not there? You're a Sikh, by God. You're a Sikh and an idiot at that!"

"Shut up!" Tirlochen lost his temper.

Mozel burst out laughing. Then she raised her arms, which were covered with a fine layer of down, and circled them around Tirlochen's neck. Swinging a little, she said, "Darling, let's go—whatever you say. Go and put on your turban, and I'll wait for you downstairs." She turned to go.

"But wait a minute," Tirlochen said, stopping her. "Aren't you going to change your clothes?"

"This is all right," she replied, her hair bobbing vigorously. And with the *khat, khat, khat* of her shoes, she left. Tirlochen could hear the sound even when she was down on the first floor. He swept back his hair with his hand and went to his flat. He changed quickly, set on his head the turban, which was already furled, then locked the door of his flat and left the building.

Standing on the footpath with her sturdy legs wide apart was Mozel, smoking a cigarette. She stood there like a man. When Tirlochen approached her, she blew a whiff of smoke in his face teasingly.

"You're disgusting!" he said irritatedly.

Mozel smiled. "This is not new. Other people have called me disgusting." Then she glanced at Tirlochen's turban. "You've done a good job with the turban—it does appear that you have a kesh."

The bazaar was completely deserted. A breeze blew timidly, as if fearful of the curfew. Streetlamps cast a feeble light. About this time, the trams usually started running and people began to appear in the streets; there would be quite a bit of hustle and bustle soon. But right now, it seemed as if no man had ever come this way and none was likely to.

Mozel walked ahead of him. Her clogs resounded on the flagstones. The sound shattered the stillness, and Tirlochen cursed her silently for not having changed into something else before she left. He was tempted to tell her to take off the clogs and walk barefoot. But sure that she would refuse to do his bidding, he remained silent.

Tirlochen was terrified. The stirring of a single leaf made his heart beat violently. But Mozel walked on, unafraid and exhaling cigarette smoke casually, as if she were out on a leisurely stroll.

At the crossing a policeman roared, "Ai, where are you going?!"

Tirlochzen recoiled in fear. Mozel approached the policeman boldly, shook her hair, and said, "Oh, you didn't recognize me—Mozel," adding, with a finger pointed towards a gully, "there, my sister lives there—she's sick—I'm taking the doctor to her."

While the policeman studied her face, she took out a packet of cigarettes from somewhere and offered one to him. "Here, smoke," she said.

The policeman took the cigarette. Mozel removed from her mouth the cigarette she had been smoking and handed it to the policeman. "Here, light it."

The policeman drew on the cigarette. Mozel winked her left eye at him and her right eye at Tirlochen, and dragging her clogs noisily, she walked off towards the gully through which they had to pass in order to get to Kirpal's mohalla.

Tirlochen was quiet. But he could sense that Mozel was deriving some strange pleasure from her defiance of the curfew. She liked playing with danger. She had become a problem when she went with him to Juhu. Fighting the gigantic waves of the ocean, she would go far out while he watched her anxiously, afraid that she might drown. When she returned, her body would be blue and bruised, but she did not seem to care.

Mozel walked ahead of him. He looked about fearfully, half-expecting someone with a dagger to appear. She came to a halt. When he caught up to her, she made an attempt to reason with him.

"Listen, Tirloch dear—it's not wise to be so scared. If you're afraid, something is bound to happen. Believe me, I know what I'm talking about."

Tirlochen remained silent.

When they had crossed one gully and were at the gully beyond which Kirpal Kaur's mohalla lay, Mozel came to a standstill. Not far from them, a Marwari's shop was being systematically looted. She studied the situation for a moment. Then she said, "It's all right," and they resumed walking.

A man carrying a large tray over his head bumped into Tirlochen. It was apparent to him that Tirlochen was a Sikh. He reached inside his salwar belt swiftly, but Mozel came forward, swaying on her feet as if drunk, and pushed the man away.

"Ai, what are you doing?" she mumbled in a drunken tone. "Killing your own brother? I want to marry him." Then she turned to Tirlochen, "Karim, pick up the tray and put it back on his head."

The man withdrew his hand from his belt and gave Mozel a lewd stare. He then leaned forward and poked her in her breasts with his elbow.

"Have fun, sali, have fun," he said. He picked up his tray and was gone.

Mozel touched her breasts. "Not disgusting—everything goes—come on."

She started walking again, faster this time. Tirlochen followed, increasing his pace.

They crossed the gully and came to Kirpal Kaur's mohalla. "Which way now?" Mozel asked.

"The third gully. It's the corner building," Tirlochen answered nervously.

Mozel turned in that direction. It was very quiet. Although this was a well-populated area, not a sound could be heard, not even that of a child crying.

When they came to the gully, they witnessed a riot in progress. A man ran out of one corner building and disappeared into the next building. Several moments later, three other men emerged from the same building, looked about briefly, and then dashed into the other building. Mozel stood still. She motioned Tirlochen to withdraw into the darkness. "Tirlochen dear," she whispered to him cautiously, "take off your turban."

"I can't take it off, no matter what happens," he replied quietly.

"As you wish, but don't you see what's going on out there?" She was annoyed with him.

Both of them could see what was happening. There was trouble, trouble of a very mysterious nature. When two men came out of the left building with sacks on their backs, Mozel shuddered, shaken to the core of her being. A dark-red liquid dripped from the sacks. She nervously chewed her lips, thinking about what to do next. After the two men disappeared beyond the far end of the gully, she turned to Tirlochen.

"Look, this is what you have to do. I'll run towards the corner building, you come running after me, fast, as if you're pursuing me—understand? But we must be quick."

As soon as Tirlochen indicated that he understood the plan, Mozel darted off in the direction of the corner building, her clogs echoing noisily on the flagstones. He ran after her. In a few minutes they were both inside the building, at the foot of the stairs. He was out of breath, but she seemed fine.

"Which floor?"

"Second," Tirlochen answered, anxiously wetting his lips. He followed behind her. There were large spots of dried blood on the stairs; he grew faint when he saw them.

When they arrived at the second floor, he went down the corridor and knocked gently on a door. Mozel stayed by the stairs.

He knocked again and, with his mouth close to the door, whispered urgently, "Mehnga Singh Ji, Mehnga Singh Ji."

"Who is it?" A small, thin voice was on the other side of the door.

"Tirlochen."

The door opened slowly. Tirlochen beckoned to Mozel. She ran to him, and they both went in quickly. She saw a slim girl who looked terrified. Looking at her closely, Mozel saw that she had fine features and a beautiful nose, which was red from a cold. Mozel hugged her, and taking the hem of her own dress, she wiped the girl's nose with it.

Tirlochen blushed.

"Don't be afraid. Tirlochen has come to take you away from here," she told Kirpal Kaur lovingly.

"Tell Sardar Sahib to get ready quickly," Tirlochen said, "and Mataji too, but hurry up."

Suddenly, they heard shouts from the floor above—shouts of triumph and screams of fear.

A small, stifled scream escaped from Kirpal Kaur's throat. "They have got them."

"Who?" Tirlochen asked.

"Never mind that now." Mozel grabbed Kirpal Kaur's arm before she could speak. "It's just as well. Now take off your clothes."

Before Kirpal Kaur had a chance to respond, Mozel went up to her and took off her shirt in one quick move. Dazed and shaken, Kirpal Kaur hugged her naked body with her arms. Tirlochen turned his face away. Then Mozel removed her own dress and slipped it over Kirpal Kaur's head. She herself was now completely naked. She loosened Kirpal Kaur's salwar belt and pulled the salwar down.

"Go, take her now," she ordered Tirlochen, adding, "but wait." With that she proceeded to undo Kirpal Kaur's plait. "Go, get out of here quickly."

"Come," Tirlochen said hastily. He was about to leave when he stopped suddenly and looked at Mozel. The soft down on her arms stood on end due to the cold.

"Why don't you go?" Mozel asked in exasperation.

"What about her parents?" Tirlochen said haltingly.

"To hell with them! Just take her and go."

"What about you?"

"I'm coming."

Just then they heard men's voices on the stairs. The sounds were soon followed by a loud banging on the door. It seemed the men were intent on breaking it down.

Kirpal Kaur's crippled father and blind mother were in the other room, moaning.

Mozel reflected for a moment, shook her hair, and said, "I can think of only one thing now. I'll open the door—"

Kirpal Kaur suppressed a scream in her dry throat. "The door—," she gasped.

"I'll open the door," continued Mozel. "You run after me, I'll go up the stairs…You follow me…These men at the door will forget everything and come after us…"

"And what then?" Tirlochen asked uneasily.

"Your, what's her name, will use the diversion to get away, and no one will bother her in that dress."

Tirlochen explained the whole situation to Kirpal Kaur as fast as he could. Mozel screamed loudly, opened the door, and fell over the men outside. Taken by surprise, they quickly moved aside as she ran up the stairs. Tirlochen went after her.

Mozel was climbing the stairs blindly, the clogs still on her feet, and the men, who seconds ago were attempting to break down the door, turned and pursued her and Tirlochen. Suddenly Mozel's foot slipped; she came stumbling down the stairs, her body hitting every stone stair and the steel banister and landing on the cement floor.

Tirlochen descended the stairs in a hurry. Bending over her, he saw that her nose was bleeding and blood was trickling from her mouth and ears. The men were now gathered around them. Everyone was watching Mozel's naked and fair body, which was covered with bruises.

"Mozel, Mozel!" Tirlochen exclaimed, shaking her arm.

Mozel opened her large, Jewish eyes, which were now red and swollen, and smiled.

Tirlochen removed his turban from his head, unfurled it, and covered Mozel's body with it. Mozel smiled again, winked at him, and said as blood bubbled from her mouth, "Go and see…if my underwear is still there or not—I mean…"

Tirlochen left her and went inside Kirpal's flat. Mozel tried to look at the men standing around her.

"He is a Miyan bhai…but a really mean and ruthless one…I call him Sikh…"

Tirlochen returned. He indicated by a look that Kirpal Kaur was safe. Mozel breathed a sigh of relief. With that, blood gushed out of her mouth.

"Oh, damn it…," she whispered and wiped her lips with her down-covered wrist. Then she addressed Tirlochen. "All right, darling, bye-bye."

Tirlochen wanted to speak, but the words were caught in his throat.

Mozel pushed Tirlochen's turban away from her body. "Take away… this religion of yours." And then her arm fell lifelessly over her robust breasts.

Translation from Urdu by Tahira Naqvi

Farewell

The hushed watches of the night were shattered by a military patrol vehicle tearing past Victoria Park.

Section 144 and a curfew were both in force. There were riots between Hindu and Mussulman. Each was at the other's throat with billhooks, pokers, knives, and sticks. Everywhere assassins were at work, striking clandestinely under cloak of darkness. Looters were on the rampage too, and the shades were haunted by their yells of deadly delight. The bustees were burning. Sporadic screams from dying women and children added to the monstrous atmosphere. On top of everything came the panicky soldiers on patrol: they fired blindly in any direction to maintain a semblance of law and order.

At a particular spot two lanes converged. A dilapidated rubbish bin lay overturned there. Behind it, using it as a shield and crouched on all fours, was a man. He dared not raise his head. For a while he lay as if lifeless, trying to distinguish the cries in an uproar some way off. "Allah Ho Akbar!" or "Bande Mataram!"? He could not be sure which they were.

All of a sudden the rubbish bin seemed to move slightly. Every nerve in the man's body tingled. His teeth were clenched, his limbs stiff with apprehension and dread. Several moments passed…The night remained still.

Maybe it was a dog. To drive it away, the man shifted the rubbish bin slightly. The silence deepened. Then the bin moved again, and this time the man's fear became mixed with curiosity. Extremely slowly, he raised his head—and opposite him there rose another head. A man! From each side of the bin the two creatures stared at each other, stunned. Their hearts had almost stopped; their eyes locked in a violent contagion of fear. Neither could afford to trust the other. Each thought the other was a murderer. Their eyes were narrowed, expecting an attack; but no attack came. In both their minds the same question reared its head: *Hindu or Mussulman?* Depending on the answer, the outcome might be fatal. Neither creature had the courage to voice the question; nor could he turn and run. The other man might jump him with a knife.

Minutes passed. Both men fidgeted with doubt and discomfort. Finally one of them shot the question, "Hindu or Mussulman?"

"You say first," came the reply from the other side.

Neither was willing to reveal his identity. Their minds were riddled with suspicion. They let the question lie, each having thought of a new one. "Where's your home?" called one.

"This side of the old Ganges. Shubaida. Where's yours?"

"Chashara, near Narayangunj. What d'you do?"

"I've got a boat. I'm a boatman. You?"

"I work in a cotton mill."

Once more, silence. Peering through the gloom, each tried to see the other, scrutinize the clothes he was wearing. The rubbish bin and the darkness obscured the view. Then the men heard the uproar again—this time much closer. The frenzied shouts were clearly audible. The mill worker and the boatman trembled in terror.

"They're not far now," cried the mill worker in a state of panic.

"Yes, let's go, let's get away from here," called the boatman in a voice that was equally strained.

But the mill worker objected, "No. Don't get up, whatever you do! Want to die?"

The boatman's suspicions were refreshed. What evil designs did this fellow have? The boatman stared hard into the eyes of the mill worker, who stared back and said, "Just stay where you are, just as you are."

The boatman felt pricked by these words. Why was this man trying to stop him? Grave doubts clouded his mind. "Why should I wait?" he called.

"Why? You need to ask?" replied the mill worker in a low, charged voice. "I've just told you. D'you want to die?"

The boatman did not care for the tone of the question. All kinds of unpleasant possibilities jostled in his mind and made him resolute. Why hang about in this dismal alley for a moment longer?

His obstinacy alarmed the mill worker. "I don't like your behaviour," he called. "You haven't yet told me what you're doing around here. Suppose you go off and bring your lot to finish me?"

"What the hell do you mean?!" the other man shouted, momentarily forgetting where they were.

"It's the truth. You don't seem to understand how people's minds work." Something in the mill worker's tone reassured the boatman slightly. He heard him add, "If you go, d'you think I want to stay here alone?"

The racket of the crowd receded. The lethal hush returned. As time went by, the two men imagined they were awaiting death. Crouched on opposite sides of the rubbish bin in this dark alley, they brooded, thinking of their homes, their wives, their children; whether they would ever get back to them in one piece, and whether, if they did return, those faces would still be there to greet them. These riots had come from nowhere, out of the blue, without the smallest warning. Overnight, the gossip and banter of the marketplace had turned into killing and bloodshed—enough blood to make Mother Ganges herself red. How could men turn so merciless so suddenly? The human race was truly cursed! The mill worker let out a deep sigh. The boatman followed suit.

"Have a smoke?" asked the mill worker, taking a biri from his pocket and holding it out. The boatman, out of sheer habit, pinched the rolled-up tobacco a few times, twirled it in his ear, and only then stuck it firmly between his lips. The mill worker tried to light a match. He had not realised that his clothes were soaked, and so were his matches. He threw away the dud stick in disgust.

"Damned matches are wet," he said and pulled another one out of the box.

The boatman impatiently got up and crouched beside the mill worker. "I'll light it. Give me the box," he said. He virtually snatched it from the mill worker. After a couple of failures, he got a match to go.

"Allah be praised! Here you are—quickly, take it."

But the mill worker sprang up as if he had seen a ghost. The biri between his lips drooped and fell. "You are a…"

The match flame died. Both pairs of eyes widened with mistrust and anxiety in the darkness. There was a profound pause.

The boatman abruptly stood. "Yes, I'm a Mussulman," he said. "What of it?"

The mill worker replied in a frightened voice, "No—nothing, it doesn't matter. I was only…" Glancing at the bundle beside the boatman, he asked, "What's in there?"

"Some clothes for my children and a sari. Don't you know that tomorrow is Id?"

Was that really all there was? The mill worker's doubts persisted.

"You think I'm lying? You don't have to believe me. See for yourself." He held out the bundle.

"No need for that. Sorry, friend. It's all right. But you never know these days, do you? You can't trust anyone. Don't you agree?"

"That's true. I hope you're not carrying anything?"

"I swear to God I haven't even a needle on me. All I want is to reach home with my life." The mill worker shook his clothes as if to prove his words.

Both men sat down again next to each other. For some while they inhaled their biris deeply, and did not speak. "Tell me," the boatman said reflectively, as if chatting with one of his family or friends. "Tell me what all this killing's about?"

The mill worker kept up with newspapers and had some notion of politics. With some warmth he replied, "The fault's with those League types of yours. They've started all this in the name of freedom struggle."

The boatman was stung. "I don't know anything about all that. I'm only asking, what's the point of all this killing? Some of your people die and so do some of ours. How can it benefit the country?"

"That's what I'm saying. The whole thing's not worth a damn." The mill worker made a gesture of hopelessness with his thumbs. "You may die, I may die, our families may become beggars. In last year's 'riot,' they hacked my brother-in-law into four, so my sister became a widow and landed on my shoulders with all her children. To me it looks as if the leaders give the orders from the comfort of the top floor, and leave us to do the fighting and the dying."

"It's as if we're not human beings at all, but stray dogs. Why do we snap at each other and bite like this?" The boatman wrapped his arms round his knees and sat hunched in impotent rage.

"You're right."

"Does anyone ever think of people like us? Are the fellows who started this riot going to provide my meals? Will I get my boat back? It's probably sunk at Badamtoli Ghat by now. That rich zamindar Rup Babu—his manager used to get into my boat every day to cross the river to the courthouse. That man was as generous as Hazrat: five rupees for the fare, and five for the tip—ten in all. He covered my entire monthly expenses. Will a Hindu babu like him ever step into my boat again?"

The mill worker was about to say something when they heard the march of heavy boots. There was no question: the boots were about to enter their alley from the road. The two men eyed each other with dread.

"What do we do?" The boatman had grabbed his bundle.

"We must escape. But where to? I don't know the city very well."

"Anywhere to get away," said the boatman. "We don't want to be beaten up by the police for nothing. I don't trust those bastards."

"I don't either. But which way? They're coming."

"This way." The boatman pointed towards the southern end of the lane. "Let's go. If we can get to Badamtoli Ghat, we don't need to worry anymore."

Their heads bent, they ran without stopping to catch their breath, crossing numerous lanes until they reached Patuatuli Road. Deserted, the road stretched beneath bright electric lights. They peered out anxiously from the side street: could someone be lying in wait for them? Too bad; even if someone was, they could not delay. Scanning both ends of the road, they ran straight on in a westerly direction. They had not gone far when they caught the *clip-clop* sound of a horse's hooves behind them. Glancing back, they saw a mounted policeman some way off, riding towards them. They darted into a narrow lane used by sweepers.

The horse swept by at a fast trot, its rider's revolver at the ready, each hoofbeat jerking at their hearts. Only when the sound had become faint did they dare to peer out.

"Stick to the edge of the road," said the mill worker.

And so, clinging to the walls of houses and buildings, they advanced in spurts as fast as they could.

"Stop!" whispered the boatman. The mill worker pulled up, taken aback. "What is it?"

"Over here." The boatman took the mill worker behind a pan shop. "Look over there."

The mill worker followed the boatman's finger and saw a shed about a hundred yards off with a single light burning in it. Adjacent to it, on a high verandah, ten or twelve policemen with rifles stood at attention. A British officer was addressing them, gesticulating through a haze of pipe smoke. Below the verandah, a policeman held the reins of a horse, which tattooed the ground restlessly.

"That's the Islampur outpost," said the boatman. "If I go a bit further down the lane to the left of it, I reach Badamtoli."

The mill worker's face was grey with fear. "What then?" he mumbled.

"You stay here. There's no point in your going to the ghat. This is a Hindu area; the ghat's in Islampur—Mussulman territory. Spend the night here, then go home in the morning."

"And you?"

"I have to go," said the boatman in a voice choked with worry and fright. "I can't stand it any longer, friend. It's eight days since I heard from my family. Only Allah knows how they are. Somehow, I have to get into that lane. If I can't find my boat, I can still swim across."

"Are you mad?!" cried the mill worker. He gripped the boatman's shirt. "How will you ever make it?" His voice was passionate.

"Don't try to stop me. Don't. You must understand: tomorrow is Id. By now my children and their mother will have seen the new moon. They'll be looking forward so much to new clothes and hugs from their father. My wife will be pining for me. I have to go, brother. I can't wait." His voice faltered.

The mill worker felt agonised. His grip on the boatman's shirt slackened. "What if they catch you?" His voice was hoarse with fear and pity.

"They won't, they won't get me. Stay here, don't get up. I'm going. I won't forget tonight. If Fate wills, we two will meet again. Farewell."

"I also will never forget it. Farewell."

With a few stealthy steps, the boatman was gone.

The mill worker stood up and waited, stock-still with suspense. The thumping of his heart refused to slow. He was all ears, praying that God would keep the boatman from peril.

Minutes passed in strained silence. The boatman had been gone some while. How his children would be delighted by their new clothes, and how that would please the poor fellow! The mill worker sighed. The boatman's wife would probably fall upon his chest and weep tears of loving relief. "You have escaped the jaws of death," she would say. A small smile played upon the mill worker's lips as he thought about the reunion. And what would the boatman do then? Then he would—

"Halt!"

The mill worker's heart missed a beat. Men in heavy boots were running nearby. They were shouting something.

"The bastard's trying to get away!"

The mill worker edged out far enough to glimpse a police officer with a revolver leaping down and running into the lane: he fired twice, splitting the night. The mill worker heard both reports, saw the blue sparks of both bullets. He was so tense he bit his finger. Then he saw the officer jump on his horse and race down the lane. And he heard the death cry of the fugitive.

In his dazed imagination, a picture of the boatman floated up. To his chest he was clutching the new clothes and sari for his children and wife. Gradually they turned crimson with blood. He heard the boatman's voice speak to him: "I couldn't reach them, brother. My darlings will drown in tears on their festival day. The enemy reached me first."

Translation from Bengali by Krishna Dutta and Andrew Robinson

Teresa (second row, far left)
Karachi Club

Teresa (center), cousins Alec and Kitty
Athaide, and uncle Fred Vas
at New Year's celebration
Karachi Goan Association Hall,
circa 1942

from *Sleepwalkers*

This is Lucknow.

With the partition of the country, the mohajirs migrated from Lucknow to Karachi. And, here too, as soon as they regained some balance, they raised the old Chowk of Ameenabad. Here too, tilting their caps in the Lukhnavi style, several streets converge upon the square all at once, as if the whole world were flocking here. When not an inch of space remained in Ameenabad, the mohajirs spread themselves around it. And, in this way, all of Lucknow in Karachi was peopled. Not just the old city, but also the new one born from the womb of the old, was soon spreading its spirit of playfulness over the suburbs. They say people come and go, places stay where they are. But, in this case, the mohajirs had transported an entire city within the folds of their hearts. With some came the bricks of their houses; some carried entire homes intact. Some brought a whole gali, and others transported the bustling main road beyond the gali—whatever they could contain in their hearts! As soon as the mohajirs recovered their breath after reaching Karachi, the entire city emerged from their hearts, brick by brick. Who knows what remains at the spot where this city had earlier stood! Here it has acquired such splendour that any visitor to Karachi is repeatedly asked, "Have you seen Lucknow in Karachi?"

In the dying hours of the night, when the silent lanes of Ameenabad are lit with the eerie glow of colourful lamps, people lying deep in sleep in the pitch dark of their homes roam about the bustling Chowk as if it were day. In the beginning, Manwa Chowkidar would constantly bang his lathi on the road, wide-eyed with fear and astonishment as he stared at the dazzle around him…The entire Chowk is deserted; who on Allah's earth do I keep bumping into in this dead silence?…What was even stranger was that, within a few days, he actually began to see apparitions. In fact it so happened that it was only rogues and crooks that the Chowkidar could not spot. He could clearly see all the people who had walked to the Chowk in their sleep.

"Arre bhaiya, why are you coming at me like that?" Manwa Chowkidar had leapt back the other night as he bumped into someone. But then, to his amazement, he realized that it was his very own Deewane Maulvi Sahab. He greeted him courteously, "Assalam-alaikum, Maulvi Saab!"

"Walaikum-assalam, Manwa." Deewane Maulvi Sahab paused for a moment, pulled out a two-rupee note from his pocket, and thrust it into Manwa's hand.

"Much obliged, Maulvi Saab! May Allah always grant us your benign shadow!" Even as Manwa was kissing his fingers after saying "Aameen," Deewane Maulvi Sahab vanished into thin air.

"How can that happen, Manwa Chacha?" asked Azizo, the chaiwala, holding out a glass of tea to Manwa Chowkidar.

"Arre bhaiya, if it can't happen, where did this two-rupee note come from?" Manwa took out the new note and showed it to him.

"Who knows? That could have been some ghost or spirit!"

"So what if he was a ghost! He was, after all, our very own Deewane Maulvi Sahab." Manwa Chowkidar paused to sip his tea. "Forget the others, Ajijo, I even saw *you* going towards the bazaar."

"But I was enjoying khwaabe khargosh then, you know!"

"That's exactly what happens! People are out in the streets while they're sleeping in their homes."

"Your mumbo-jumbo is beyond my understanding, Chacha! If people are really walking in the streets while asleep, I'll keep my tea business open even at night."

"I see Deewane Maulvi Saab so clearly in the crowd every night, Ajijo."

"What strange stories you tell, Chacha!"

Deewane Maulvi Sahab's name is actually Nawab Mirza Kamaluddin, but he is known as Deewane Maulvi Sahab both at home and outside. He is so used to it that if anyone were to call him Nawab Kamaluddin, he would think that the poor fellow had mistaken him for someone else.

While the other mohajirs have created another Lucknow in Karachi, Deewane Maulvi Sahab believes that he continues to live in the old Lucknow, just as before. At first, many of his friends tried to convince him that he had gone away. But even in the old Lucknow, whenever Deewane Maulvi Sahab left the city, he would be restless till the time he came back to it. No matter where he went, his journey was always from Lucknow to Lucknow.

His wife, Achhi Begum, often says, "We had hardly regained our breath after reaching Karachi, when Deewane Maulvi Sahab started pestering us to go back to Lucknow. And, if some good soul asked him what, after all, was left in Lucknow, pat came his reply: Lucknow!"

"Now, what do you do with this?" asks Achhi Begum, continuing her commentary. "Our children are here, our relations are here, and all our friends as well. So what's left in Lucknow? Nothing but Lucknow! What in

Allah's name would we do there? But who could make Deewane Maulvi Sahab understand this? He wanted to go there precisely because his Lucknow exists only in Lucknow. And where Lucknow is, there must he be."

"Then how did you manage to hold him here?"

"Would he be called deewana if your Deewane Maulvi Sahab were to heed my words?!" Achhi Begum herself had given this name to him. No wonder then that when strangers call him by this name, Deewane Maulvi Sahab feels they are his own people. "But all that is over now, bhai. We never returned to Lucknow. Lucknow came to us here."

"Lucknow came here?"

"Of course! What else? It was burnt to ashes, but whatever was left of it followed us here. Such a shrunken little face it had. It was tinier than the smallest section of Ameenabad. Deewane Maulvi Sahab rushed to embrace it, sobbing as he did."

"And then, Begum Sahiba?"

"All of our Lucknow here knows the rest of the story. The ruined Ameenabad began to blossom again. A branch here, then a branch there, and one by one all its branches sprouted. Our Lucknow came alive, exactly as it had been. In fact, prettier than its earlier self."

"Our Deewane Maulvi Sahab never insisted on going back after that?"

"Only the mad know the ways of the mad! Such was his condition that whenever we would ask him to arrange for our visas, so that we could go back and offer prayers at the graves of our ancestors, he would immediately say, 'Have you left your brains in the grazing fields? Do you believe the graves of our ancestors are located in some foreign land? Arre bhai, we only have to go and offer prayers. Come, let's do it right away.' But, seeing me flustered, he would soften and say, 'My dear Begum, how far do you think our ancestral cemetery is? It is just a couple of streets away. Right behind Nazeerabad is Chhote Mamun ka Maqbara, and to its right, a stone's throw away, is the cemetery.' By then I would be imploring him, 'I don't feel well, Deewane Maulvi Sahab! I don't want to go today.' But he would be adamant. 'Come on. Let our enemies be indisposed. So what if you are feeling slightly unwell? Remember, postponing a pious duty is as bad as committing a sin.'"

Achhi Begum also talks of how Deewane Maulvi Sahab believes the whole of Lucknow to be out of its mind. He says, "These are strange times. Even in one's own city, one feels stifled, as if one were in an alien land." And he goes from house to house, counselling everyone, "Arre Mian! Turn to Allah and offer namaaz five times a day with your heart and soul. Can there be a greater misfortune than not feeling at home in your own house?"

"But Maulvi Sahab—"

"Oh no, Mian. Ifs and buts won't do! When the whole city is confronted with the same fate, the situation becomes very grave. Who knows—the entire city may have incurred the wrath of Allah for a collective sin!"

"But listen to me, Maulvi Sahab…"

"What should I listen to, Mian? *You* should listen to me and turn to Allah at once."

The old settlers of Lucknow in Karachi even find some truth in the utterances of the eccentric Deewane Maulvi Sahab. They wonder, "If this is not the wrath of Allah, then why are things as strange as they are? Even after recreating a whole Lucknow, exactly as it was, over this long period of time, why do we still have this gnawing sense of being strangers in our own homes?"

It is not as if the mohajirs have not made any economic progress. In fact, they have outsmarted not only the Sindhis but the other local Pakistanis as well. Through sheer hard work and ingenuity, they have grown to dominate business, industry, and even the bureaucracy, at both the provincial and national levels. The roads of Karachi have opened up in all directions. Meerut, Malihabad, Azamgarh, and Allahabad can be reached in no time at all.

Four or five years ago, when a cousin of Deewane Maulvi Sahab's came to visit him from the Lucknow in India, his mind split open in wonder. "Quibla Maulvi Sahab, what can I say? I am beginning to feel that the real Lucknow is, in fact, here. And it is not you who have migrated from our place to this, but it's we who have moved from here to there." Expecting to be lauded for his observation, Deewane Maulvi Sahab's cousin looked at him.

"We haven't moved anywhere, Bhai!" Deewane Maulvi Sahab said, suspecting that he was stuck with another one of those lunatics. "Coming and going is the business of tourists like you. Anyway, the same place cannot be situated in two locations. Our Lucknow is the only Lucknow. We don't recognize any other Lucknow. Do you understand?" he said, proffering his silver case to the guest, along with a paan with special zafrani tobacco in it. "And, listen. You may find it hard to believe me, Bhai, but you cannot refute the truth. Natives do not just represent their land, but also become the native land. If you have any doubts, shall I open my mouth and show you something? Come, come closer, sir: one of Nawab Asifuddaula's thumri mehfil is in progress in my throat! *Hee, hee, hee!*"

Translation from Urdu by Sunil Trivedi and Sukrita Paul Kumar

Teresa (left) and Kitty Athaide,
Teresa's cousin
Gandhi Gardens, Karachi, circa 1940

Teresa (right) on graduation
excursion with friends
Nainital, Uttarakhand, India, 1944

Teresa (center) with friends
Karachi, circa 1945

*Eric, Teresa's brother, in British
Indian Army uniform*
1942

On Writing Sleepwalkers

On a visit to Karachi in the mid-eighties, I found I had come to a wonder-land. All its people were walking, talking, or whatever, in deep sleep. What was most amazing was that the wonderland looked very familiar! There were so many Uttar Pradesh towns there—situated, I felt, even in the same geographical dimensions. As for the people—they spoke the chaste Urdu that reminds one of pre-Partition days, when it was spoken more for aes-thetic pleasure than for communicating. I would often turn to look ques-tioningly at my host, Muhammad Ali Siddiqui, a fellow writer in Urdu. The literary critic in him would shrug his shoulders and say, "Well, I would be grateful if *you* could explain our melodrama to me."

Ali is, in fact, the original of Ishaq Mirza, whom I conceived before any other character in *Khwabrau* (Sleepwalkers) and whose forthright bearing provided me with the ending of the novel for which I had to work out the beginning. I found Ali completely involved, like Ishaq, in the here and now—unlike most other Karachi mohajirs, who cannot live their present except in the past tense.

Ali took me to Amroha, Gorakhpur, Meerut, even Malihabad. You won't believe what followed. Before he ventured to take me into the thick of Karachi, he abruptly stopped and said with a gleeful sneer, "From here we shall go forth and witness the grandeur of our great Lucknow…"

As in India, so in Karachi. The scene led us into the same stationary hubbub of Ameenabad of Lucknow. Roads come here, leisurely sauntering in from numerous directions, each with its cap tipped slightly on one side of the head. And just as they spot one another at the Chowk, they push themselves forward to become permanently frozen in an embrace. The immense Chowk presents the same clusters of poori-bhajiwalas, kabab-walas, mithaiwalas. And when you have had a bellyful of these delicacies, a light-footed itrawala will approach you respectfully from nobody knows where. Ali eyed me, enjoying my disbelief. "Your whole Lucknow has walked away here into our Karachi, hasn't it? I wonder what's left there."

"The Punjabis," I told him, "who insist on speaking their Urdu in Pun-jabi!"

Once, well past midnight, Ali and I happened to visit a restaurant in the Lucknow of the mohajirs. The restaurant was as astir with activity then as it must have been in its peak hours. My friend remarked that "Lukhnavis" were in the habit of walking out of their dreams to come straight to the Chowk. He assured me that these sleepwalkers would keep popping in till the small hours. *Khwabrau* was thus born in my mind. And months later, when it became ripe for delivery, I prepared myself for what I knew would be a hassle-free labour.

People ask, Why did the mohajirs forsake their homes in India to migrate to Karachi?

And, why, when your home is on fire, don't you flee it to go elsewhere? Isn't this also how millions of Punjabis, who habitually knew a Hindustani to be one from outside Punjab, suddenly woke up from a nightmare to find themselves in Hindustan? A short story of mine, "Panaahgah" (The Shelter) seeks to depict how post-Partition communal clashes cast their shadows as far as today. In the story, middle-aged Mirasen is the only Muslim inhabitant left behind in a village in Hindustani Punjab after a terrible communal riot. She is disgraced, beaten, repeatedly raped. The poor ignorant woman does not even know where all of her kinsfolk have gone. "Why, we have packed them off to Pakistan!" her erstwhile non-Muslim friends jeer. "Why don't you follow them?" Her kith and kin have actually been temporarily moved to a refugee camp in a neighbouring town. Mirasen is one day found, unconscious with fever and fatigue, by the kindly Sarpanch who takes her in his oxcart to the camp. In the last lines of the story, she opens her eyes late in the evening in the pale electric light, and a young Hindu doctor of the camp affectionately asks her how she is. "Don't be scared, ma," he adds softly, "you have arrived safely." The illiterate Mirasen, moved by his care and kindness, says, "Please inform my people I have reached Pakistan too."

The fact of the matter is that the migrants from India moved—wherever, whenever they did—to "Pakistan," or "the sacred refuge." But it is interesting to note that Nawab Mirza's wife in *Khwabrau*, for one, has fearful associations with the word "Pakistan." She is afraid because her husband has to pass through "a Pakistani corridor" every day on his way to and from work. So while Mirasen is happy to have reached her Pakistan while still in India, Achhi Begum is apprehensive of a "Pakistani corridor" in her "Lucknow" in Karachi. The problem cannot, as we realize when we consider it in all its complexity, be resolved with a few impassioned strokes. Here I should perhaps also draw your attention to Sain Baba, a native of Sindh in *Khwabrau*. His poverty has made him a perfect refugee in his own land, running from town to town in search of his Pakistan. Deewane Maulvi Sahab pities the Sindhi Sain, believing in a rush of pure and plain madness that Sain has had to travel all the way from his native Sindh to their Lucknow for mere food and shelter. The problem is thus intricate enough to be solved only with compassionate understanding.

Deewane Maulvi Sahab's emphatic belief that he has been continuously living in his old Lucknow all these years is perhaps pathetic; yet if this belief alone can serve as a divine cure for his malady, why shouldn't we grant him the privilege of madness? But when a sudden bomb explosion at Nawab Mahal takes away the lives of his wife, eldest son, and daughter-in-law, you find that the madman is no longer mad. He weeps bitterly on the shoulders of his Sindhi cook and comes out of his madness to discover that he is, after all these years, in Karachi. However, as we soon come to realize, it is only the nature of his madness that has changed. Now he believes that he is in Karachi to visit his son Ishaq Mirza and that he must hasten back to Achhi Begum in Lucknow.

Ishaq Mirza, his younger son, has always been aware of the trick that contemporary history has played with the mohajirs. He knows too well the reality of the myth of the Indian Lucknow in Karachi. And even though affection makes him indulgent towards the belief of his father, he is of the firm opinion that the Lucknow of Karachi can never be dragged back to its Indian origin and that the children who grow up here will have to suffer another mohajirat. This is why, when Deewane Maulvi Sahab asks his grandson, Salim, to get ready to go back to Lucknow, the lad, running after his ball, answers, "But *this* is Lucknow, Bade Abbu!"

I feel tempted to give a brief account of the situation. For the situation itself is what inspired me to attempt the novella. I dedicated it to my friend Muhammad Ali Siddiqui not merely as a gesture, but also because he provided me with my favourite character in the novel: Ishaq Mirza. Ali loves his Amroha in India, but would rather live in the Amroha of his children in Karachi, for they know no Indian Amroha except in their grandmother's tales.

Another friend, Anwar Sadeed, an eminent Urdu critic, has always wondered why *Khwabrau* was not written by a Pakistani. But then, isn't it natural that an Indian survivor of the tragic events of the history captured in the novel should be able to reproduce the anguish of the migrant sensibility and experience?

Like my Deewane Maulvi Sahab, I too had to flee my native land—Sialkot in Pakistan—during the din of Partition. Unlike the old man, I was then in my early twenties; yet as a child of very simple, unschooled old parents, I felt I had suddenly turned grey while taking charge of our dire circumstances beyond the borders in distant Bharat, with which we were familiar only through the slogans and speeches of political bigwigs. Suffer I did no less than Deewane Maulvi Sahab, the suffering having driven the old man out of his wits, and me to an insane pursuit of premature sanity. Anyone rooted securely for generations in the old country named anew could not have been in more sympathetic concord with migrant life than I was. Muhammad Ali Siddiqui once took me to a thickly peopled wayside in Karachi and pointed to a gigantically calligraphed MOHAJIR, on a board as huge as the whole plaza where it had been fixed. I realized what he meant by doing that, and voluntarily associating it with my own Indian experience, I turned away rather madly.

I am reminded of another incident that supports my argument. A German Indologist visited me with her husband about the time I had just completed the novella. Reading a few pages of the manuscript while I was busy talking to her husband, she suddenly let out what sounded like a sob.

"Why?…" Alarmed, I asked her in my most persuasive voice.

"But this is *my* story," the tear-stricken lady, restraining herself, said. "This is the story of all of us living on either side of the Berlin Wall. Let me tell you what happened to our family…"

I knew for certain that she was not feigning interest in my book. She had indeed gone through the same terrible experience in different circumstances. So, shall I say, it is not always the events but the emotional impact of events that accounts for literary authenticity. Except for the emotional felicity available to a writer, his writing will, despite possessing absolutely correct details, fail to be creatively substantial. I do believe I am no other than Deewane Maulvi Sahab of *Khwabrau,* and living here in India, I did experience every detail of his life in Pakistan. In this specific context, therefore, my dear friend Anwar Sadeed should regard me as a fellow Pakistani.

Alec Athaide, Teresa's cousin,
with his wife, Phyllis
Karachi, 1943

Yolande (Ken's wife), Matilda
(Teresa's aunt), Ann deCruz (Matilda's
granddaughter), Ken, and Teresa
at Ken's family home shortly before
Matilda and Teresa left Karachi
1948

Greyholme, the home built by
Matilda's son, Bude, and lived in
by the extended family
Cincinnatus Town, Karachi

Where There Is No Frontier

When, after fifty-one years, Abdur got down apprehensively from the second-class compartment of the train at Azimabad station, the winter sun was starting to decline in the western sky. The sunlight had lost its shine and was the colour of faded turmeric, and the north wind gusted like a mad, unbridled horse.

His full name was Abdur Hussein. He was sixty, of medium height and slender build. There were heavy shadows under his eyes, and he had prominent jawbones. His eyesight was no longer strong, and he wore heavy-framed glasses. His whole body bore the marks of age: his skin was rough and wrinkled, and his hair and beard mostly grey.

Abdur was wearing a very crumpled pajama and a sherwani, over which he had a long-sleeved woollen pullover. Even that was not enough to stop the indomitable cold of north India, so over the pullover he had a thick woollen shawl wrapped around himself. On his feet he wore heavy sandals. He carried a large leather suitcase in his right hand and, in the other, a holdall containing his pillow, a thin mattress, a pair of blankets, a bedcover, and sundry odds and ends.

Two years after Partition, when he was nine, Abdur and his family left Azimabad for West Pakistan and settled in Karachi, where they lived in the very crowded part of the old city, a locality that became a colony for Mohajirs, the Urdu-speaking Muslim refugees from India.

He had two reasons for coming back to India after fifty-one years. One was to go to Ajmer Sharif; the other was to come to Azimabad and visit his elder sister, Fatima, who had remained behind when the family went to Pakistan after Partition. Many people had told them that they would have no security in India and that their future would be bleak, so it did not make sense for them to risk staying. However, Fatima's father-in-law, Sheik Badruddin, was a dogged character who said simply that he and his family would not be leaving his country, the land of his birth, for anywhere. Let happen what may.

Before Partition and for some time after, there had been clashes between Hindus and Muslims that had culminated in arson, bloodshed, and murder. No person of either community would trust anyone of the other; there prevailed only mutual hatred, malice, and suspicion. Once the terror had reached a height for the Muslims and groups of them started leaving for West Pakistan, Badruddin still did not succumb to mistrust of others, believing that not all men had lost their humanity.

It was not possible for an ordinary man like Abdur to travel from Pakistan into India at the drop of a hat. After days of running around and experiencing all sorts of harassment, he had almost given up hope when he was given a fifteen-day visa. Having left Karachi by plane, he had to travel by train from Delhi to Ajmer Sharif. From there he had come to visit Fatima in Azimabad. Returning the same way he had come, he would have to go back to Delhi and take the plane to Karachi.

Abdur had arrived in India some seven days back. When he was leaving home, people had warned him again and again that Muslims, especially Pakistanis, were unsafe in India. In the seven days since arriving in India, he had done a lot of traveling by train, bus, and taxi, but so far he had had no reason to believe that there was any threat to him at all. India was a huge country with millions of people, and no one had even looked at him twice. However, for the few days that he would be there he would have to be careful. He would not neglect the warnings of his neighbours in Karachi.

Abdur got down from the train and waited, looking all around with immense wistfulness in his eyes. He was not alone, as many other passengers had got down from the train too, and a good many people all over the platform were waiting with their luggage to go to various destinations. The whole station concourse was bustling.

When his family had relocated to Karachi, Abdur had been terribly nostalgic for Azimabad, but after a few years he no longer felt that way. Thousands of other Muslim families had left India and crossed the border with them, and because he had a new country, new friends, school, and his studies, the insignificant town of Azimabad in some corner of Uttar Pradesh started to become as vague as a remote star. At the end of the winter day he returned, however, all his memories started to come back, one after the other.

Abdur recalled the one-storey red building of the station of fifty-one years earlier and its platform spread with brick dust. Since then, there had been some additions. The platform in those days had been bare, but at one end of it there was now an imposing shelter, set up to offer passengers protection from the rain and the intensity of the sun. Abdur also noticed, close to the ticket counter, a big stall where tea was available and many types of sweets were on display in a glass showcase; above the showcase were big glass jars with a variety of biscuits and savoury items, and beside the jars was a stack of loaves of bread. The tea stall too had not been there before.

Fifty-one years back, Azimabad had been an insignificant station with only a couple of up trains and a couple of down trains running through in a whole day. There would be a bit of activity when the trains came in, but for the rest of the time the entire station concourse would remain quiet and still, as though sunk in a profound sleep. Both up and down trains used to run along a single line, but now another pair of tracks were laid out, and on the other side of the line a new platform, also with a shelter, had been built.

As he stood at the station, it seemed to Abdur that since Partition there had been a great increase here in the number of people and their hustle and bustle and constant come and go. He was reminded of Karachi and how many people were there when his family arrived after Partition. In fifty-one years, there had been a population explosion, and dense crowds were everywhere all the time. Indeed, all over the world people were increasing like insects, so why should Azimabad be any exception?

Abdur brought himself out of his reminiscing. He looked at the passengers on the platform for a few moments but did not recognise any face, though it soon occurred to him that the people he knew in Azimabad when he went to Karachi would have changed so much that he would not be able to recognise them anyway. Moreover, how could he say how many of the people he knew then were still alive? And even if they were, there was no reason to think that they would have all come to the station right then. And if anyone should remember him, was there any resemblance at all between his boyhood appearance and the way he looked now? Surely no one in Azimabad would know him.

Abdur waited no longer but moved with the throng towards the gate.

When he had arrived in India some seven days back, he bought a postcard from a post office in Delhi and wrote a note to his elder sister, Fatima, telling her that he would very soon be visiting her, but he was not able to say with certainty on what day he would arrive. She would probably send one of her sons to the station. But would the man be able to recognise Abdur? Fatima's eldest son had been only one when they had left for Pakistan. Who could say what that one-year-old boy looked like now? Anyhow, if no one came to pick Abdur up from the station, he would have no trouble finding Fatima's house in the northern part of the town. And now as he set foot in Azimabad, the old picture of its streets and its various localities started to appear before his eyes.

The ticket collector, wearing a black coat, was standing at the gate. After giving him his ticket, Abdur walked a few yards away to the flight of stone steps, and although they had all been damaged by the constant tread of feet, they were still much as they had been at the time of Partition. On his way down, Abdur remembered that there had been altogether twenty-five steps; he counted them, and the number was still the same. Memory, with its secret storehouses, is a strange thing.

When he reached the bottom of the steps, Abdur was struck by how busy it all was. At the time of Partition, there had been a narrow brick-dust road here, on one side of which were three or four shops with tarpaulin awnings and cracked tin roofs. The shops sold tea or paan and biris. On the other side, a few tongas would stand, waiting for passengers. The tonga drivers and their horses would doze for almost the whole day, as though they had been weighed down by the deep and unending indolence of this remote place. The appearance of the area had totally changed. The old brick-dust road had been sealed and enlarged so that it was ten times wider, and on both sides were rows of shops as far as the eye could see. Four or five feet of the road had been taken over by the shopkeepers for the display of their wares, while in the shops, crowds of people buzzed around like flies. The scene was exactly the same as that of the station area in any mofussil town in Pakistan, and in this regard there was no difference between the two countries.

Abdur noticed a line of tongas waiting under some luxuriant pipal trees. At the time of Partition, there would not have been more than three or four tongas; now there were at least ten. There were also many autorickshaws under some trees on the opposite side. Who could say when they had come on the scene, for there had been no autorickshaws when Abdur's family had left India. Old Karachi swarmed with autorickshaws, but Abdur did not really like to travel in them, and so he went to the tonga stand under the pipal trees. He hired one and climbed up with his suitcase and his holdall, and the middle-aged driver set off.

The road was a confusing turmoil of hordes of pedestrians, bullock drays, autorickshaws, tongas, vans, handcarts, and so on. Brandishing a whip that hissed in the breeze, the tonga driver kept on shouting at the top of his voice, "Come on, get a move on! Get out of the way!" And it was not only him; other drivers of tongas, autorickshaws, and vans all called out in the same manner as they forced their way through the traffic. It took fifteen or twenty minutes to get clear of the station precinct, and then the road was a lot less busy.

Azimabad town was quite a way from the station. Abdur recalled clearly a brick-dust road joining the station with the town; they were now travelling along it, but it was no longer how it used to be. Fifty-one years ago, there had been vast stretches of stony land with bushes and jungle on each side. Since then, the jungle had been cleared, and in its place were countless big houses and an occasional temple.

The sun had now sunk in the west and was obscured by the taller houses. The dim reddish glow that lingered in the sky would last only a few more minutes and then the winter evening would come down. The arrangements were almost complete, for the day was no sooner coming to its end than the dew was falling softly all about and the north wind was like the blade of a knife, cutting at exposed parts of the body.

However, Abdur had not noticed the decline of the winter's day in this mofussil town of Uttar Pradesh. Suddenly he called to the tonga driver, "Hey, brother!"

The driver, wrapped in a grey blanket, looked over his shoulder and said, "Yes?"

"The town has changed quite a lot, hasn't it?" Abdur said.

"Oh, yes."

Gesturing to both sides of the road, Abdur said, "Once all that was open land."

The tonga driver was a very courteous man who knew how to be respectful to his passengers. Looking in front of him, he answered, "Yes. Now you won't find a hand's breadth of open space in this town. Just houses and houses." He paused for a moment, then went on, "To my mind the town's become too big!" He was very likely an uneducated man, given his pronunciation of "town" as "tone."

"As the population grows, so does the town," said Abdur.

"True."

Around the neck of the spirited horse drawing the tonga was a string of brass bells that, with the rhythm of the animal's movement, made a sweet, melodious sound. Sitting on the thick piece of sackcloth placed over the hard and cold seat on the timber decking, Abdur felt that in this ancient carriage he was being taken back to an existence now fifty-one years past. It was a strange thing that, having come such a long way from distant Karachi to see Fatima, he should recall the faces of Ramu, Lachhman, and Dhanua. He thought of so many others too, whose names he had forgotten. All of them had been his friends and playmates in the same class at the Azimabad primary school.

As Abdur thought of Dhanua, an image of his friend's face suddenly appeared clearly. He recalled how long back Dhanua's father, Lajpat Singh, and his mates had started a riot in Azimabad just before the Partition. Despite the friendship of the sons, Abdur's family was not spared, and those men tried to burn the family's house down. Who knew if Lajpat Singh was still alive? If he were, how would he react to Abdur's sudden arrival from Pakistan? Deep down, Abdur felt very ill at ease.

Having set foot after a long time in the land of his birth, Abdur found all kinds of thoughts invading his mind; no sooner had one gone than another came. His anxiety over Lajpat Singh did not last very long, however, as he recalled two tonga wallahs, Fakira and Hanif. Fakira was a truly fine fellow. Sometimes, if he did not have any passengers, he would let Abdur and his friends get up onto the tonga, and he would take them on a round of the streets of Azimabad. Hanif, though, was terribly quick tempered and peevish, as though every few minutes the blood was rushing to his head. He would not let Abdur and his friends even come close to his tonga, and if they did, he would let out a stream of abuse. However, Abdur and his friends were very persistent, and while Hanif was looking ahead, perhaps driving the tonga, they would quietly go behind and swing from the decking. But Hanif had ten pairs of eyes and could sense all that was going on, and without even turning around he would brandish his whip at the back while the tonga kept going.

"Brother!" Abdur called.

"Yes?" the tonga wallah answered immediately.

"Do you know Fakira and Hanif? They must be very old. Are they still alive?"

"Who are they?"

"A long time ago they drove tongas in this town."

The driver thought for a few moments and suddenly, as though he had just remembered, said, "Oh, yes, I remember. Uncle Hanif and Uncle Fakira stayed in the old quarter of the town. But they both died ten or twelve years ago."

Hearing of the death of two men familiar to him in his childhood made Abdur feel a little sad. When his family went to Pakistan, Hanif and Fakira would not yet have been forty. If they had died ten or twelve years ago, they would have been at least seventy-four or seventy-five—not a short span of life. Most people do not live as long. Nevertheless, he still felt heavy hearted for the two tonga wallahs.

A little river called the Motiya flowed through the middle of the town of Azimabad. When they came to it, Abdur was dumbfounded. In his boyhood days, a sturdy timber bridge over it joined the two parts of the town. Pedestrians, tongas, cycle rickshaws, bullock and buffalo drays, and a few motor cars all used it to go from one side to the other. But not a splinter of that old timber bridge remained. In its place was a concrete bridge three times as wide, with footpaths and a row of lampposts on each side.

As they crossed the bridge, Abdur asked, "I say, brother, when did this bridge replace the old one?"

"About thirty, thirty-five years ago," said the driver.

Abdur asked no more questions as he looked wistfully at the bridge. It seemed that very little remained of the Azimabad of his childhood.

The driver turned around and said, "Can I ask you something?"

Abdur was a little surprised. "Yes, yes. Go ahead."

"Listening to you speak, it seems that you're returning to this town after a very long time."

"I am."

"Did you live here?"

"Yes."

"Where do you live now?"

The tonga wallah's curiosity was innocent and there was nothing suspicious in the questions he was asking, but in a flash Abdur was reminded of his neighbours' repeated warnings that he not let anyone know, as far as was possible, that he was a Pakistani.

Abdur retreated for a moment. He had lived in India until he was nine years old, and in that time he had never set foot outside of Azimabad except for a visit once to Agra and Delhi. After going to Karachi, what little connection he had had with India faded in time so that he now knew almost nothing of the country. Of course, he had heard the names of a few big cities, and on arrival from Karachi he had landed in Delhi, where he had once gone in his childhood. Aside from Delhi, he knew only such names as Calcutta, Bombay, Madras, Cuttack, and Bangalore. Almost in a panic then, Abdur said, "I live in Calcutta." He tried for the life of him to sound natural lest the driver should be in any way suspicious.

"Calcutta's not all that far away," said the tonga wallah, "yet you're coming here after so long a time!" He sounded quite surprised.

It suddenly seemed to Abdur that the man was becoming nosy, cross-examining him like a lawyer. What if he should carelessly answer some question and so create difficulties for himself? He would have to stop the man. Casually, Abdur said, "There are so many problems with my business…" He did not go on any further.

Cordially the tonga wallah asked, "Do you have any family here—father, mother, any relatives?"

To have answered the tonga wallah truthfully would have invited many other questions, some of which might have made Abdur quite uncomfortable. Quietly and indistinctly, he muttered something incomprehensible. The driver guessed that he was not going to get an answer to his question, and he said nothing more.

The tonga had crossed the bridge and gone over to the other side. Here the road ran through the most privileged quarter of Azimabad. Inside the large compounds were grand mansions of a bygone age, and in front of these were flower gardens, lawns, and pebbled driveways. Fifty-one years ago, each home had a carriage pulled by a healthy horse with a shiny coat; in only a few was there a motor car. The upper-class neighbourhood was much the same as it had been before, except that it had grown many times larger.

Apart from just one Jankinath, Abdur could not remember the people to whom these houses once belonged. He remembered the name of Jankinath because two years before Partition, the English District Magistrate had come to Jankinath's house from the district town. Abdur had heard from his father that the white saheb was a high-ranking officer and that such an important man had never before been to Azimabad.

There had been great excitement in the quiet, insignificant little town. Jankinath-ji, dressed in an expensive coat and trousers and wearing on his head a turban of five yards of cloth, had gone directly to the station, along with the other important people of Azimabad. In order to prevent the dust of the town from getting onto the shoes of the District Magistrate, a red jute carpet had been spread over the entire platform and the steps leading down to the road, and to impress such a historical event on the memories of the people of Azimabad forever, Jankinath-ji had brought four musical bands from Allahabad. Abdur's father had told him that a Muslim chef from a famous hotel had also been brought in.

Abdur remembered how Jankinath-ji had taken the DM to his own house in an open carriage drawn by six horses. An attendant dressed in a splendid uniform stood on a platform at the back of the carriage, all the while holding a colourful silk umbrella over the DM. Abdur could still remember the scene, for in those times the visit of an English DM was a truly grand event in such a small town, and in order to see him in person the people of Azimabad had crowded together on both sides of the road. Abdur's father had taken him along.

In front of the procession were two of the bands; then came Jankinath-ji's carriage as the guide, followed by the DM's carriage in the middle, after which came a number of the distinguished citizens of Azimabad. Bringing up the rear of this splendid cavalcade were the other two bands.

Within three months of the DM's visit, Jankinath was awarded the title of Rai Bahadur. One night on returning home, Abdur's father had broken the news in a voice full of pride and excitement, for there could never have been a Rai Bahadur in Azimabad up until then. In his childhood days, Abdur was not able to appreciate how much honour was attached to the title and to the one who received it, but it had seemed to be something quite momentous.

Abdur wondered if Jankinath was still alive. He stopped himself from asking the tonga wallah lest his curiosity should provoke an unwelcome question in return. He then noticed that evening had started to fall. Lights were on in the houses, the rows of streetlights were lit, and the cold was more intense.

They reached the locality at the far northern end of Azimabad with its very many houses; one part of it was a Muslim quarter, the other Hindu. The locality was much the same as it had been fifty-one years before, and Abdur had no trouble recognising it. He got down from the tonga with his suitcase and holdall, paid the fare, and had a good look around at the maze of unprepossessing houses of the old locality, the Muslim quarter much duller than the Hindu one. Even on this winter evening, many people were in the streets. Abdur remembered that Fatima's father-in-law's house was very close, about a five-minute walk from the main road, and that a little further in was Abdur's old family home.

Many narrow lanes led into the Muslim quarter, but Abdur quickly realised that after all these years he had no idea which one he should take to get to Fatima's house. Fatima's husband's name had been Sheikh Ziaul. If Abdur mentioned his name, surely someone or other would be able to point out the house to him. He was just about to ask someone on the street when two men came out from an alley on his left. One of them was his age, heavy looking and of medium height; he had a bushy moustache and wore a dhoti and a full shirt, over which was a warm shawl, and on his head was a woollen cap. He was evidently a Hindu. His companion was in his mid thirties, thin, and frail looking; he had a longish face, big eyes, sharp nose, and a tidy, well-trimmed beard. He wore a pajama and long kurta, over which was a thick woollen sweater, and a round cap was on his head. It could be assumed that he was a Muslim.

The two men walked straight up to Abdur. The elder man—the Hindu—looked at Abdur and kept his eyes on him for a few moments. Then he asked, "Are you Abdur Hussein?"

Abdur was taken aback. He said, "Yes, I am. But I do not recognise you."

Immediately the man cried out, "You old owl! You ass! I'm Dhanno—Dhanua!"

In their childhood, Dhanua had been rather skinny and frail. Who would ever have thought that fifty-one years later he would have put on so much weight! There was not the slightest resemblance between the boy of those days and the Dhanua of today. However, one thing had remained the same: the intensity of his expression of emotion. He was always loud, for he could not speak without shouting.

Abdur could not have imagined meeting his boyhood friend in this way. Yet he was very much taken by Dhanua's heartiness, which momentarily returned him to their childhood. Abdur embraced him, saying, "After so many years, we are meeting, Dhanno!"

"So many years!" Dhanua—or Dhanpat—said, "We've now grown old. Who would have thought that I would ever meet you again in this life!"

There was a pause. Then Dhanpat, indicating the young man beside him, said, "Of course, you don't recognise him. He's Latif, sister Fatima's younger son, your youngest nephew."

When Abdur and his family had left for Pakistan, Latif had not yet been born, and now, when the long journey of Abdur's life was drawing to a close, he had come to India without any knowledge of this nephew.

Latif bent to touch his uncle's feet, and Abdur raised him up and held him close. He said, "My boy, may you live for a hundred years."

A few moments later, Latif picked up Abdur's suitcase and Dhanpat took the holdall. Abdur objected, but Dhanpat exclaimed, "Hey, you old owl, you're a guest in India. Please let us welcome you. Come on."

They went into the alley opposite Latif first, followed by Abdur and Dhanpat walking side by side.

Dhanpat said, "Since sister Fatima got your letter, Latif and I have been going to the station two or three times every day. But there are seven or eight trains a day coming here from Allahabad, and we didn't know which one you'd be coming on. We were both going again just now when we saw you getting down from the tonga. But if you had sent a letter letting us know, then—"

"I didn't know how long I would be at Ajmer Sharif, so how could I tell you on what day I would leave there for Azimabad?"

"Oh, I see," said Dhanpat, slowly nodding his head.

Abdur asked, "My appearance has changed utterly, like yours, so how did you recognise me after all these years?"

"I didn't. I just guessed." Dhanpat hurriedly explained that he knew everyone in Azimabad and that Abdur was expected to arrive at any time, any day. When he saw a man of his age getting down from a tonga, it occurred to him that there was an eighty percent chance it would be Abdur.

Abdur smiled.

Then Dhanpat said, "Now tell us all about yourself. What work do you do in Pakistan? How many children have you got? Your wife—"

Abdur interrupted his friend. "You can hear all about me later. But first tell me about yourself."

Dhanpat gave a rapid two-minute account not only of himself but of various things about the town of Azimabad. After Abdur and his family had left, Dhanpat had not gone very far with his education and had left school after twice failing eighth class. After spending a few years as an unemployed layabout aimlessly wandering, he eventually trained as a motor mechanic at his father's insistence and then opened a garage. He had made good money. He had a son and a daughter. The boy had passed B.A. and now worked in a government position, living in Lucknow. The girl was married and lived with her in-laws in Allahabad. There were no real problems in his family, though the health of his wife and father were a worry as they both suffered from this disease or that.

Abdur was so overwhelmed with emotion at seeing his old friend after many years and by Dhanpat's affectionate generosity that he had momentarily forgotten Dhanpat's father, the Rajput kshatriya Lajpat Singh, and those other men who, at the time of the riot just before Partition, had set fire to Abdur's house. So many people like Lajpat had been the reason for his family's going to Pakistan, people who nurtured immense anger and hatred for Muslims. Their murderous and violent looks at the time of the riot were indelible in Abdur's memory. It had seemed then that they would rip him and his family to shreds, but somehow, by the mercy of Allah, the family had survived. However, Abdur's fear had lingered for a long time after moving to Karachi.

In fact, Abdur was stung by the news that Lajpat Singh was still alive, and a strange pang of fear erupted inside him.

Dhanpat continued, not looking at Abdur, telling him that none of the prominent citizens of those times was still alive. Rai Bahadur Jankinath, the big businessman Mahavirprasad Shrivastav, and the government lawyer Baburam Gupta and all their ilk were now dead, but all of Abdur's close boyhood friends were still alive. Ramu had made millions as a contractor and lived in the grand mansion he had had built in Lucknow, coming to Azimabad for a few days once every year or two. Lachhman had got his degree in science and taken up a position in Delhi with a noted pharmaceutical company. Baiju, of course, was still in Azimabad and had a number of warehouses beside the Motiya river that stocked rice, paddy, wheat, sesame, linseed, and mustard seeds. It was a family business that Baiju now supervised.

Dhanpat also remarked that the old times had completely changed. Apart from the riot, Azimabad had gone a long time without any disturbance. It had been a peaceful town, free of agitation, through which the stream of life flowed slowly. However, after a few years, bloodshed, highway robbery, and bank holdups increased remarkably, and for this the political leaders who came after Independence were very much to blame. They gave refuge to ruffians and gun-wielding thugs who helped them hold on to power. At election time, these scoundrels cast fake votes, the genuine voters not going near the voting booths for fear of the pistols and bombs. Those who created the parliamentarians would get away with murder and robbery, and the leaders would not lift a finger. Should the police arrest any of these hired thugs, a phone call to the station would ensure his immediate release. The leaders had given them licence to do as they pleased.

Dhanpat was still talking when they reached the house of Fatima's father-in-law, an old-style, two-storey home. Through the main door was a paved courtyard, on one side of which were a bathroom and a kitchen. Facing three sides on both storeys were many other rooms.

The house had been hazy in Abdur's memory, but now everything was starting to come back to him. Fatima's father-in-law had had it built just before her marriage. The new house had been painted crimson, and the doors and window frames green, and it had had a sparkling appearance. How he used to enjoy coming here from time to time after his big sister's wedding! But the house was no longer what it once had been. The plaster was coming off various parts of the walls, exposing the brickwork; the cornices were broken; and in one place, the head of a banyan sapling was poking through. And there were so many cracks in the courtyard! The house had gone a long time without proper maintenance, and its days seemed numbered—with luck, maybe ten or twelve years.

Lights were burning in all the rooms as they crossed the courtyard and entered the main part of the house. There was an amazing stillness all around them; yet once there had been so many people in that house, and all the time, the noise of children running about resounded from the ground floor to the roof. Now there seemed to be no one but the three of them, although the sound of sizzling coming from the kitchen meant that someone was cooking.

Inside was a wide passage, on the left of which were three rooms and on the right of which was the staircase leading to the upper floor. Many of the steps had become damaged and uneven. Going up the broken staircase behind Latif, Abdur suddenly felt anxiety welling up inside. He had come to see Fatima for the first time since he had left for Pakistan as a nine-year-old boy, a long fifty-one years ago.

Latif led him and Dhanpat into a huge room that Abdur recognised as the bedroom of Fatima and her husband, Sheikh Ziaul. Electric lights were burning from the tops of the walls on two sides. As far as Abdur could remember, the decor of the room had not noticeably changed. As before, there were three or four bulky almirahs, an old-fashioned dressing table, a few cushions, a couple of chairs, and the like. Right in the middle was an immense crafted bed, beside which were three or four small, low tables. A few feet away was a television set on a high stand.

Under a thick layer of dirt, the furniture was dark and dull. Evidently, it had not been polished for quite a long time.

The grubby bed was made up on a mattress a foot thick; an elderly lady was lying on it and had a blanket over her. She had a thin, emaciated face, pure-white hair, a broad brow, and a dull look in her eyes. Seeing the three men, she turned aside and groped beside the pillow for her glasses, put them on, and said in a weak voice, "Oh, Dhanno and Lati, you have come!" Apparently, Lati was the pet name of Latif.

"Yes, Mother," said Latif.

Now wearing her glasses, the lady—Fatima—said, "There's someone with you. Who is it?"

In a gently jocular tone, Dhanpat said, "Oh, Sister, you ask who? Can't you recognise him?"

Fatima slowly raised herself up and fixed her gaze intently on Abdur's face for some moments, as though searching. She then took a breath and said, "Is it you, Munna, come from Pakistan?"

How many years had it been since Abdur had heard his pet name! After the deaths of his mother and father, no one had called him by it, and he had quite forgotten about it. But Fatima had not forgotten.

Abdur looked straight at Fatima. When his family had left India, there was an album amongst their chattels. It contained photos of Fatima's wedding, of the wondrous fairy princess his sister had seemed to him then. And now before him was this aged, bedridden, frail lady, like a heap of ruins. The blood of the same parents ran through the veins of both of them, yet how remote was the woman. He was Pakistani, she Indian; between them was not only a fifty-one-year estrangement, but also a virtually impenetrable frontier.

As he looked at this ageing and frail old woman, his heart ached terribly, and from its depths there emanated something like a howl that seemed to gather into a lump and stick in his throat, so his breathing was stifled. It was as though by some strange and mystic force he had crossed the frontiers of time and geography and was now returning to his childhood.

Nevertheless, he tried to speak, but at first his throat seemed choked. He almost ran and sat beside Fatima, and then with great difficulty he gave voice to his words. "Yes, Sister, I am indeed your Munna."

Embracing Abdur's head with her two frail and trembling hands, Fatima burst into sobs. Through her tears she said, "You remembered me after all this time! I've grown very old. It won't be long before I'll be no more I'll be under the ground." Her body writhed in a cascade of sobbing.

Abdur was infected by Fatima's emotion. He had, indeed, endured much tumult in the last fifty-one years. Riots, murders, arson, Partition, leaving India and going to Pakistan—it had all been a continual struggle for survival, one that had hardened him. He did not cry easily, but at that moment he felt that his eyes were bursting with tears. His voice choking, he said, "Don't cry, Sister. Don't cry."

But Fatima's crying did not stop; rather, her tears flowed even more.

After a short while, Fatima settled down a little and took her hands from around her brother's head. Under the strain of her sobbing, her breathing had become heavy. Abdur said, "You are getting distressed, Sister. Lie down now."

But Fatima remained sitting up. Catching her breath, she said, "After all these years I am seeing you again. How can I lie down?"

"I'll stay beside you. You can talk lying down." With great affection, Abdur supported his elder sister by the shoulder and helped her to lie down. Taking her frail hand in his own, he asked, "How did you get like this?"

It was Latif who answered the question, explaining that Fatima had had a stroke three years back. On top of that, she had developed a liver ailment and shortness of breath. Indeed, he couldn't reckon the number of ailments that had come to occupy his mother's weak body.

Alongside Latif, Dhanpat spoke up. "Look at this," he said, pointing to a bedside table on which there were bottles of various kinds of medicines and countless packets of capsules and tablets. "Your elder sister survives by the doctor and his medicines."

Abdur nodded slowly and sadly. He said nothing.

"Abdur," Dhanpat said, "I can't stay any longer. I have to get back to the garage. I'll come again early tomorrow morning." To Fatima he said, "Goodbye, Sister. After all these years, you now have your brother, so don't cry anymore. You'll only make yourself sick."

Once Dhanpat had gone, Abdur asked, "Does he come here every day?"

"Not every day," said Latif. "Usually twice a week, to see how we are getting on. He looks after us."

Fatima said, "That time when I was so sick, he took me to the hospital. I was unconscious for three days, and he stayed there with me day and night. He also set Latif up in business. I can't tell you how much he has helped us. We rely on Dhanno so much. There's no one like him."

Abdur was dumbfounded. The son of Lajpat Singh, who had started the riot in Azimabad and tried to burn down their house, was now the stalwart of Fatima's home! Before Abdur could say anything, Fatima said, "You have come such a long way on the train, you must surely be tired. No more talk now, while you go and wash your face and hands and change your grubby shirt. Then come back and have some tea with me." She asked Latif, "Has the bed been made up in Uncle's room?"

Latif inclined his head. "Yes," he said.

"Tell Bano to put some hot water in the bathroom and then to make tea and puris and bring them up here. Tell her to bring some sweets too."

Abdur did not know Bano, but he did not ask about her. He would surely meet her sooner or later.

Latif left the room and came back in a few minutes. Fatima said to her son, "Take Uncle to his room now. Give him some fresh soap and a towel and show him the bathroom."

Picking up Abdur's suitcase and holdall, Latif took him to a room on the right. He put the luggage on the floor and switched on the light. It was a very big room, though not as big as Fatima's, and was exceptionally clean and tidy. In addition to a sturdy and freshly made up bed on one side, were an almirah, some wicker stools and cushions, a wall mirror, a table, and a chair.

Latif said, "This is your room."

Abdur guessed that the room had been spruced up especially for him. He sat on the chair, took off his shoes and socks, and put them to one side. He opened his suitcase, and as he was taking out a shirt and pajama to wear about the house, it occurred to him again how extraordinarily still the whole place was. Thus far, he had not seen anyone other than Latif and Fatima, though there was someone called Bano, as yet unknown.

For a time after Partition, there had been some correspondence with Fatima's family, which then became irregular and eventually died out. Through it, however, those family members who had moved had learned that Fatima had two sons and two daughters. Of course, the first son, Niyaz, had been born while Abdur's family was still in India; the other three had been born after they left. They had also got a letter telling them of the death of Fatima's father-in-law, Sheikh Badruddin, but Abdur could not remember any news of the death of her husband, Ziaul, reaching Karachi. He had no knowledge of who his nephews and nieces were, how they were, and what they were doing.

Abdur told Latif to sit down and asked him, "Is there anyone other than you and your mother staying in this house?"

"No," said Latif. He told him that his elder brother, Niyaz, had gone to live in Munger after his marriage. He was heartless and selfish and did not visit the house in Azimabad. The two sisters were married; the elder one, Nurbanu, lived in Rae Bareilly, and the younger, Mumtaz, lived in Saharanpur. However, the two daughters were so busy that they could hardly ever visit.

There was a brief pause, then Abdur asked, "How far did you get with your education?"

"I passed matriculation," Latif replied.

"What work do you do—service or business?"

"I have a small business. I get stainless-steel utensils from a big merchant in Allahabad and sell them here at five-percent commission." Latif considered for a moment, then said, "It was Uncle Dhanno who took me to meet the merchant. He stood surety for me and provided the capital so that the business could get established. All my savings had been spent on my sisters' weddings, so I had to borrow. Of course, I've paid him back."

In Fatima's father-in-law's house—as in Abdur's family home—there had never been strict observance of purdah, and in their younger days Abdur would often take Dhanpat there. Everyone from Sheikh Badruddin down had liked him very much. Even after Abdur had gone to Pakistan, Dhanpat's coming and going alone to the house had in no way been restricted; later, during hard times, he had always been by Fatima's side and had put Latif on his feet, even though there was no blood connection between him and Fatima's family. Even their religions were different. Abdur's heart was full of gratitude to Dhanpat.

"You've not married?" Abdur asked Latif.

"I did, but—"

"But what?"

Looking downcast, Latif said, "The marriage didn't last."

"Why not?" Abdur was a little surprised.

Latif told him that he had married a girl from a wealthy home, one used to luxury. She wanted this, she wanted that, and Latif found it impossible to satisfy his wife's cupidity. The biggest problem was her unwillingness to live with her mother-in-law, an aversion encouraged by her own family. However, Latif could not even think of leaving his mother, and consequently there developed unrest, petty squabbling, and acrimony until eventually the relationship broke down.

After a pause Abdur said, "You are still young. You have a long life ahead of you. Find a nice girl from a good family and get married again."

Latif explained that there was no certainty that marrying again would fill the family with joy or bring a smile to his mother's face. Who could say that the same kind of troubles would not start up once more? Better the way he was than that.

Abdur could see that the experience of the first marriage had made Latif wary and unwilling to tread that path again. Abdur would have liked to see his nephew happily married, but what could he do about it? He had come to this country for just a few days; once he had returned to Karachi, the memories of Azimabad would grow dim and the concern he had felt for Latif probably would fade too.

The sound of a woman's voice came up from the ground floor. "Latif-bhai! I've put the hot water in the bathroom."

Although he could not see her, Abdur guessed that the woman must be Bano.

Latif opened an almirah on his right and took out some soap and a fresh towel. "Come on, Uncle," he said.

Having washed his face and hands and changed his clothes, Abdur went back with Latif to Fatima's room. As before, his sister was sitting up on one side of the bed. Almost immediately a big stainless-steel tray bearing puris, halwa, and gulab jamuns was set down by Bano on a fresh white towel laid out beside Abdur on the bed.

Bano had a strong, hard appearance and must have been a little over forty. She was wearing a thick shawl over a cheap chintz salwarkameez. Her skin was of a copper colour, and there were smallpox scars on her fleshy face.

Fatima pointed to Abdur and said to Bano, "This is Uncle, who has come from Pakistan." Then she said to Abdur, "She is like a daughter to me. Four years she's been here now, looking after all the bother of the house. We couldn't survive a day without her."

So Bano was the housemaid, a courteous woman of gentle nature. She bowed and greeted Abdur with "Adab," then said, "I've heard all about you from Latif-bhai and Auntie. We've all been looking forward to your arrival."

Abdur smiled.

Fatima said to Bano, "What are you giving Uncle for dinner tonight?"

"There's some meat, fish, vegetables," Bano replied.

"Prepare it well. Oh, and make some kheer. But before you put it all on the oven, give Uncle some tea." Fatima paused. Sadly she said, almost to herself, "I see my brother after all these years and I can't even cook for him…"

Bano had gone.

After a little while of eating in silence, Abdur said, "I've heard everything from Latif. It's very sad, Sister. I can understand your daughters not being able to come and see you. Girls don't have that freedom after they get married. But why hasn't Niyaz come to Azimabad since his marriage?"

Fatima remained quiet for a while. Then, tapping her forehead with her finger, she said sadly, "I don't blame him. It's my fate."

Abdur sensed that Fatima would make no complaint about her eldest child. After a few moments he said, "And Latif's marriage broke down. He needs a family."

"I've said so many times. But he doesn't agree. What can I do then?"

"How will he get by when you have gone?"

"There's nothing I can do about that. What must be will be."

In other words, Fatima had committed everything to fate. This was very likely part of her becoming old, sick, and frail. All of Fatima's will, all her spirit, had been spent.

Again Abdur was about to say something, but Fatima went on. "You've heard all about us. Yet even though we were born of the one mother, I know virtually nothing about you. I heard the news of Father's and Mother's deaths, but tell me about Asma and Nazzu." Asma and Nazzu—or Nazim—were their sister and brother, who also had gone with their parents to Pakistan.

Abdur told her about them as he went on eating. After Partition, the family went with countless others across the border and straight to Karachi. Nabab Hussein—the father of Abdur, Fatima, and their siblings—and hundreds of thousands of Indian Muslims like him had the idea that if they could reach the land of their dreams, Pakistan, they could hold the moon in the palm of their hands. Their joy knew no bounds as they looked forward to the big mansions that were being made ready for their accommodation. But as soon as they set foot in Karachi, they were sent to a refugee camp and their dreams were shattered.

However, Nabab Hussein was not one to be kept down. He was an exceptionally honest, enterprising, and hard-working man. While staying in the refugee camp, he set about working to restart his life in his new country. With the aid of a government loan, he opened a small cloth shop in the market of old Karachi. He was not willing to remain in the refugee camp, so as soon as he had arranged the finances, he rented two rooms in an old barrack-type house and moved in with his wife and children. The children were then enrolled in school.

Within a few years, the business had grown and its income had increased, so Nabab Hussein left the small shop and opened a big one. With some money he had saved, he bought a house. However, as soon as he had got his family established, he developed a fever and died after a few days. Abdur had just completed his matriculation, Asma was in Class Nine, and Nazim was in Class Seven. They were all thrown into uncertainty.

Abdur had been a very good student. He had thought that he might go as far as a master's degree, but his wish was not to be fulfilled. After mourning their father's death, he took over the shop in order to support the family. His business grew from one shop to three. He had Asma married once she had completed her matriculation. Nazim passed his B.A., took a job in government service, got married, and now lived in the government quarters. Of course, Abdur got married himself after Asma's marriage, but not long before his wedding, another tragedy struck with the death of their mother. Abdur had one son and a daughter. The boy was doing a master's degree in science, and this year the girl would present for her B.A. final examinations, after which her marriage would be arranged.

Although Fatima had got the news of her parents' deaths, she had not known anything about her brothers and sister. She said nothing for a long time, then asked, "Nazzu and Asma are in Karachi then?"

Abdur nodded slowly. "Yes," he said.

"Do you see them?"

"Oh, yes. They visit on holidays. I visit them too."

"They're all well?"

"Yes."

"I really long to see them. But it won't be in this life. Will you tell them to come here if they can?"

"Of course I will."

Somewhat distractedly, Fatima said, "There are often reports in the newspapers of unrest in Karachi."

Abdur explained that Karachi was a big port city and that it had its experience of bloodshed and gunshots. There was, of course, the Sunni-Shia rivalry, but there was also the unwillingness of the original residents to accept on fair terms the Urdu-speaking refugees who had come from India. Although a long time had passed since the birth of Pakistan, they still would not break bread with those who had settled there after fleeing India. As a result, there was continuing mutual mistrust and unrest as well as political turmoil, strikes, mass arrests, police shootings, agitation.

Fatima looked anxious. "None of you have been attacked, though?"

"Don't worry, Sister," said Abdur. "We had to learn to live with all of this as soon as we got there."

Again there was silence. Then Abdur went on, "In Karachi we often hear of serious attacks on Muslims in India. It seems that anyone could be killed at any time. You have no fear of that then?"

Latif was sitting on a chair beside them. He told Abdur that the turbulence created by the destruction of the Babri Masjid had spread to Azimabad, where, after the bomb blasts in Bombay, the situation had become volatile and riots had broken out. The Muslim locality had been targeted. However, Dhanpat and many men like him had put a stop to that. There were also several political parties that had organised peace marches. At that time, Dhanpat and others spent many days defending the Muslim quarter.

"But—," Latif said.

"But what?" asked Abdur.

"Though they don't actually say it, there are many people who don't want us to stay in India. Pakistan was established as a separate state for Muslims—and they say we should go there."

Abdur suddenly felt very concerned for Latif and his people. He said to Fatima, "Sister, I haven't seen you in such a long time. I wasn't aware of all this. If you approve, when I return to Karachi, I will try to bring you and Latif to us there." He did not know what the necessary procedure was or even how possible it was to bring two Indians across the border, but what he said carried with it his fear and anxiety.

Fatima said, "But just a little while ago, you said that they don't like Indian Muslims. You've been there a long time, so it's all right for you. But if we suddenly turned up, would they be happy about that?"

Abdur was a little embarrassed. He could not think of anything to say.

"There's no need to worry," said Fatima. "Just as there are bad men here, there are also good and honest ones—much more so. I trust in them." She paused for a moment, then said, "After Independence, my father-in-law and my husband wouldn't let any of us leave the country. As long as I live, I'll stay in Azimabad."

There was a resolve in Fatima's tone that was not to be resisted. It was as though she had taken on the doggedness of her father-in-law and husband. She would not leave her country to go anywhere.

A thought suddenly occurred to Abdur, and he said, "Not just Niyaz, I won't have met any of my other nephews and nieces before leaving. I made some guesses and brought salwar-kameez-dopattas, Pathan kurtas, and some cloth for trousers and shirts. I'll give them to you tomorrow. You can pass them on."

Abdur had heeded the warnings of his neighbours in Karachi and had kept quiet about visiting Ajmer Sharif and visiting his elder sister. But when he awoke the next morning, he felt emotionally overwhelmed and restless. He had been born in this town and had spent the first nine years of his life here; not only had he lived here, but his father and his grandfather and his grandfather's grandfather—five generations—had been born, had grown up, had been educated, and had worked in Azimabad. Having come back here after so long, who could say if there were any chance that he would ever return? So he decided that he would look around the town and would visit the house that his family had left behind.

Abdur washed himself, had some tea and breakfast, and asked Latif, "Do you have any pressing work today?"

"Why do you ask?"

"I'd like you to come to our old house with me."

"Certainly. You're here for just a few days; I'll come with you."

"It won't be any disturbance to your work?"

"No. I have someone to look after things. From time to time, I'll drop in to check up."

But just as they were about to leave, a great number of people from the Muslim quarter, ranging from young boys to old men, suddenly appeared, all of them with boundless curiosity on their faces. Somehow the word had got around that Nabab Hussein's son had come from Pakistan. Latif brought the older ones inside and offered them seats, while the younger ones crowded outside the door and children peeped through the windows.

One frail-looking old man who must have been eighty or even eighty-five said, "My name is Jan Mohammed. Nabab Hussein was my friend. I heard that your father and your mother had both died. I was very sad to hear it." He paused for a moment, then continued. "Son, I knew you in your childhood so long ago. Your appearance has changed completely."

Abdur was unable to recognise Jan Mohammed, but he could hardly say so directly. He smiled and said, "Uncle, I have now turned sixty. I couldn't look like a boy forever."

"True…" The old man slowly nodded his head.

Another old man asked, "How are you all getting on in Pakistan?"

"We manage," said Abdur.

The other men put to him question after question concerning the state of things in Pakistan, what the people from Azimabad were now doing, who was doing what work, and so on. Abdur told them what he had told Fatima about Pakistan the night before. He also mentioned that the majority of those who had left Azimabad had settled in Karachi and were working in business or service professions. A few families had gone to Lahore, but Abdur had no connection with them and could not say how they were.

In the midst of all the hubbub of their conversation, Dhanpat arrived. He pushed through the crowd into the room and said to the men of the Muslim locality, "What's all this? You've already got news of Abdur?"

As one, they answered yes, then said that they had been hearing about things in Pakistan.

Dhanpat could see, from the way in which Abdur was hemmed in, that he would not be able to easily get away. Yet Dhanpat had decided to take him around the town and, if they had the time, to take him to his own house and his garage.

Trying not to offend anybody, Dhanpat said respectfully, "Uncles, please don't be angry. Abdur will be here for a few days and will go to all your houses. But now, please be so kind as to let him take leave of you."

On hearing Dhanpat's words, the old men insisted that Abdur visit them all and share a humble meal with them. Were they not able to entertain the son of Nabab Hussein, their regrets would know no bounds. Abdur calculated that if he accepted the invitations of so many men, he would have to stay in Azimabad for at least twenty days, and there was no possibility of that. However, as a means of getting away, he promised to eat at all their houses.

After the men had gone, Abdur raised his eyebrows in a look of amusement and asked, "And what was your purpose in driving them all away?"

Dhanpat replied, "I was rescuing you. Otherwise, who knows how long you would have remained captive!" He paused for a moment, then said, "Are you going to just sit here in the house? Come, let me show you the old town."

"I've already asked Latif to do just that. I had no idea that you would come back so early. Just as we were thinking of going out, all the men arrived. But I want to go and see our old house first."

"All right. Let's go then."

The three of them left after taking leave of Fatima.

In Abdur's boyhood, most of the roads in the Muslim quarter were unpaved; only on one or two was there any asphalt. Now all the roads were sealed. On both sides, the houses were so close together that they touched each other.

Many of those who had come to greet Abdur had not returned to their own homes but were chatting in groups on the road. Seeing him again, they pursued him like jackals. Women of various ages looked curiously through the windows of every house, and those people who were sitting on the front veranda or courtyard getting some of the winter sun called out a few words, having guessed that the companion of Dhanpat and Latif was the son of Nabab Hussein, who had come from Pakistan.

It was about a fifteen-minute walk through narrow, winding lanes from Fatima's house to Abdur's old family home. The house was not as it had been before. When Abdur's family had left for Pakistan, it had had two storeys, but now it had another top floor. The whole place had recently been painted, and the smell of fresh paint still hung around the doors and window frames. The front courtyard was very much the same as before. There, an old man with a quilt wrapped around his body was half-lying on a charpoy while five or six little children were making a racket all around him. From the outside, it could be guessed that a good many people lived in the house.

Dhanpat took Latif and Abdur up to the old man and called to him, "Uncle Akbar!"

The old man quickly sat up, supporting himself on his hands. He was over eighty, but his movement was by no means impaired, and his eyesight too was quite good. Seeing the three of them, he said, "Oh, Dhanno, Lati. I see you have brought someone with you."

"Yes. This is Abdur, the son of Nabab Hussein," said Dhanpat.

"Which Nabab Hussein?"

"The one who was the owner of your house."

"You mean the one who took his wife and children to Pakistan after Independence?"

"Yes."

Akbar was quite taken aback. He looked straight at Abdur and asked, "You've come from Pakistan?"

"Yes, I have," answered Abdur.

Suspiciously, Akbar asked, "You've suddenly come to India?"

Abdur could guess at the cause of the old man's suspicion. Before leaving for Pakistan, Abdur had heard that one Akbar Ali had given some cash to his father to live in their house. It must, indeed, have seemed very suspicious that the son of Nabab Hussein should suddenly turn up so many years later.

Before Abdur could answer him, Akbar Ali again asked, "Have you all come back to India?"

In other words, the old man was worried that Abdur had come back to India to settle in the house. Abdur smiled to himself and said, "No, uncle. There is no possibility of our returning here." He then explained the reasons that had brought him to India.

Akbar Ali's worries dispersed, and it suddenly occurred to him that he was not being exactly hospitable to the son of Nabab Hussein. In a fluster he said, "Why are you standing up? Sit down, sit down!"

They sat down very close to one another on the charpoy. The children had become quiet and stood at a distance, looking attentively at the unfamiliar Abdur.

Akbar Ali said to the children, "Go and tell your parents to come here to me right now."

The children ran off. Then Akbar's three sons and their wives, accompanied by the children, came out of the house and stood near the charpoy.

Akbar Ali introduced Abdur to them all and said, "This house once belonged to his family. Now, fifty-one years later, he has come from Pakistan to visit the home of his forefathers." He paused, then said, "But first, give him tea and sweets. Then I will show him the house myself."

Although he had eaten breakfast not long before, Abdur could not avoid eating again. The wives of Akbar Ali's sons brought balushai, laddus, and spiced hot tea. He had to have it all.

When Abdur had finished his tea and sweets, Akbar showed him around the house. Abdur could remember very clearly which room had been his, which had been his brother's, which had been his sister's, and which had been his parents'. As he looked at it all, a tremendous wave of nostalgia welled up in his breast.

Latif and Dhanpat did not accompany them, but remained sitting on the charpoy in the courtyard. After Abdur came back and was about to take his leave, Akbar Ali suddenly remembered something. He called Abdur over to a corner of the courtyard and said to him in a low voice, "It is good that you have come from Pakistan, son. There is a rather urgent matter—"

Abdur was taken aback. "What matter?"

Akbar Ali told him that, before going to Pakistan, Nabab Hussein had given him the right to the house for about ten thousand rupees, but had not had the property registered by the court. Nabab Hussein had been in too much of a hurry to get away with his wife and children. Afterwards, of course, Akbar Ali, through bribes and stratagems, had had the house put in his name. However, to his mind there remained a hitch: what if the title deed was with Nabab Ali and one day his sons returned and wanted their house back? Then there would really be a problem.

Abdur said, "Father never told me any of this. The deed to your house is not with us either. You don't have to be concerned about that, uncle. If I ever return to India, I won't want the house back." He paused, then said,

"Apart from that, we are foreigners. Why would an Indian court pay any heed to us?"

"I believe what you say," replied Akbar Ali, "but what about your brother and sister—"

"They won't want it either."

"But I have one request to put to you."

"What request?"

Akbar Ali told him that if he would write on a stamped affidavit that he and his brother and sister would never claim title to the house, then Akbar Ali could die free from worry.

"I will do as you ask," said Abdur. He had heard that many Hindus did not want those who had left India to return. Now he could see that there were also some Muslims who were not likely to welcome them back either.

Abdur, Dhanpat, and Latif walked out from the old house onto the main road and took a tonga. Indicating Abdur, Dhanpat said to the tonga wallah, "My friend here has come back to Azimabad after a very long time. We want to show him the town."

"Right," said the tonga wallah.

As it had seemed to Abdur when he had come from the station the day before, Azimabad had grown tremendously. He had no idea how many new neighbourhoods there now were. He noticed two big parks, a girls' college, a big hospital, a couple of fine nursing homes, even a sports stadium—none of which was there fifty-one years ago.

And so the noontime passed in sightseeing.

Looking up at the sky, Dhanpat said, "We should stop now. I'll drop you two home, and in the afternoon I'll come and take you to my garage."

Dhanpat let Latif and Abdur get down at the main road in front of the Muslim quarter and went on his way. Three hours later, he came back to take them to his garage, which was in the middle of the town at the Chowk Bazaar.

In Abdur's boyhood days, the Chowk Bazaar was very small. It had little shops on each side. Under a high roof, the vegetable sellers, fishmongers, and butchers were all spread out, and on each side were several old one- or two-storey tin buildings. But now the place was barely recognizable to Abdur. The old buildings had been pulled down and new ones put up. There was also a rather grand supermarket, as well as a line of many shops, banks, a post office, private telephone booths, a Xerox office—more than Abdur could take in. To one side was a vast courtyard where about a hundred scooters, jeeps, and private cars were parked.

Dhanpat's garage was on one side of the Chowk Bazaar. Inside a tall shed was a workshop for cars, autorickshaws, and scooters and, next to it, a well-appointed office with a desk, chairs, and a telephone. Dhanpat took Abdur and Latif to the office, where they sat down. He told one of the men working in the shed to bring tea and biscuits and then called to the neighbouring shopkeepers to come and meet Abdur. Some of the people who had brought their cars in for repair also wanted to be introduced.

There was a tremendous curiosity about Pakistan. Abdur answered their various questions as he had those of Latif, Jan Mohammed, and others in the Muslim quarter. However, a few discordant voices were among them: "What do you want in coming back to India, Mian?" "We have a billion people in India. Don't try to burden us with any more."

As he listened to all this, Abdur's face became pale. But Dhanpat exploded. "What are you all saying! He hasn't come here to put any burdens on anyone. His sister is in India, as are his nieces and nephews and other relations. He has come to see them. After a few days, he'll be going back."

"It's best that he does," said a few of them.

Having shut up the garage at eight that night, Dhanpat was taking Abdur and Latif home. He said, "Don't worry about what those people said. They're just a pack of ignorant pigs."

Abdur was not offended by it. He shook his head slowly and said, "There are also such people in Pakistan. Let anyone from India go there—he too will be unwelcome."

It was about twenty minutes by tonga from the Chowk Bazaar. On their way, Dhanpat suddenly remembered something. He said, "Oh, I forgot to tell you."

"What was that?" asked Abdur.

"I was telling my father about you. He asked me to bring you to our house. When will you come?"

This startled Abdur, and he saw once again the image of Lajpat Singh setting fire to their house fifty-one years before; he felt beset by a strange sense of panic. Why should the man be inviting him? No, he would not meet that man at all, though he did not say that to Dhanpat. Abdur remained silent for a little while, then said, "I am in Azimabad for only a few days. I'll go and see uncle before going back to Karachi."

"But you must eat with us when you come."

"All right."

Once a day, Dhanpat went to Fatima's house to try to get Abdur to go with him to his house; in an endeavour to avoid this, Abdur took up the invitations of the old men of the Muslim locality, though he had originally thought not to accept anyone's.

Dhanpat was greatly put out. Becoming angry, he said, "What is it with you? I've told you how my father sends me every day to bring you to our place. Why do you have some objection to coming to our house?"

With an embarrassed look, Abdur said, "Don't be angry, Dhanno. The old men of the locality keep at me so much, I can't say no to them."

"I have been asking you too."

Abdur did not respond except to take the hand of his old friend in his.

Then, in no time at all, came the day for his return to Karachi. His visa would expire in a few more days, and he would have to be on the plane to Pakistan.

Abdur had decided to catch the local three-o'clock train to Allahabad and then take the Delhi Mail. He would arrive in Delhi the following evening, spend the night at some hotel, and the next day do some shopping. He would have to spend that night too in Delhi, and the next day he would fly to Karachi.

He had already announced the time of his departure, and since morning, the atmosphere in the house had been glum. Now and then, Fatima would break into a feeble sobbing. Taking her two hands, Abdur said, "Don't cry, Sister. I'll come again." But as he spoke, his voice ran dry and he felt a strange discomfort welling up inside him. Latif was a manly man and did not cry like his mother did. Nevertheless, his face was marked by a profound melancholy.

Dhanpat had said the day before that he would return around one thirty, and he and Latif would take Abdur to the station and put him on the train to Allahabad.

Abdur was still uncomfortable with Dhanpat. Dhanpat no longer insisted on Abdur's going to his house, though it was clear that he was terribly disappointed. However, Abdur still had not told him why he would not go.

Later in the morning, Fatima brought out from the almirah a jewel box and took out of it an old necklace, an emerald, a few rings, and some earrings and said, "Take these and give them to your family."

Abdur was taken aback. "No, no, don't give these to me."

"Can't I give something to my own brothers' and sister's children if I like?"

Abdur explained that he was a foreigner and unable to take away any gold or jewellery or anything of value. He would have to surrender it at the airport.

With a sorrowful look Fatima said, "They're my things. Why can't I give them to my own family?" And covering her face with her hands, she began to cry again.

Abdur had great difficulty consoling his elder sister. He explained that it was the law and he could not thwart it. It would be especially dangerous for him to take gold and jewellery out of the country.

Dhanpat arrived just before one o'clock. By then, Abdur had packed his suitcase and holdall and had had his lunch.

"All ready?" asked Dhanpat.

Abdur nodded. "Yes."

"Come down with me for a moment."

"Why?"

"I need you to."

Dhanpat went out with Abdur to the alley in front of the house. An old man was sitting in an autorickshaw there. He was in his mid-eighties, and it was obvious that he was very frail.

Indicating Abdur, Dhanpat said to the old man, "Father, here is Abdur."

Abdur had not thought that Lajpat Singh himself would come. His heart started to thump.

Lajpat got out of the auto and, taking Abdur's hand in both of his, said, "I sent word through Dhanno time and again, but I know why you never came. Son, a long time has passed since Independence. We were not in our right minds then. I treated your family appallingly. I used to think then that if the Muslims left, it would be for the good of India. Later, with a cool head, I came to see the injustice of that. I wanted you to come to our house so that I could say this to you. You didn't come, so I had to come to you."

Abdur could only look at him, stunned. Was this the same Lajpat Singh who one day had set fire to their house?

Lajpat went on. "After you had all gone, I told Dhanno to look after whoever had remained in the Muslim quarter, especially your sister and her children."

Abdur tried to speak, but his words would not come out.

Lajpat continued. "My son, you have all suffered so much on my account. Now, more than fifty years later, no one can do anything about it. Forgive me." Catching his breath, he said, "Next time you come to India, be sure to come to my house."

Abdur mumbled, "Of course I'll come, Uncle."

Because of his continuous talking, Lajpat was quite out of breath and could not remain standing any longer. He added, "Son, I have grown very old. My body is very weak. I have suffered from fever for the last fifteen years, and it now troubles me greatly. I must go home and lie down. Good-bye..."

Abdur remained standing there for a while after Lajpat Singh's autorickshaw had gone around the bend in the lane and out of sight. He felt that he would have to return to India—not just for Fatima and her family, but for this man too.

Translation from Bengali by John W. Hood

from *Basti*

Yar Zakir!

I first send you the usual salutations. I'm fine, and I hope everything's well with you too.

You must be wondering at my foolishness: "What a time that wretch chose for writing a letter, what a time for him to send word that he's well and to ask how I am!" I too realize how many years it's been that I haven't written—nor have you. And now, in this unsuitable time, I've suddenly thought of you, and am writing to you. Considering how disorganized the mails are, I'm not even sure that this letter will reach you. But nevertheless I'm writing. And after all, why? I'm about to tell you. First, you should know that I've transferred myself once more into a new department. Now I'm with the Radio. One benefit of coming here is that I've pretty well escaped from the boring business of files. Here we deal with people, not with files. Compared to files, it's more difficult work, but never boring.

Yar, since coming here I've met a strange girl. The thought never entered my head that I might run into her. A wheat-coloured complexion, delicate features, slender figure, medium height, an honest and sincere manner; I always see her in a white cotton sari. She parts her hair in the middle and wears it in a plain braid, but sometimes a lock comes loose and falls on her forehead. Her behaviour is always reserved. She's quiet and melancholy. Yar, her simplicity and sadness together have ravished my heart. You don't have to pause when you read those words. First hear the whole story.

From time to time, I have to go to the newsroom. That's where I encountered her. Previously, I'd seen her in passing, around the office. I knew she was an announcer. I'd heard her name too. But I still wasn't especially curious about her. Simplicity at first says nothing to a man, then gradually sadness becomes a spell. She used to quietly go to the newsroom, find out the news from Dhaka, and go away. The news was usually disturbing, but not a trace of anxiety was permitted to show in her face. It was my guess that she was inwardly very worried by the news. One day I asked her, "Bibi, do you have some relatives in Dhaka?"

Teresa Vas
circa 1948

"Yes, my mother and sister are there."

"Are you getting letters?"

"The last letter came two weeks ago. Since then I've written two letters. I've sent a wire too, but no answer has come."

"But what will you learn from the news on the radio?"

"At least I can get an idea how things are in the city."

"Then please come to my office. All the Dhaka newspapers come to my desk."

After this, she began to come to my office. She came every day, looked through all the Dhaka newspapers, and went away.

"Where is the rest of your family?" I asked one day.

"Some in Karachi, some in Lahore, some in Islamabad."

"And here?"

"There's no one here any longer."

"You're the only one here?"

"Yes, I'm alone in India."

One Muslim girl who stayed alone in the whole of India—this seemed a strange thing to me. I know whole families left, and one person would stay behind. But this person was usually an old man. These old men who stayed on alone were not held back by the thought of their property, but by the thought of their graves. There was no problem about property: people could go to Pakistan and enter a claim, and by entering false claims they could even get a larger property in return for a smaller one. But no one can enter a claim for a grave. In Vyaspur, that Hakimji from the big house, you remember? His whole family went off to Pakistan. He stayed in the same place and continued to take sick people's pulses. I asked him, "Hakimji, you didn't go to Pakistan?"

"No, young man."

"And the reason?"

"Young man! You ask for the reason? Have you seen our graveyard?"

"No."

"Just go sometime and take a look. Each tree is leafier than the next. How could my grave have such shade in Pakistan?"

I laughed inwardly. Yar, you Muslims are wonderful! You're always looking toward the deserts of Arabia, but for your graves you prefer the shade of India. Seeing the old people who had stayed behind here, I realized what great power the grave has in Muslim culture. But did the thought of graves hold this girl as well? The idea bewildered me. One day I asked her, "Your whole family has gone to Pakistan. You didn't go?"

"No, I didn't go."

"And the reason?"

"It isn't necessary for everything to have a reason."

"It isn't necessary—but anyway?"

"Anyway, if I'd gone to Pakistan, it wouldn't have made any difference. I'd have been alone in Pakistan too."

I looked closely at her face. "What town are you from?"

"Rupnagar."

"Rupnagar!" I was startled. "Why, you're that Sabirah?" This reaction of mine confused her. But I didn't leave her in confusion long. I hastily asked, "You know Zakir?"

In reply, she looked at me carefully from head to foot. Then she said slowly, "I see, so you're that Surendar Sahib."

After that she became absolutely silent. I too was silent, in confusion. Then she went away. The next day she didn't come. The day after she didn't come either, but now this girl had a new meaning for me. Now for me she wasn't a radio announcer, but an evocation of a lost friend. I went and got hold of her and abandoned formality. "Sabirah! Are you angry with me?"

"For what?"

"No matter what the circumstances, it's necessary to tread carefully around someone else's emotional life."

She made no reply to this, but the next day she came and examined all the old and new Dhaka newspapers with close attention. And from then on she made a habit of coming at a regular time, going through the Dhaka newspapers, chatting a little, drinking tea, and going away. Once or twice I mentioned your name, but each time she either said nothing or changed the subject. So I'm careful now, and I don't mention your name. But I know that when we meet, we aren't just two, for a third person is invisibly present with us. Perhaps she meets me for that man's sake. The Dhaka newspapers are secondary now. One day I asked, "Sabirah, don't you have any plan to get married, or anything?"

"None."

"And the reason?"

She hesitated, then said with a wan smile, "Look, you've stepped out of bounds now."

"Sorry," I apologized.

"It's all right," she said with the same wan smile, then fell silent.

Zakir, this Sabirah of yours seems less like a girl than like a historical relic! Yar, don't take it amiss, your history in India has progressed very awkwardly. First your conquerors came—so forcefully and tumultuously that their horses' hooves made the earth quiver, and the clashing of their swords echoed in the air. Then the political leaders appeared, and thundered out their power. The great Mughal emperors Babur, Akbar, Shah Jahan, Aurangzeb. Then Sir Sayyid Ahmad Khan, Maulana Muhammad Ali, Muhammad Ali Jinnah, and all the others—and after them, your Sabirah. A silent melancholy girl, staying on alone in the whole of India. I don't know whether your history is unique, or whether the histories of all cultures progress like this. "First the sword and spear—and finally?" Didn't your "elder statesman" Iqbal have his gaze fixed on this final stage? This stage too is a part of the destiny of the group. Yes, it was the day of Id. I saw Sabirah coming out of the studio. I was a bit surprised to see her on that day. "What, you? You didn't take the day off today?"

"No," came the short reply.

"Then please celebrate Id here, and give me a treat."

"Of course, come into my office."

Entering her office, she ordered tea and sent for cake. She was pouring the tea, and I was wondering if any Muslim was actually on duty in an office on the day of Id. Most office workers didn't even stay in the city for the day. Even the day before, they slipped away from the office early and got their train tickets and went straight to their own towns. And girls? Girls celebrated Id even more enthusiastically than men did. Drinking tea, I gathered my courage and asked, "Sabirah, you didn't go to Rupnagar?"

"Rupnagar?" She looked at me with surprise. "Why should I?"

"You people have the custom of not spending Id away, but going home to celebrate Id."

"Perhaps I've already told you my family situation. There are now none of us left in Rupnagar."

I fell silent. Then, drinking tea, I asked casually, "Don't you even have any distant relatives there?"

"Even my distant relatives have all gone. Rupnagar is empty."

"What a strange thing," I murmured.

"Won't you have some more tea?" She interrupted me, and without waiting for my answer began pouring tea into my cup. Drinking my tea, I threw in one more question: "Since you came to Delhi, have you never been back to Rupnagar?"

"No."

"It's strange. How long has it been?"

"A long time. In the early fifties my brother-in-law's letter came from Dhaka, saying that he had a job and we should come. In those days I'd just been offered a position by All India Radio. I left for Delhi. My mother and sister set out for Dhaka. They were the last batch that Rupnagar sent to Pakistan."

"And you decided to settle in India?"

"Do you really have to ask?"

At this answer, I should have kept quiet, but I ignored her politely sarcastic tone and said, "What I mean is that if you had gone to Pakistan..."

I paused briefly, and she interrupted me in a sharp tone, "Then? Then what would have happened?" And she gave me such a look that I didn't have the courage to finish my sentence at all. You'll understand what I wanted to say.

Yar, how strange it is that the same town becomes more meaningful than before for one of its inhabitants, who has left the country, so that he dreams about it; while for another inhabitant all its meaning disappears, so that even though he's in the same country, he never feels any desire to see the town again. How meaningful the journey to Pakistan made Rupnagar! And how severely Sabirah was punished for staying in India, that for her Rupnagar became meaningless. I think my fate is the same as Sabirah's. And sometimes I feel that in my childhood I must have offended some holy man, and he cursed me: "Son, your native land will no longer let you see her." So the town of Vyaspur doesn't let me see her. When I go there, the town seems to ask, "Where is the other?" And when I can't find an answer, she closes her door against me. That constant eagerness I used to have for my vacation to come so I could run to Vyaspur—that eagerness is now utterly gone. Last June I went there, after a long time. It was late in the month. The rains hadn't started yet, and the afternoon heat was at its height. In the middle of the afternoon, I began to feel once again my old itch to wander, and I set out. From one lane to another, from the second lane to a third. Yar, every lane asked me, "Where is the other?" I felt that I no longer had any kinship with these lanes, as though all of them were angry with me. I passed through Rimjhim's lane too. The doorway looked absolutely desolate. Rimjhim's mother sat alone in the doorway, with her half-naked body and withered youth, spinning. I left those lanes and set out toward our school. It was the vacation, so the school was closed. I passed through the empty verandahs and went toward the field. Suddenly my eye fell on the mango tree by the chapel. I went and sat in its shade. Yar, how much time we used to spend sitting in its shade, throwing bricks at the green mangoes to make them fall! This time too the branches were full of green mangoes. I had an overpowering desire to throw bricks at them and make them fall. But yar, my hands were somehow paralyzed. They didn't move to throw a brick. I sat in silence, watching the green leafy branches laden with green mangoes. Then a green mango fell in front of me with a little thump. What was this? At the time, there was no wind blowing and no flock of parrots perched in the tree. Had our mango tree recognized me? I felt melancholy and stood up. If the lanes, birds, and trees don't recognize you, you're sad, and if they do recognize you, you feel melancholy. You go around looking for a neem tree (did you ever find one?), and here the neem, tamarind, mango, pipal trees are all still in their places. But when they see me, they turn into strangers. When one tree recognized me, I felt melancholy.

My dear friend, for me there's now nothing but melancholy. You must have earned something since you've gone there. Staying here I haven't earned anything; I've only wasted my life. Yar, the hair at my temples is absolutely white. How is the hair at yours? I'll tell you one thing more—

and this is the saddest thing of all. Yesterday when I was drinking tea with Sabirah, my eyes fell on the parting in her hair. How elegantly straight a parting she had made. I saw that among the black hairs one hair was shining like silver. So, my friend, time is passing. We're all in the power of time. So hurry and come here. Come and see the city of Delhi, and the realm of beauty, for both are waiting for you. Come and join them, before silver fills the parting in her hair, and your head becomes a drift of snow, and our lives are merely a story.

    That's all,
    Surendar

Translation from Urdu by Frances W. Pritchett

Iris Dias, Teresa's cousin
Manori Island

Teresa (front row, second from left)
with friends and family
Manori Island, circa 1950

Kitty Athaide (second row, far right),
Teresa's cousin
Bandra, circa 1950

Rebirth

The dwelling place of the household goddess had a circular thatched roof like a miniature barn. When such a roof showed signs of leaking, Jugin of Bhatshala village would be summoned to repair it. Jugin was an old hand at shrine building, long famous for his workmanship. Five years ago he had constructed the frame for the tiles on the cowshed near the shrine, using rafters made of palmyra wood. Though his eyesight had become a little dim, there was still no one to match his handiwork. It was always Jugin who created the showy crown of thatch atop the deity's humble abode. He was an artist as much as a craftsman. Who else but he could fashion such a crucial thing? People's faith in him went deeper still. The lady of the house, Shudharani, believed that Jugin's crown was so splendid that Goddess Lakshmi's auspicious owl perched on it at night. The source of her faith was her lifelong devotion to Lakshmi.

At her shrine, the puja offered to Lakshmi was straightforward. A brass pitcher full of water stood permanently by the outer step of the temple door. Every Thursday, in the evening, Shudharani in company with five other married women performed the puja: they ululated fittingly, smeared vermilion on each other's partings, and then Shudharani herself distributed to the others flowers and food offerings—the prashad. Everything was done correctly: a lamp burned, incense smouldered as the women, saris hooding their heads, prostrated themselves before the goddess. The sandalwood and vermilion marks on the mango leaves tied to the branch in the pitcher gradually dried up in the warmth; and the air lay heavy with the perfume of sprinkled Ganges water. No bell sounded, though; theirs was a silent puja, like a meditation. Neither was the image of the goddess sacrificially immersed. Each aspect of the ritual was simple, timeless, and sacred. Jugin had observed it countless times; he knew its every gesture.

As well as being a shrine builder, Jugin was a folk poet, an accomplished one. He liked to compose songs and rhymes for the boys to sing at the Paush festival in winter. Which people chose to sing them there—or at the autumn harvest festival Nabanna—had never for a moment bothered Jugin Sheikh. He saw nothing wrong in the Muslim boys of Bhatshala singing his songs at a Hindu festival and collecting aubergines, pumpkins, bananas, and other fruits and vegetables from each house. Even when he was building an abode for Lakshmi in the courtyard of Shudharani's house, he never thought of the fact that though his first name was Hindu, his surname revealed him to be a Muslim. And yet today, he somehow felt everything inside him was being partitioned, all his true feelings being uprooted.

While watching him as he wove together straws, Shudharani had suddenly remarked, "Jugin, your name is not right for you, Jugin."

The remark's unexpectedness puzzled him. He said respectfully, "But Didi, which of us really has the right name? Is Bhatshala rightly named? The village is full of poor Muslims, but it hardly has a grain of bhat—and yet it has a fancy name: Bhatshala, 'full of rice.' I composed a funny song about it once, some twelve years back. 'The rice pot sounds boom-boom: / bhat in Bhatshala—no room. / Poets are out of verse, / they hang their heads and curse; / a noose is hardly worse.' *Ha-ha!* That's why we rely on you, Didi. With a lot of struggle, I can make ends meet by building shrines—even today, when work is scarce."

As Shudharani began to reply, a loudspeaker started up at the Brahmapada temple in nearby Shivkalitala. Despite the earliness of the hour, a shrill voice began to sing kirtan—devotional songs to Krishna—continuously. Jugin had heard something about this the night before on his way to Shudharani's. A group of kirtan singers had come from Maheshpur, led by a certain Bashab Chandra Das. Once upon a time, Jugin knew, Das had played young heroes in itinerant theatre troupes; now, recognising an opportunity, he had formed a kirtan group of his own. These days, religion was no longer the benign expression of exalted ideals, no longer a matter of graceful contemplative behaviour. Instead, it was a whirlwind of intoxication, a furious blast of emotion, like a desert simoom. Jugin, in his simplicity, had not grasped what lay behind the change, but he had certainly felt its impact. He began to regret his name, his Hindu name. The loudspeaker was pouring forth, blaring its insane sound in every direction, like the wind. Why? Jugin did not know. He thought to himself, *Didi's correct: my name isn't right for me.* And yet, hadn't his hand built the crown of the divine abode, shaped it like the shikara of a temple? Would anyone remember that once he had finished? That a Sheikh had designed the shrine and that its pinnacle was the labour of a poor Muslim poet? Lakshmi's owl, her golden vehicle, perched there, didn't it? How could the owl be so foolish as to disobey the commandment not to touch anything Muslim? Surely the owl did not believe in it. But did Shudharani believe in it? This year, Jugin felt, Shudharani had changed. This year he ought not to have worked for her, he found himself thinking.

Climbing to the crest of the roof, he set about plaiting the straw with slips of bamboo, parting it and tying it with knotted string as if it were hair. As his hands worked, his eyes strayed to the road. A gang of boys in khaki shorts and white cotton shirts were running towards the market, carrying sticks and swords. Jugin knew what they were up to. In the courtyard of the Temple of the Twenty-two Goddesses at Chakkalitala, they would practice with these weapons. A couple of boys from Shudharani's house who had just finished some rice left over from the previous night ran out after the others. They carried a sinister tin falchion. The adult men of the house were yet to return from their nighttime visit to Brahmapada. There, in the dead of night, the bald-headed ochre-clad swami, the mahant of the temple, would have given them secret mantras. There was holy war—jihad—in Hinduism too: this fact Jugin had only recently perceived. Never before had he seen Hindus brandishing their weapons like this—like Muslims at Muharram. Whom would they fight? The Muharram procession? The idea made Jugin's sweet old face ashen with worry. What was really afoot among the Hindus? They seemed besotted, as though they had taken leave of their senses.

Various kinds of rumour had been reaching his ears. Things had been said on the radio and printed in the papers. Those who were in the know were talking. The incident at the Babri mosque-cum-temple had raised the temperature of such talk. Mr. Jirat, the schoolmaster at Shankarpur, had explained things at length the other day in the mosque. Now it was being said that Emperor Shahjehan had built the Taj Mahal on top of a ruined temple. What did that matter? Everything used to be Hindu, of course, but why were Hindus suddenly wanting to remind everyone of that fact? Were they trying to tell Muslims to leave their country? Jugin at last grasped the truth. But if he left Bhatshala, where would he go? If the Hindus could provide him with a land of rice and curry, that would be fine! It was only because there was no bhat, no food, to be had in Bhatshala that he had come to Didi's village, Gouripur. But look at her now: how grim she seemed! His throat felt dry. *Where can I go?—tell me that. All these sticks and swords threatening us all day, trying to scare us away, and at night who knows what kind of conspiracy being hatched? How can you want to send us away, Didi, when we've lived together so many years? Is that what you want in your heart, Didi: Jugin to go?*

His train of thought brought his hands to a stop, so profound was his agony. A shaft of pain was boring into him. He said aloud, "Why blame my name, Shudha Didi? Everything springs from my birth. When I was born, my mother's cord was found wrapped around me—like a sacred thread! My mother and my aunts were awestruck. Other people looked at me and felt the same. I was a Brahmin, reborn. A Hindu baby had floated into my mother's womb, either in error or on some mysterious current. 'Take special care of your newborn,' they all advised my mother, 'as long as he lives.' Didi, whether you think such a sign is auspicious or not, you must admit I make beautiful straw crowns for your temple. My mother certainly believed I was the son of a Hindu."

"How can that happen, Jugin! It's just one of those stories. There's no rebirth for Muslims—you know that," Shudharani said.

"Not for Muslims," said Jugin, "but for Hindus there is. I cannot explain these mysteries, Didi. No God—Hindu or Muslim—will come and vouch for my being a Hindu; and yet we all know, don't we, that who gets born in which womb is God's will. Tell me this: do all newborn babies come with sacred threads wrapped around them?"

"You should not say such things. In your religion it is really immoral. I don't believe a word!" Shudharani had become solemn.

Jugin replied, "No one can control our beliefs, Didi! To me your eyes look like the eyes of Suleyman, but you will definitely rebuke me for saying it. I've never seen such eyes anywhere."

"What kind of eyes?" Shudharani frowned.

"The eyes of Suleyman. Sweet, dark brown as catechu. How did you come to have such eyes?"

"Who? Suleyman? Who is he?"

"A Muslim emperor. A prophet. The eyes of your Goddess are black—I wonder where your brown eyes come from. Allah must be responsible," Jugin concluded contentedly.

Shudharani was sceptical. "More of your stories! I don't believe any of them."

"Believe them or not, Didi, but you will never come across anyone who is totally Hindu or totally Muslim. You have Muslim eyes, and I have Hindu hands. Otherwise, how could I make crowns for shrines like this? If the crowns are not Hindu, how could Lakshmi's owl perch on them: he'd get wind of the difference! Ponder what I say: we are in the hands of Allah at birth. We are all of mixed race, Didi."

Having spoken, Jugin went back to his work, interweaving the straw with renewed energy. But Shudharani began to grumble. "Eyes of Suleyman—fancy that! Who says so! How absurd! I will not give you any more prashad from today, Jugin. I'm warning you. And no water for your midday prayer either. You can go to the mosque for it. You've been cheating me all along, asking for wages just when you feel like it. And taking advantage of a woman's generosity to get prashad, pretending to be Hindu. No more! I won't help you anymore. I won't call you anymore after this, I'm telling you. I don't need you after this. You can leave, go away!"

The uttering of these words pained Shudharani strangely. Unable to restrain herself, she retreated inside the house and muffled a sob. Hers was a patriarchal household, and this year her sons had made strong objection to employing Jugin. People were saying it was a profane act to let a Muslim build the dwelling place of a goddess. The sons had berated their mother, flashed angry looks at her; in their eyes the Muslims were barbarians and intruders. Not only that; hadn't they once slaughtered Hindus in such numbers that the weight of dead Hindu sacred threads had come to 74 1/2 maunds? That was why Hindus inscribed 74 1/2 at the head of a letter. How could this fact be forgotten? Shudharani had attempted to reason with them. "Was that Jugin's fault? He's never killed a Hindu. He's a poor man, almost dying of hunger rather than killing anyone! You're making a scapegoat of him: don't rob Udo to pay Budo." A war of words had followed. Finally, Shudharani had rolled her eyes in mockery and said to her son, "This business of 74 1/2—why revive an ancient story? You should be writing the names of gods on letters—not the weight of some old sacred threads. Your culture's sunk rather low, hasn't it, Kailash?"

Her obstinacy had prevailed, and her sons had kept off Jugin. But what further arguments and disputes would follow, God only knew. For the time being, Shudharani had ceased to speak to Jugin in her usual pleasant way, ceased to give him prashad or water for his prayers.

At midday, silent and glum, with head bowed, Jugin went helplessly to the local mosque and said his prayers. When he returned, he resumed his work, concentrating hard.

Thursday evening came. The puja was performed in front of him. He received no prashad. *Why should he? Are my eyes Muslim eyes that I should take pity on him?* Shudharani asked herself. *I'm a Hindu through and through, from the nails on my toes to the tips of my hair. That's what I want to be, a good Hindu, just as our priests—our mahants—have instructed us. Jugin doesn't know that's what we are here. He must not come here anymore. I must make this absolutely clear to him.*

Jugin did not eat well that night. He lay down, but sleep would not come; instead he lay brooding, as if he was about to die. Didi would not call him again. The affection had gone out of her eyes. And affection is the essence of everything. When it goes, men become stones. Clearly she no longer trusted him. He thought, *She sees designs in every word I say. My only motive for coming to her is to get some handfuls of food—nothing else. Oh well, I shan't go there anymore. But it really is too bad that she did not believe the word of my mother.*

A tear welled up quietly in Jugin's eye. He remembered a rhyme he had known since he was a child; it told the one hundred and eight names of Lord Krishna. He began to say it softly:

> *His father Shri Nanda named him Nander Nandan—*
> *Paradise-born One.*
> *Yashoda his mother named him Jadu Bachadhan—*
> *Darling Sweet Son.*

"That was out of her affection for him, Didi." Jugin continued:

> *His teacher Upananda named him Thakur Gopal—*
> *Lord of the Cowherds.*
> *The boys of Braja named him Shundar Rakhal—*
> *Most Handsome Cowherd.*

His friend Shubal named him Thakur Kanai—
Noble Lord Krishna.
His friend Shridam named him Rakhalraja Bhai—
Brother Cowherd King.

"The faith of the cowherds—it has been usurped by the priest, by the mahants. That's what's wrong, Didi."

The sage Kanva named him Dev Chakrapani—
Lord of the Universe.
His guardian Banamali named him Baner Harini—
Fawn of the Forest.

"Yes, Didi; the forest fawn, the owl, the peacock—vehicles of the gods and goddesses—they are all good creatures. Theirs, theirs is the true religion."

Translation from Bengali by Krishna Dutta and Andrew Robinson

*How Many Pakistans?*_____

What a long journey! I don't understand why I keep thinking about Pakistan again and again—why it troubles me so much.

Salima, have I ever been unkind to you, hurt you? Why are you then so unfair to me and so unjust towards yourself? You laugh. I am sure that your laughter is full of poisoned arrows. It is certainly not touched with the fragrance of the mehndi flowers that suffuse the night as the wind blows over them. The wind! The very thought of it amuses me. You used to tell me that I was "touched" by the winds that had swept across our days! Do you remember, Salima?

I am sure that you remember those days. Women never forget anything. They only pretend to forget. Otherwise it would be difficult for them to go on living. It is strange to think of you as either Salima or merely another woman. I would like to think of you only as Bano. The same Bano who used to bring me mehndi flowers. Your breath seemed to mingle with their fragrance. You would blow on the flowers as if to say, "Only when the wind blows over them do you know how fragrant they are!" To tell you the truth, Bano, I was "touched" by that wind—intoxicated by it. But now I hesitate to call you Bano. I wonder if you would ever again care to be reminded of that name. What does that name mean to you now anyway?

That night, I really did want to climb those stairs to your room once again and ask you a question, remind you of something. But then I said to myself, How could you have forgotten it? It was impossible for you to have forgotten anything.

O God! You don't know how many Pakistans were created along with that one Pakistan. In how many hearts, in how many places! The creation of that one Pakistan solved nothing. It merely confused everything. Now nothing is what it seems to be.

That night too everything was confused. I don't know if it was the voice of the peepal tree in the backyard or of Badru Miyan that had cried out, "Kadir Miyan!...Sala Pakistan has been created...O sister, Pakistan has been created!..."

How terrifying was that moonlit night! You were lying naked in the courtyard downstairs, Bano. Bathed in moonlight! The leaves of the peepal tree in the backyard were rustling in the wind when Badru Miyan's voice seemed to rise from the very depths of Hell. "Kadir Miyan!…Sala Pakistan has been created…O sister, Pakistan has been created!…"

Let me tell you about the three stages of my life's journey. During the first stage, I was intoxicated by the fragrance of Bano's mehndi flowers. The second stage was completed when I saw Bano lying naked in the moonlight. The third stage began when she stood before me at the door, holding the frame with both her hands, and asked, "Is there someone else?…"

Yes, Bano, there was someone else…

Bano, after that single, terrifying moment of bewildering silence, why did you laugh? What had I done to you? Were you seeking revenge? On me? On Muneer? Or was it on Pakistan? Whom were you trying to humiliate? Me? Yourself? Muneer? Or…

Oh, why does Pakistan come between us again and again? How does that nation concern us? Alas, Pakistan is the name of the reality that separates the two of us. It's the truth that falls between us like an abysmal silence. It's the void between our families, our friends, and our communities that makes us insensitive to each other. Pakistan is a dark, blind space—a space without feeling, a space where the sufferings of others are no longer sufferings, and the joys of others are not joys. Perhaps Pakistan is that barren and still place where there is no wind or breath to stir the fragrance of mehndi flowers. It must be so. Otherwise, why should I have been forced to leave Chinar and wander like a dervish?

Do you remember in Chinar where the mehndi flowers used to bloom along the wall of the Mission School? We would take the path that led from the school to the peepal tree at the bank of the Ganga and, sitting on the broken walls of Raja Bhartrhari fort, eat imli.

How can I forget the evening when Zamin Ali, the compounder, told my father, "I know it's not true, but how will you convince people? Send Mangal away for a few days. If he stays here, everyone will gossip about his affair with Bano. Marriage is out of the question. It may lead to communal riots."

You can't imagine how shocked I was when I heard that. Did I have to leave Chinar? I was, however, compelled to…Oh, how beautiful were the nights in Chinar! The waters of the Ganga; the boats going to Kashi; the ruined walls of Brathari's fort!…And the courtyard of the checkpost at the banks of the river where I used to wait for you—wait for you to come—wait and wonder if you would escape from those narrow lanes at last, from those alleys of mud and drain water, and reach the banks of the Ganga. You never did escape!…I waited…and waited…

When did we suddenly cease to be children? We didn't realize that our innocent meetings had become the subject of gossip. We had grown up, and our friendship was regarded with suspicion.

We didn't suspect that our love would create communal tensions in the village. How did that happen, Bano? Why did that happen? But, of course, you wouldn't have an answer either.

We never met again after those days.

Slowly, the three stages of my life's journey passed. At none of the stages did we have the chance to stop and talk to each other. Not when the fragrance of the mehndi flowers had intoxicated us, or when I saw you lying naked in the moonlight, or when you stood at the door holding the frame with both your hands and asked, "Is there someone else?"

Mehndi Flowers, Chinar, My House, Our Love…

The red-brick road used to meander past my house to the main bazaar, run along the bank of the Ganga, and go right up to the gate of Bhartrhari's fort. It used to make a sharp right turn at the checkpost. There was another path, which was unpaved. Dirty water used to flow across it in small rivulets and disappear into the sands of the Ganga. That path led to the house in which you lived, Bano.

Beyond Bano's house was land full of mud and drain water. The Mission School lay on the other side of that land. It was once a British bungalow. It was surrounded by a hedge of mehndi flowers and a field of wild dhatura plants. Those dhatura plants used to cause me anxiety. When there was communal tension in the town because of us, Bano had somehow managed to meet me at the checkpost and say, "If the maulvi and his followers continue to harass me, I'll eat dhatura leaves and commit suicide. Don't you dare to leave the town without me. If you do, remember that Gangaji flows nearby. So, think before you…"

We didn't talk much that day. She left. I couldn't tell her about the turmoil in my house. Every day someone or the other threatened my father in the streets of the village. Everyone was afraid that I would be killed or that the Muslims would suddenly attack our house.

Pakistan had already been created in those days, Bano! Your father, however, continued to write his *Bhartrhari Namaha:*

> *Long ago I became a wanderer, Mother.*
> *From a wanderer, I became a fakir.*
> *The last days of this faithless one*
> *Will be unhappy.*
> *I leave my people behind.*
> *Take good care of them.*
> *Having become a fakir,*
> *I have ruined my Kingdom.*
> *I have left it desolate.*

People used to say that your father, the drillmaster, had lost his senses and that was why he was writing his *Bhartrhari Namaha*, the life of a Hindu saint-poet. "He isn't a Turk—he is a local labourer, a damned low-caste convert!" It was then that we learnt that a true Muslim had to be a descendent of some Irani-Turani! That the Muslims of Chinar were not real Muslims! People used to keep their distance from the drillmaster. But when they heard of my affair with you, they all took up arms as if they were true defenders of Bano!

I know, but you don't, Bano, that the drillmaster had no objection to our affair. But he was helpless and had to say, "I'll do whatever the Maulvi Sahib asks me to do." Once, your father even visited mine secretly and wept bitterly. Even after that day, however, he continued to write his *Bhartrhari Namaha,* though he didn't have the courage to read it out loud to anyone. The day I was forced to leave the town, I learnt that he hadn't abandoned his work on *Bhartrhari Namaha.* The clerk of the checkpost had slipped a piece of paper into my sweaty hand when I had gone to take my leave of him.

It was a terrifying night. Murder was in the air. Everyone was apprehensive. Nobody knew when the village would begin to resound with the cry "Ya Ali, Ya Ali" and when people would begin to slaughter each other. Even the Ganga was flooded. The peepal tree on its banks trembled. The wind was fierce. The ruined fort was full of strange whispers. My father and half a dozen Hindu youths—yes, I must admit that, Bano—escorted me to the station so that I could leave the village alive.

At first, everyone had advised me to go to Jaunpur and stay with my uncle. But then someone, I don't know who, decided that I should go to Bombay and try to get a job in the railway workshop at Kurla where another uncle of mine was employed.

What a dreadful night it was, Bano! How humiliated I felt as I made my escape. Conflicting thoughts pounded in my brain. At times I thought that I should go back to my house, pick up a hatchet, and kill all those Muslims of yours—paint the streets red with blood and win you. And if I failed at that, then I should kill you and drown myself in the Ganga.

But I was also ashamed and scared. I knew that though the drillmaster had no objection to our affair, he had kept quiet. I also knew that he hadn't abandoned work on his *Bhartrhari Namaha.* If he hadn't continued to write it, perhaps there wouldn't have been so much opposition.

The air in the village had been poisoned. It was as if a venomous snake had bitten each of the villagers. Father had been warned that I shouldn't show my face in the village the next morning, which triggered discussions well into the middle of the night. By the time they ended, only one train was running: the goods train to Mughal Sarai.

Yes, I was escorted to the station by half a dozen Hindu youths. We avoided the main bazaar and took the path that ran past the ruined fort. The road was dark. The clerk of the check-post lit our way with a lantern and managed to slip a piece of paper into my hand. It was then that I discovered your father was still working on his *Bhartrhari Namaha.*

> *Why have you become a mendicant*
> *And given up friends, soldiers, and courtiers?*

Why have you adopted a life of poverty
And left behind both narcissus and poppy?
Why have you worn robes of saffron
And taken off expensive shawls of silk?
Why do you wander from door to door,
Singing God's name,
And go far from Kamroop, Dhaka, and Bengal?
Why have you left us in your madness
And abandoned your Kingship?

It was madness perhaps. Silks, shawls, narcissus, and poppy—they were all real. But peepal, akh, mehndi, and dhatura were no less real than the narcissus flowers, Bano!…So was Pakistan real…What could we have done with Pakistan!

There were lots of people at the platform with us. The goods train left at two thirty in the morning. My father was upset and despairing. Everyone was scared and felt humiliated. Perhaps that was why they were all very angry. It seemed as if there might be communal riots even after I left the village. God help us, I said to myself, if these Hindus start a riot on their way back from the station! Pounce upon the Muslims as they sleep and cut them to pieces!…How difficult it is for a Hindu to be a Hindu, Bano! As soon as a man becomes a Hindu, he loses something precious.

How painful was that parting! There was a slight chill in the air, and the stone floor of the platform was very cold. The Vindhya Hills in the distance and the palm trees across the railway tracks watched us silently.

What can I say now? I had never imagined that I would be driven out of my own house like this. No one who has been humiliated and driven out of his own village can ever be at peace again. I can still recall those lanes where Bano lived. I used to wait for her at the check-post for what seemed like eternity and then walk through those lanes looking for mehndi flowers scattered on the ground. They would mark the spot Bano had reached, and beyond which she had been prevented from going by someone who had called her back, or questioned her, or forcibly stopped her.

The truth is that Pakistan pierced my heart like a sword that day. I know that people had been forced to convert, had changed their names, had been killed…Shame, fear, anger, tears, blood, madness, love—all these were burnt into my soul that day. To tell the truth, even if I had been able to possess Bano after that day, it would have been worthless. I still would have been unable to recover the past…Bano had been locked up in her house…The wind had ceased to blow over the mehndi flowers…

The train left, and I began to wander from place to place like a dervish. I knew I could never return home again.

I was sure that Bano's father couldn't have continued to live in Chinar without feeling suffocated. But I learnt nothing about Bano's fate, except that she hadn't drowned herself in the Ganga. That she was alive some-where—happy, unhappy, anxious. Perhaps in someone else's bed. In love. Praying for her husband's health like any honest wife. Colouring her hands with mehndi. Looking after her children. Joyous perhaps; full of regrets for the past perhaps…But I was certain she would never forget that moment when time had suddenly stood still for both of us, that moment when a nation called Pakistan had been created, that moment of unceasing tor-ment…

Well, Bano, what happened was fated. I reached Mughal Sarai. I then went to Allahabad and from there to Bombay. My uncle found me a job in the Kurla railway workshop, but after a few weeks, I moved to Pune. I got a job in the workshop of a hospital where artificial limbs were manufactured. I was convinced that neither your family nor mine would be able to con-tinue living in Chinar. But I never imagined that my father would send me news of the migration of such a large number of other families as well.

The fact of the matter is that Chinar as we knew it had been destroyed. When something like Pakistan comes into existence, a vital part of one's being dies. The crops no longer grow. The sky is torn into bits. The clouds no longer bring rain. The winds cease to blow.

A few years later, my father wrote to me that, along with the families of eight Muslim weavers and two Hindu carpenters, he had left Chinar in search of the fields, the rain, the wind, and the sky. They had moved to Bhiwandi. I didn't know that Bano's family had migrated with them. What job could a drillmaster have found there? I wondered about that. My father's move to Bhiwandi did make sense, for he was a cotton merchant. Everyone must have suffered a lot in the beginning.

My father's letters were deliberately vague. In none of them did he men-tion that he lived with your family in the same house in Baja Mohalla, that your family occupied the ground floor and he the rooms upstairs. Did the drillmaster agree to that arrangement out of a sense of guilt? The others who had migrated with them lived in either Bengal Pura or Nayee Basti.

I really did want to come and see you, Bano. But to tell you the truth, I was still very angry. And when I heard that you were in Bhiwandi and had got married, I was very upset. Besides that, my father had subtly hinted to me that I should stay away from Bhiwandi for a while. He said that he had much regard for the drillmaster and didn't want him to feel embarrassed or mortified by my presence. The drillmaster, he insisted, was blameless in the whole affair.

What an awkward situation it was! How could I have lived in the same house with you?

I was torn by conflicting thoughts and feelings. Suppose I had been unable to contain the anger I had suppressed for so long?

What would have happened if Pakistan, which had been smouldering inside me, had burst into flames?

Or if I had tried to prevent you from sleeping with your husband?

Or if I had driven him out of Bhiwandi, just as I had been forced out of my house?

Or if I had lost control over myself one night and broken into your room?…

Of course, my father and the drillmaster had convinced themselves that they were blameless. But what about me? They had lost nothing. I was the only one who had suffered. Since the day I was forced to leave Chinar, I have been wandering from place to place with a mask over my face, gloves on my hands, and a dagger in my belt…

But, Bano, there were communal riots even in Bhiwandi—not because you and I loved each other, but because the two communities had no love for each other. I was shocked when I heard about the riots. I didn't know what would happen. Five years earlier, I had been accused of causing trouble; but this time, I wasn't around…I had stayed away from Bhiwandi deliberately. I was afraid that I would cause a riot if I saw you again…

But when, at last, I did see you…

Moonlit Night and Bano

I reached Bhiwandi about ten days after the riots. As I entered the city, I saw the charred remains of houses, like gaping black holes, between tall buildings. There was nothing but ash, rubble, and dust everywhere. The air smelt of smoke, of recently extinguished fires. It was sharp, acrid, and pungent, and it scratched and clawed its way deep into the body. Bano, you must have smelt it too.

When I arrived at the bus station late in the evening, everything was quiet. There were a few policemen standing idly beneath a large cinema poster. Most of the buses were empty. There were no passengers going to Sange Minar, Ali Bagh, Bhorwarda, or Sinnar—not even Shirdi.

Under the shed of the local bus stop, I saw a few more policemen. They were huddled under it like gypsies. Were it not for their guns, which were stacked together like sugar cane, I wouldn't have known they were policemen.

The roads were deserted. I saw a few people walking aimlessly on the grounds outside the dak-bungalow where the Collector had set up his office. There were no taxis to Thane or Kalyan.

Perhaps you knew how it was to walk through riot-torn cities. I didn't. Desolate streets. A strange, eerie silence. A blankness. One either sees nothing or notices everything with an uncanny attentiveness. Why does one become either wild or acutely sensitive? Especially when one isn't personally involved.

Even in a small town like Pune, it is difficult to find out how to get to Baja Mohalla. Well, I somehow found my way to it and even located the house, but it seemed empty. Can human beings endure such silence and stillness?

To tell you the truth, Bano, for a moment I thought that if I hadn't left Chinar, it would have become silent and still too. Then I thought about you, Bano. How could I face you? I lost my nerve. For a moment, I felt as if I hadn't left Chinar and you hadn't aged at all.

The door of the house was open. I walked in without making a noise and found myself in a courtyard. There were two pots of water in a corner. Near them were two shadows. One woman was naked from the waist up. The other was sitting in front of her and was massaging her breasts. Startled, I stepped back into the street again.

As soon as I stepped out, I saw the drillmaster. He recognized me at once, but didn't know how to greet me. For a while, he stood puzzled and uncertain. What could he have said to me or asked me? I came to his rescue and asked him, as if he was a stranger, about my father.

"He left for Chinar two days ago," he replied.

"Two days ago?" I couldn't think of anything else to say.

"Yes, he didn't want to stay here. A few other families went back with him," he said.

Immediately I understood why my father had gone back to Chinar and why the drillmaster had declined to. After all, the reasons my father had left Chinar were different from those of the drillmaster—or from mine. The drillmaster had been exiled by history, and those whom history exiles can never return…I had been forced to leave by a few people only.

Since my father was no longer in the house, I didn't know what to do. There were riots in the city. Where could I have stayed? It was impossible for the drillmaster to invite me to stay with him. After all, you were in the house. Yet, how could the drillmaster have left me standing in the street like a stranger? He still had a sense of decency.

"Did my father take all his things with him?" I asked.

"No, most of them are still here," he replied.

"Did he lock his house?"

"Yes," he replied and then, after some hesitation, added, "I have a duplicate key."

"I would like to stay in his room for the night. I have to go back tomorrow," I said. I had no choice. Where could I have gone in that strange city?

He left me standing alone in the street and went inside. A moment later he returned with the key and a candle. He led me upstairs, opened the lock, gave me the key, and said, "Have you had something to eat?"

"Yes," I replied and went inside.

"Let me know if you need something," he said as he walked downstairs. The biographer of Bhartrhari was shrewd enough to say "Let me know" instead of "Come to the door and ask."

Everything was very quiet.

I pulled my cot up to the terrace so that I could escape the oppressive heat of the room. Or was it in the hope of seeing you, Bano!…It was a moonlit night. The air was still. I decided to sleep on the open terrace.

What a strange night it was, Bano! You didn't know I was upstairs. I wonder what the drillmaster told you. If the police hadn't come the next morning, you wouldn't have ever known…

I waited for a long time for the sound of footsteps. I did hope that you would come upstairs, but after a while, I calmed down. After all, I thought to myself, a wife's place is beside her husband.

The peepal tree in the backyard was bathed in moonlight. I had placed my cot in a spot that allowed me to look down into the courtyard. But what I saw was dreadful.

Bano was lying on a cot in the moonlight. Her blouse was open, and her saree was pulled up to her waist. Her breasts were full, like balloons. She was convulsing with pain and thrashing about like a fish out of water. Once in a while, a fountain of milk squirted out of her breasts. Milk streaked down her stomach and glittered like mercury in the moonlight. A big drop of milk lay in the depression of her navel, like a pearl.

"Hai Allah!" Bano moaned.

"Try to sleep, Bano," I heard her mother plead.

"They are bursting," she wailed, squeezing her breasts hard with both her hands.

"Let me help," her mother said. She started massaging Bano's breasts gently. Streams of milk squirted from them. Bano continued to moan and weep. Her naked body was soon bathed in milk, and it glittered in the moonlight.

Bano's mother frequently wiped her breasts with the hem of her saree and then squeezed the milk out of it into the drain nearby. A thin stream of milk slithered through the drain like a white snake.

Oh, Bano! What I saw shocked me.

Agitated, I paced up and down the terrace late into the night. I lay down only after I saw that Bano had finally covered her breasts with her saree and gone to sleep. What a nightmare that was! I saw breasts full of milk hanging from the sky!…

I had just gone to sleep when I was awakened by a knocking on the door in the backyard. I thought I heard someone wailing, "Qadir Miyan!…Sala, Pakistan has been created!…O sister, Pakistan has been created!…" After a moment's silence, I thought that I heard the same voice cry out, "Qadir Miyan, now we'll tie ehram here itself and perform talbiya. This is where we'll perform Haj…All right, Qadir Miyan?"

Had I not seen the peepal tree in the backyard, I would have said that the voice had risen from the depths of Hell, and I would have run away… But what a strange nightmare it was…Blood rained from the sky, corpses walked in the streets, fountains of blood spurted out of chopped heads, naked bodies danced in the flames…

Then the leaves of the peepal tree crackled in the wind. They sounded like clerks typing in a hospital. The sound was familiar. Everything else was horrifying.

The next morning my head felt heavy. My eyes were red. My hands and feet were numb. I had to get up early because the police wanted to ask me some questions. The drillmaster had woken me up. He was trembling with fear.

"It's the police," he said. "They are asking about you."

"Why?"

"They make inquiries about every outsider."

I was furious. Tell me, Bano, when I was forced to leave my house, why didn't the police come to ask me why I was leaving?

Pakistan, Bano, is the fragmentation of man…It is the refusal to consider the whole man…

I understood that when the police took me away for questioning early in the morning.

You and I, Bano, had become victims of Pakistan. We had been entrapped by it…

At the station, the police asked me all sorts of questions. Why had I come to this area?…What could I have told them? Why does a man wander from place to place? The police would have really harassed me had the drillmaster not come to my rescue. He told them everything about me. The fact that Master Sahib was a Muslim was of great help. The testimony of a Muslim was the best proof of innocence that a Hindu could have. But I did wonder if Master Sahib hadn't committed the same mistake he committed in the past, when he continued to write his *Bhartrhari Namaha*.

After the police released me, your father and I sat down on a log lying nearby. Neither of us knew what to say to the other. The silence became oppressive.

The drillmaster was the first one to speak. "Badru has gone crazy," he said. "He has been sitting under the peepal tree since the riots broke out. All his looms were burnt. Did you hear him call out to Qadir Miyan last night?"

There were three or four other people sitting at the Teenbati crossroads. Perhaps they had gone to the police station to stand bail for someone or to give information. They looked depressed and afraid. The maulvi was telling those who were sitting around him, "The Prophet has said that the trumpet shall sound thrice. At the first sound of the trumpet, people will begin to tremble with fear. Terror will grip their souls. At the sound of the second trumpet, everyone will die. And when the trumpet sounds the third time, everyone will stand before the Lord to be judged. That is how it shall be. The first trumpet has sounded…"

"Are you still writing your *Bhartrhari Namaha*?" I asked Master Sahib.

"Yes," he said, and then he recited the following lines:

I am only a wanderer,
Staying here for a night!

Talk, let the night pass quickly,
And the sun rise again!

After he finished the verse, he looked around. There were wild yellow flowers growing in the cracks of the wall nearby; birds were hopping in the tall and thick grass growing all around. The flutter of wings, yellow flowers…The Master Sahib watched them in silence for a while.

I broke the silence and asked, "Last night…"

"Yes, that was Badru. He has gone mad. All his looms were burnt. Since then, he has been sitting under the peepal tree and screaming curses," Master Sahib said.

"In the house…," I asked, gathering courage.

Master Sahib then told me the entire story—he told me what had happened to you, Bano. You had given birth to a child in Dr. Sarang's Nursing Home three days before the riots erupted. The rioters then set the Nursing Home on fire. Pregnant women had jumped out of the second storey to save themselves. Some women had even thrown their newborn babies out the windows. Two women had died. Five children had been burnt to death. Bano's baby had died when she had thrown him down into the street. There was a massacre. Bano had somehow managed to escape and reach home safely. Now her breasts were full of milk, and she was in agony.

"It's time I went back to Pune," I said, trying to find an excuse to get away.

"Go to Chinar if you can, to see your father," the drillmaster said.

"Why, is he not well?"

"No. He lost an arm during the riots. Our house was attacked. We would all have been slaughtered were it not for him. He ran out into the streets and confronted the goondas. Someone struck his arm with a sword and severed it. Blood spurted out from his amputated limb. Your father picked up the arm and fought the attackers with it till he fell down unconscious. The goondas threw fire bombs into our house and ran away. Your father lay in the street with his severed arm clutched in his other hand… We took him to the Military Hospital. He was released eight days later. The day after his release, he left for Chinar."

We sat in silence for some time.

The birds were still hopping in the grass.

"He said that he would get himself bandaged in the Chinar Hospital. O God, have mercy upon us!" The drillmaster covered his eyes as he said that.

Where was I? In what kind of world? Who were these people? Was I amongst human beings? Was I living through a nightmare?

The drillmaster and I walked back home. I went upstairs. Later I heard Bano and her husband, Muneer—Master Sahib and his wife—arguing with each other.

"I don't understand why you insist on staying here," Muneer said.

"You won't understand!" Bano shouted in reply. "I must give birth to a child in this country, on this very earth. Only then will I leave."

When I leaned over the balcony and looked down into the courtyard, I saw Muneer trembling with rage and screaming, "Do what you like! Sleep with anyone you want to! Find someone to give you a child!"

"You can't anyway!" Bano screamed back at him.

I was shocked. Were they talking about me?

I was wrong. A moment later, Bano added, "You are impotent because you sell your blood to get money for drink."

Muneer slapped her.

"Don't I know?!" Bano said, showering curses on Muneer. "Every time you go to Bombay, you sell your blood. Then you lie in bed and shiver all night."

It was terrible to hear you curse and weep, Bano! Each one of us was in agony; each one of us had made his own Pakistan. We had all been disfigured. Mutilated. Crippled. We were only half alive!

What a dreadful moonlit night it was. I stole out of Bhiwandi in the same way I had left Chinar. I took a taxi to Thane.

The air was full of the bitter smell of ash; breasts full of milk hung from the sky; fountains of blood spurted out of bodies standing at the crossroads…

Thane! From Thane, I went to Bombay by bus and, from there, took a train to Pune. There I lay in bed with a fever for several days.

What an awful age we live in…And what a strange creature man is! Disfigured, crippled, bloodied, he continues to live.

Bano, can you imagine what passes through a man's being when, in his loneliness and agony, he hears the voice of a woman ask, "Is there someone else?" Can you guess, Bano?

Is There Someone Else?

About five months later, I received a letter from my father. He had returned to Bhiwandi. His cloth business wasn't doing well because of the Sindhis and the Marwaris. The market was sluggish. Nor were all the looms working. Because he had lost one arm and had begun to walk a little crookedly, the people in the marketplace had begun to call him tonta. He was rather amused by that. He also wrote that Muneer had left for Bombay with Bano. No one knew whether they were still in Bombay or had gone to Pakistan. The drillmaster had gone mad. He had now begun to do his drill exercises at home and to write the story of Brathari at school.

If I had not gone to Bombay that day, Bano, I would never have encountered you…What a painful meeting it was! I felt so ashamed of myself.

You must have thought that I visited prostitutes often. To tell you the truth, Bano, I do visit prostitutes. I do so because of you.

I was in Bombay for a few days. I had interrupted my journey to Bhiwandi. After I reached Bombay, I lost heart and wondered what I would do in Bhiwandi.

At the station I met Kedar, a friend of mine who had stayed with me in Pune and was then living in Bombay. He suggested that we spend the evening together.

You had nothing to do with that evening, Bano.

Kedar and I had a few drinks at a pub in Colaba. Then we walked till we reached the Handloom House. We turned into the lane that runs by its side.

If I go back there now, I'll recognize the lane, but at the moment I can't recall the neighborhood. We walked down that lane for a while and then took a right turn. Perhaps there was a cigarette shop at the corner. A few cars were parked in the lane. It was, I think, a neighborhood where Bohra Muslims live. It was very clean. The building had a lift. The staircase was also very clean. Kedar and I climbed up the stairs. After walking up five floors, both of us were out of breath. We could smell food being cooked in one of the apartments. Kedar stopped in front of a door and rang the bell. The flat didn't seem to be carefully maintained.

The door opened. We were greeted by a Sindhi. He was wheezing. He took us into a room and made us sit down on a plain sofa. The Sindhi was gasping for breath so badly that it seemed as if he would collapse and never regain consciousness.

Kedar and the Sindhi disappeared into another room. A few minutes later, I heard Kedar's laughter.

I was restless and uncomfortable. I stood near the window to get some fresh air. I could see dirty rooftops everywhere.

The Sindhi returned. He was still wheezing. "Beer," he rasped, "will you have some beer?"

"Yes," I replied.

He sent a boy to get a bottle of beer. He didn't drink any himself.

"You," he asked asthmatically, "Bombay..." He wanted to know if I lived in Bombay.

"No, I live in Pune."

"Visit?" he asked, panting heavily.

"No, I had some work here."

"Are you a businessman?"

"No, I had some personal work. I am on my way to Bhiwandi."

He continued to sit next to me and breathe heavily. I was getting impatient. But Kedar soon reappeared. When the Sindhi saw Kedar standing before him, he got up with a start. I too got up. All three of us stood silently in the middle of the room. Kedar paid for my beer.

Suddenly, the door of a room opened and a woman handed Kedar a bunch of keys. Seeing me standing next to Kedar and the asthmatic Sindhi, she asked, "Is there someone else?"

I turned around to look. It was you, Bano. You were standing there in a blouse and a petticoat, holding the doorframe with your hands and asking, "Is there someone else?"

Yes! There was…There was someone else…

There was a moment of agonizing silence. You had recognized me. There was a contemptuous, a venomous smile on your lips…or did I imagine it?

Were you taking revenge? Against me, Muneer, or Pakistan? Or were you taking revenge against yourself?

I left and went downstairs. Kedar followed me.

I wanted to climb up the stairs again and ask, "Bano, was this fated to happen?"

Where should I go now? Where should I hide? There are Pakistans everywhere. Where can I find the kind of life I desire? How can I live an undivided life?

Bano! Pakistan is everywhere. It inflicts wounds on you and me. It humiliates us. It defeats us every time…

Translation from Hindi by Vishwamitter Adil and Alok Bhalla

Teresa (second from right) with friends
London, 1950

Cool, Sweet Water

The war is over. The trenches that had been dug everywhere have been filled up. The houses that had been reduced to rubble by the bombs are now being rebuilt. When the war started, it was autumn; then came winter, and now it is spring. People appear as busy and happy as they did before the war. Businesses that had slowed down are doing well once again. Who knows if people still remember the agonies of war now that six or seven months have passed? The hustle and bustle of life make you forget everything easily. But what can I say about the others? As far as I'm concerned, even now when I see moonlight caressing the earth, it seems that it has lost its shimmer; I feel as if the moon is still complaining about our neighbouring country. If someone proclaims that the moon says nothing and hears nothing and all this is just nonsense attributed to poets and writers, then that's all right; these are matters that are related to the imagination. I am a writer; the emotions that I experience in relation to the moon are unusual. When I heard that the Russian spaceship *Luna 9* had landed on the moon, my respect for the reach of man's intelligence increased, but a sigh also arose from a corner of my heart. I looked again and again at the moon, and believe me, my frail eyesight managed to catch sight of the Russian flag on the moon's surface. I was also able to see the corpse of the old woman with the spinning wheel; her spinning wheel had been smashed by *Luna.*

Who knows what will happen after man's conquest of the moon? What will the gains be, what the losses? But all I feel at the moment is that the people who inhabit the earth have lost everything. Any attempt to associate the moon with images of beauty bewilders me; in my imagination, no lover appears weeping in remembrance of the beloved in the light of this shimmering ball of love and passion. When I compel myself to imagine this scene, I begin to ponder the kinds of metal available on the moon and I wonder what chapters regarding man's preservation and destruction will be written with the aid of those metals. Who knows when the surface of the moon will become a battlefield.

I was still drifting in the darkness hovering over the image of the moon when the Russian flag was also planted on Venus, the star that is the first to appear on the sky in the evening. How can I now look at someone's shining eyes and proclaim that they are filled with stars? How will I say, "You people, when you are tired of enduring the hardships of this world, you will have no beautiful vision left. You will talk of the metals found on the moon instead of sitting in the moonlight and conversing about the beloved, and when you are tormented by thoughts of the beloved at night, instead of counting the stars you will think of building a bungalow on Venus"?

Oh yes, where did I begin and where have I rambled to? I was saying that to this day I see the moon as a doubter. Even now when I hear the firecrackers go off in the neighbourhood at a wedding, I am reminded of the boom of guns and the explosions of bombs. I go into the kitchen and see the lantern hanging by a nail on the wall, and I still remember the seventeen days of darkness. We made each other out in the light of this lantern, bumped into furniture as we walked around, and so many times suffered bruised knees, cuts on fingers. No one has wiped clean the glass chimney of this lantern. I don't want it to be cleaned ever so that I can remember that the nights of war are pitch dark.

I love peace, I hate war. But I love that war, as much as I love peace, that is fought for freedom, for honour, for the survival of one's country.

Oh yes, so I was saying that the war is now over, but as long as I live, my memories will live with me. Now how can I forget the eight-year-old boy who was flying a kite on the roof of the house next door? There were so many planes flying that day that one couldn't hear a thing. Even though I knew these were our own planes, my heart trembled with fear and foreboding. I screamed to the boy, "Come down from the roof!" He said, "When the enemy's planes appear, I'll bring them down with my kite. I'm not afraid like you."

For a moment my trembling and pounding heart was stilled, but in the very next instant, when another plane flew overhead and the frightening sound of the siren echoed, I screamed fearfully, calling out for my son, Parvaiz, who was nowhere to be seen. I couldn't leave the house because I was afraid my daughter, Kiran, might get scared. Thank God, Parvaiz was in the other room, studying. Leaving his books in the other room, he came to be with me. I don't know what was wrong with me in those days. I kept a constant watch over the children. I wanted to cleave my chest and hide them in there. I wanted to protect them from the shadow of war. Again and again I remembered a scene from a film in which there were corpses everywhere after a bombardment and, walking among them, a child, crying for who knows whom. For some reason, when I had Parvaiz and Kiran by my side, I was besieged by an overwhelming desire to protect them. I kept thinking of the young boy who had been flying a kite on the roof. Was he still flying the kite? Oh God, what is this strange passion for freedom, which has never been vanquished by anyone, and does it blend into the souls of tiny beings? I don't know if rulers of powerful nations also think like this or not. They probably think that big fish can swallow little fish.

They probably see very little difference between people and fish, though Viet Nam proved to the whole world that this adage, which has come out of ponds and seas, is of no account.

A few days after the war started, Zaheer decided to take the children away from Lahore so that they would not be frightened by the thundering booms that continued day and night. I resisted strongly because I didn't want to leave my loved ones behind, but the look of terror in the eyes of my dear daughter, my Kiran, convinced me that it was important to take this little creature away from here. The next day, my two children and I started off for Multan by car. Only I know how I clutched Lahore to my breast and bid farewell to it. I became very emotional at that time and began weeping. The journey was very trying; I was sitting in the car exhausted, my face hidden in the pallu of my sari. Suddenly the car came to a halt with a jolt, and when it didn't start again for a while, I raised my head to look out of the window. A long line of army trucks loaded with soldiers was ahead of us, the trucks passing one at a time because of poor road conditions. I wondered what front they were headed for and how many of them were going to return. I said goodbye to them in my heart and hid my face again, but in the very next instant, the sound of clapping drew my attention back to them. The soldiers in a truck in the rear were dancing a bhangra, and as I watched them, the soldiers in the other trucks began dancing bhangra as well. They were laughing boisterously. Some had cigarettes between their lips. There was such fervour in their clapping—oh God! I was watching them, and I couldn't believe my eyes. Oh God! Were they really going to fight cannons and bullets? I stared at them in disbelief. In truth, there was no trace of anxiety on their faces. Their faces were illuminated with the bloom of flowers.

Finally the trucks packed with soldiers got on their way, but I kept watching them until they had disappeared on the horizon, kept listening for the sound of their clapping, kept asking myself, *Am I afraid of death?* For the first time, the thought of death was like the taste of honey.

How badly one sleeps during war. It was our second night in Multan. Our hosts and all the children were asleep. I had been awakened by the rumble of planes. I got up and looked out the window and in the distance saw red lights in the sky. I thought I should wake up the hosts and ask them what this was when suddenly there was the sound of a tremendous explosion. The windowpanes rattled and the walls shook as if they were about to fall on our heads. There was no reason to make inquiries anymore. Everyone was awake and walking about. My children were calling for me. I quickly advised everyone to huddle together under the tables in the gallery.

Then there was another explosion, which was more severe than the first one. Under the tables, the children knocked into each other. I put my arms around Kiran and held her close and whispered in Parvaiz's ear, "Don't be afraid of death. You remember those dancing soldiers, don't you?" He laughed and sat up straight. But I felt he was trembling. A few minutes later, there were more explosions, but they weren't very strong, the sound now coming as if from afar. Then suddenly we heard a plane fly over the roof. I remembered all my relatives who were not with me. I experienced a deep sense of disappointment. How sad to die far away from home, in a strange place. I saw everyone's face in my imagination, but the faces disappeared in the twinkling of an eye. Soon there were two planes flying over the house. I thought of God, I prayed for this moment of danger to pass, and I felt great peace.

Gradually the roar of the airplanes became less distinct and then disappeared altogether. For a while after that, there was neither an explosion nor the sound of another plane flying over the house. Complete silence prevailed, disturbed only by the occasional barking of a dog and the sound of weeping coming from the house next door.

Moments later the all-clear siren went off, and we stood up. My hostess, who had been bending over her three-year-old child during all this, spoke for the first time. "Apa ji, how dear our children are to us. If the roof had fallen in the explosion, it would have come down on me, but Munna, snug under me, would have been completely safe, wouldn't he?" She left the room without waiting for my reply.

The children went back to sleep in no time, but I remained awake all night. I kept wondering about the place where the bombs had actually fallen. How had the innocent women and children fared there? Troubled by this thought, I hugged my sleeping children and held them close. In the dark, I thought I could see the bodies of dead children, I could see wounded children thrashing about in pain.

The night passed in torment. Early in the morning, I dressed and left with my hosts to see the places where the bombs had fallen.

Two or three miles outside of Multan, we came across a crowd of people. A great many mud homes and thatched dwellings had been razed. The women were retrieving things that were buried in the rubble. There were pots and pans scattered everywhere.

The children looked bewildered. Many of them had bandages around their heads and on their feet. Some women squatted with their hands folded, staring at the demolished dwellings as if they had lost everything, as if these were not just ordinary dwellings but palaces. The men were informing visitors that there had been no loss of life.

I stood there quietly, anxiously observing what was going on around me. Despite the large crowd, I felt as though I was isolated. But I was relieved to hear there had been no loss of life. About seventy yards from where I was standing, a group of people had gathered, and all of them seemed to be looking down at something. On questioning the steward, I found out that this was one of the spots where a bomb had landed.

Later, when the crowd had thinned, I too approached. A small crater had formed where the bomb had fallen, and sitting next to the crater was an old man with a sheet spread out beside him. Strewn about on the sheet were innumerable coins. As soon as he spotted me, the old man cried, "A donation, Begum Sahib. A well will be dug on this spot, and out of it will come cool, sweet water."

I placed whatever I had in my purse on the sheet, and the old man, as if moved to sudden liveliness, started calling out loudly:

"Cool, sweet water, sa'in, cool, sweet water!"

Translation from Urdu by Tahira Naqvi

About the Contributors

Vishwamitter Adil published English translations of Urdu poetry and fiction and was a screenwriter, director, lyricist, and film actor. He died in 2002.

Abul Bashar was born in 1951 in Hamarpur, West Bengal, India. His works include *Bhorer prosuti, Saidabai, Simar,* and *Mati chere jai.* His earliest work explores the lives of Muslim women of West Bengal. In 1988 he received the Ananda Purashkar.

Samaresh Basu was born in 1924 and spent his early childhood in Dhaka (in present-day Bangladesh). From 1943 through 1949 he worked in a factory in Ichhapore and was an active member of the trade union and the Communist Party; he was jailed from 1949 to 1950, when the party was declared illegal, and while in jail, he wrote his first novel, *Uttaranga.* In all, he wrote more than 200 short stories and 100 novels, including those published under the aliases Kalkut and Bhramar. His book *Shamba,* a modern interpretation of the Puranic tales, won the Sahitya Akademi Award in 1980. He died in 1988.

Rajinder Singh Bedi was born in Lahore in 1915 and moved to India after Partition. The author of several collections of short stories and film scripts, he is regarded as one of the most prominent Urdu fiction writers. Two of his collections of short stories, *Dana-o-Daam* (The Catch) and *Grehan* (The Eclipse), were published before Partition. His novel *Ek Chadar Maili Si* received the Sahitya Akademi Award in 1965 and was made into a popular film. He died in 1984.

Alok Bhalla has a doctorate from Kent State University and is a professor of English literature at the Central Institute of English and Foreign Languages, Hyderabad. He has published extensively on translation theory, literature, and politics and has recently edited a collection of stories, *Partition Dialogues: Memories of a Lost Home* (Oxford University Press, 2006).

Urvashi Butalia was born in Ambala, India, in 1952 and completed graduate studies in London in 1977. In 1984 she cofounded Kali for Women, India's first feminist publishing house. Her writing has appeared in numerous periodicals in India and England. Her most recent edited books are *Speaking Peace: Women's Voices from Kashmir* and *The Other Side of Silence: Voices from the Partition of India.*

Radha Chakravarty is a Reader at the Department of English, Gargi College, University of Delhi. She has translated numerous Bengali authors into English, and her essays, articles, and reviews have appeared in journals and critical anthologies worldwide. Her books of translations include *The Bankimchandra Omnibus* by Bankim Chandra Chatterji; *In the Name of the Mother: Four Stories* by Mahasveta Debi; *Crossings: Stories from Bangladesh and India;* and most recently *Boyhood Days* by Rabindranath Tagore. In 2005 she was nominated for the Crossword Translation Award.

Krishna Dutta was born and raised in Calcutta before moving to London. She is a scholar and translator, particularly of the works of Rabindranath Tagore. In addition to coauthoring his biography *Rabindranath Tagore: The Myriad-Minded Man*, she also edited and translated, with Andrew Robinson, *The Selected Letters of Rabindranath Tagore, Rabindranath Tagore: An Anthology,* and Tagore's *The Post Office, Noon in Calcutta: Short Stories from Bengal,* and *Glimpses of Bengal.*

Gulzar (Sampooran Singh) was born in Deena in 1934. He moved to Delhi after Partition and began his career writing lyrics for film and television. In 1971 he became a screenwriter and director, scripting more than sixty films and directing seventeen. His honors include the National Award (received three times) and the Filmfare Award (received fourteen times). In 2002, Filmfare awarded him its Lifetime Achievement Award for his contributions to Hindi cinema. He received the Sahitya Akademi Award in 2003 for his collection of Urdu short stories, *Dhuaan.*

Rashid Haider was born in Pabna in 1941 and now lives in Dhaka. Best known as a novelist and short-story writer, he has written extensively about the Liberation War and the lives of rural and middle-class people. A playwright, translator, political historian, and biographer as well, he received the Bengla Academy Award in 1984 and both the Humayun Qadir Prize and the Nedhushah Literary Prize in 1987.

John W. Hood is an Australian scholar of Indian culture who earned his doctorate in Bengali historiography from the University of Melbourne. He has translated numerous works from Bengali, most recently *Freedom's Ransom* by Prafulla Roy. He is also a noted scholar of Indian cinema, having written five books and numerous articles, essays, and interviews. His most recent book on Indian cinema is *The Films of Buddhadeb Dasgupta,* an enlarged and revised edition of his book *Time and Dreams.*

Intizar Husain was born in Dibai, India, in 1925 and migrated to Pakistan in 1947. A writer, critic, and translator, he has published seven volumes of short stories, four novels, and a novella, as well as travelogues, memoirs, and a volume of critical essays. In 1982 he was offered, but declined, the Adamjee Literary Award for his second novel, *Basti* (Town). His numerous honors include the Yatra Award, Pride of Performance (Government of Pakistan), Kamal-i-Fun Award (Government of Pakistan), Adabi Award (Anjuman-i-Farogh-i-Urdu, India), and the ARY Gold Award.

Kamleshwar (Kamleshwar Prasad Saxena) was born in 1932 in India and became one of the most prominent Hindi authors of the twentieth century. Along with having published several books of fiction and literary criticism, he was director of

Doordarshan, India's national television channel, and wrote numerous film scripts. He was also the editor of the Hindi daily newspapers *Dainik Jagran* and *Dainik Bhaskar* and was awarded the Padmabushan in 2005. He died in Mainpuri in January 2007.

Sukrita Paul Kumar is a former fellow of the Indian Institute of Advanced Study, Shimla, and has published four collections of poems in English: *Without Margins, Oscillations, Apurna,* and *Folds of Silence.* Her critical books include *Conversations on Modernism, The New Story, Breakthrough* (a collection she edited), *Man, Woman and Androgyny,* and *Narrating Partition.* In 1991, she became a recipient of the Bharat Nirman Award for Talented Women for her contributions to literature and art, and she received a 1993–1994 Shastri Indo-Canadian Faculty Research Fellowship. Her U.S. residencies include the Iowa International Writing Program. She teaches literature at a Delhi University college.

Saadat Hasan Manto was born in 1912 in Samrala, Punjab, and is regarded as the leading Urdu-language fiction writer of the twentieth century. Of Kashmiri ancestry, he published twenty-two collections of stories, three collections of essays, scores of plays, a novel, and scripts for more than a dozen films. He worked for All India Radio in Bombay before moving to Pakistan after Partition. Often at odds with literary censors in both India and Pakistan, he died at the age of forty-two.

Khadija Mastur was born in 1927 in Lucknow, India. She and her younger sister, Hajira Masroor, worked actively for the Muslim League in 1946, and during Partition, she and her family migrated to Lahore, Pakistan. She wrote several collections of short stories and two novels, *Aangan* (The Courtyard) and *Zamin* (Earth). She died in Lahore in 1983. For her collection of short stories *Thanda Meetha Pani* (Cool, Sweet Water), she was posthumously honored with the Baba-e-Urdu, Dr. Abdul Haq Award.

Tahira Naqvi was raised and educated in Lahore, Pakistan, and now lives in the United States. Her short-story collections are *Attar of Roses and Other Stories of Pakistan* and *Dying in a Strange Country.* She has also translated books by such prominent Urdu writers as Ismat Chughtai, Khadija Mastur, Saadat Hasan Manto, and Hajira Masroor.

Joginder Paul was born in 1925 in Sialkot and migrated to India during Partition. His mother tongue is Punjabi, but his primary and middle-school education was in Urdu. He received his master's degree in English literature and eventually became head of a post-graduate college in Maharashtra. His nineteen fictional works are widely read in both India and Pakistan, and he has won every important award that an Urdu writer can receive.

Frances W. Pritchett is a professor of Urdu and Hindi at Columbia University. Among her translated works are *Aab-e-hayat: Shaping the Canon of Urdu Poetry,* the last anthology of classical Urdu poetry, and *An Evening of Caged Beasts: Seven Postmodernist Urdu Poets.* Her works of literary criticism include *Nets of Awareness: Urdu Poetry and Its Critics.*

Mohan Rakesh was born in Amritsar in 1925 and was educated in Lahore. He was one of the pioneers of the Nai Kahani (New Story) movement in Hindi in the 1950s. His works included novels, short stories, travelogues, criticism, memoirs, and drama. Among his plays are *Ashadha Ka Ek Din* (One Day in the Rainy Month of Ashadha), one of the first plays to revive the Hindi stage in the 1960s; *Adhe Adhure* (The Incomplete Ones); and *Lehron Ke Rajhamsa* (The Swans of the Waves). He was recognized with the Nehru Fellowship and the Sangeet Natak Akademi Award. He died in 1972.

Ravikant is a historian, writer, and translator working with the Sarai Programme of the Centre for the Study of Developing Societies, Delhi. He has coedited (with Tarun K. Saint) *Translating Partition* (Katha, 2001) and (with Sanjay Sharma) *Deewan-e-Sarai* (vol. 1): *Media Vimarsh / Hindi Janpad* (Vani, 2002) and *Deewan-e-Sarai* (vol. 2): *Shaharnama* (Vani, 2005).

Andrew Robinson was born in 1957 and studied at Oxford and the School of Oriental and African Studies in London. He is a prolific author, editor, and translator and until recently was the literary editor of the *Times Higher Education Supplement.* His books include *Satyajit Ray, The Inner Eye: The Biography of a Master Film-Maker,* and *Satyajit Ray: A Vision of Cinema.* With Krishna Dutta, Robinson coauthored the acclaimed biography *Rabindranath Tagore: The Myriad-Minded Man;* also with Dutta, he co-edited and co-translated *The Selected Letters of Rabindranath Tagore* and *Rabindranath Tagore: An Anthology.*

Prafulla Roy was born in 1934 in a village in the Dhaka district. Still a boy at the time of Partition, he took up writing in 1953. The short-story collections of his that have been translated into English include *In the Shadow of the Sun* and *Set at Odds: Stories of the Partition and Beyond.* Considered one of Bengal's finest writers, he has been honored with the 2003 Sahitya Akademi Award for his novel *Kranti Kal.* Roy's work has influenced such filmmakers as Buddhadeb Dasgupta, Tapan Sinha, Biplab Ray Chaudhary, and Sandeep Ray. Numerous films have been based on Roy's stories and made in several languages.

Bhisham Sahni was born in 1915 in Rawalpindi. He is a prolific translator and author of fiction and plays. His novel *Tamas* (Darkness), translated into English in 1988, received international notice for its portrayal of the communal riots during Partition. In addition to writing in Hindi, Sahni writes in English, Urdu, Sanskrit, Russian, and Punjabi. He has translated twenty-five books from Russian into Hindi, including Tolstoy's *Resurrection,* and has received two Sahitya Akademi Awards, the Madhya Pradesh Kala Sahitya Parishad Award, the Shiromani Writers Award, the Lotus Award from the Afro-Asian Writers' Association, and the Soviet Land Nehru Award.

Tarun K. Saint teaches English literature at Hindu College, Delhi University. His area of research interest is the literature of Partition. He has edited *Bruised Memories: Communal Violence and the Writer* (Seagull, 2002) and coedited (with Ravikant) *Translating Partition* (Katha, 2001).

Sunil Trivedi is a translator and senior business executive who was educated in Calcutta and Allahabad. He is a scholar of Hindi, Urdu, Sanskrit, and English. His works include the translation, with Sukrita Paul Kumar, of Joginder Paul's novel *Sleepwalkers*.

Richard Williams has translated such works as Mannu Bhandari's Hindi novel *Mahabhoja* (The Great Feast).

Permissions

"The Train Has Reached Amritsar" by Bhisham Sahni, translated by Alok Bhalla. From *Stories About the Partition of India* (vol. 1), edited by Alok Bhalla. New Delhi: Indus, 1994. Reprinted by permission of the translator.

"Toba Tek Singh" by Saadat Hasan Manto, translated by Tahira Naqvi. From *Stories About the Partition of India* (vol. 3), edited by Alok Bhalla. New Delhi: Indus, 1994. Reprinted by permission of the editor.

"Lajwanti" by Rajinder Singh Bedi, translated by Alok Bhalla. From *Stories About the Partition of India* (vol. 1), edited by Alok Bhalla. New Delhi: Indus, 1994. Reprinted by permission of the translator.

"Incognita" by Rashid Haider, translated by Radha Chakravarty. From *Crossings: Stories from Bangladesh and India*, edited and translated by Radha Chakravarty. New Delhi: Indialog, 2003. Reprinted by permission of the translator.

"from *The Other Side of Silence*" by Urvashi Butalia. From *The Other Side of Silence: Voices from the Partition of India* by Urvashi Butalia. New Delhi: Viking Penguin India, 1998; Durham, NC: Duke University Press, 2000. Reprinted by permission of Duke University Press.

"Pali" by Bhisham Sahni, translated by the author. From *Translating Partition*, edited by Ravikant and Tarun K. Saint. New Delhi: Katha, 2001. Reprinted by permission of the publisher.

"The Claim" by Mohan Rakesh, translated by Richard Williams. From *Stories About the Partition of India* (vol. 3), edited by Alok Bhalla. New Delhi: Indus, 1994. Reprinted by permission of the editor.

"The Dog of Tetwal" by Saadat Hasan Manto, translated by Ravikant and Tarun K. Saint. From *Translating Partition,* edited by Ravikant and Tarun K. Saint. New Delhi: Katha, 2001. Reprinted by permission of the publisher.

"Whose Story?" by Gulzar, translated by Alok Bhalla. From *Raavi Paar and Other Stories* by Gulzar. New Delhi: Harper Collins India, 1997. Reprinted by permission of the translator.

"The Owner of Rubble" by Mohan Rakesh, translated by Alok Bhalla. From *Stories About the Partition of India* (vol. 1), edited by Alok Bhalla. New Delhi: Indus, 1994. Reprinted by permission of the translator.

"Father" by Prafulla Roy, translated by John W. Hood. From *Set at Odds: Stories of Partition and Beyond* by Prafulla Roy, translated by John W. Hood. New Delhi: Srishti, 2002. Reprinted by permission of the translator.

"Mozel" by Saadat Hasan Manto, translated by Tahira Naqvi. From *Stories About the Partition of India* (vol. 2), edited by Alok Bhalla. New Delhi: Indus, 1994. Reprinted by permission of the editor.

"Farewell" by Samaresh Basu, translated by Krishna Dutta and Andrew Robinson. From *Noon in Calcutta: Short Stories from Bengal*, edited and translated by Krishna Dutta and Andrew Robinson. New Delhi: Viking Penguin India, 1992. Reprinted by permission of the translators.

"from *Sleepwalkers*" by Joginder Paul, translated by Sunil Trivedi and Sukrita Paul Kumar. From *Sleepwalkers* by Joginder Paul, edited by Keerti Ramachandra. New Delhi: Katha, 1998. Reprinted by permission of the publisher.

"On Writing *Sleepwalkers*" by Joginder Paul. From *Sleepwalkers* by Joginder Paul, edited by Keerti Ramachandra. New Delhi: Katha, 1998. Reprinted by permission of the publisher.

"Where There Is No Frontier" by Prafulla Roy, translated by John W. Hood. From *Set at Odds: Stories of Partition and Beyond* by Prafulla Roy, translated by John W. Hood. New Delhi: Srishti, 2002. Reprinted by permission of the translator.

"from *Basti*" by Intizar Husain, translated by Frances W. Pritchett. From *Basti* by Intizar Husain, translated by Frances W. Pritchett. New Delhi: Indus, 1995. Reprinted by permission of the translator.

"Rebirth" by Abul Bashar, translated by Krishna Dutta and Andrew Robinson. From *Noon in Calcutta: Short Stories from Bengal*, edited and translated by Krishna Dutta and Andrew Robinson. New Delhi: Viking Penguin India, 1992. Reprinted by permission of the translators.

"How Many Pakistans?" by Kamleshwar, translated by Vishwamitter Adil and Alok Bhalla. From *Stories About the Partition of India* (vol. 2), edited by Alok Bhalla. New Delhi: Indus, 1994. Reprinted by permission of the editor.

"Cool, Sweet Water" by Khadija Mastur, translated by Tahira Naqvi. From *Cool, Sweet Water: Selected Stories* by Khadija Mastur, edited by Muhammad Umar Memon and translated by Tahira Naqvi. Karachi: Oxford University Press, 1999; New Delhi: Kali for Women, 1999. Reprinted by permission of the editor.